Psellos and the Patriarchs

Michael Psellos in Translation

Miniature portrait of Michael Psellos and his pupil Michael Doukas, MS Pantokrator 234, fol. 254 (12th century). © Holy Monastery of Pantokrator, Mount Athos. Used with permission.

Psellos and the Patriarchs

Letters and Funeral Orations for

Keroullarios, Leichoudes, and Xiphilinos

translated by
ANTHONY KALDELLIS
and **IOANNIS POLEMIS**

University of Notre Dame Press

Notre Dame, Indiana

Copyright © 2015 by University of Notre Dame
Notre Dame, Indiana 46556
undpress.nd.edu
All Rights Reserved

Manufactured in the United States of America

Library of Congress Cataloging-in-Publication Data

Psellus, Michael.
Psellos and the patriarchs : letters and funeral orations for Keroullarios, Leichoudes, and
Xiphilinos / [Michael Psellos] ; translated by Anthony Kaldellis and Ioannis Polemis.
    pages   cm. — (Michael Psellos in translation)
    Includes bibliographical references and index.
    ISBN 978-0-268-03328-6 (paper : alk. paper) —
    ISBN 0-268-03328-5 (paper : alk. paper)
    1. Psellus, Michael.   2. Authors, Greek (Modern)—Biography.   3. Patriarchs and
patriarchate—Biography.   4. Political customs and rites—Byzantine Empire—History.
5. Funeral orations—Translations into English.   6. Byzantine Empire—Officials
and employees.   7. Byzantine Empire—Politics and government.   8. Byzantine
literature—History and criticism.   9. Byzantine Empire—Social life and customs.
I. Kaldellis, Anthony.   II. Polemis, I.   III. Title.
    PA5355.Z5P73   2015
    189—dc23

                                                                2015017672

∞ *The paper in this book meets the guidelines for permanence and*
durability of the Committee on Production Guidelines for Book Longevity
of the Council on Library Resources.

Contents

Preface

This volume was created fortuitously. In 1998, Anthony Kaldellis translated the long letters to Keroullarios and Xiphilinos and part of the funeral oration for Leichoudes. More recently, Ioannis Polemis translated the funeral orations for Keroullarios and Xiphilinos in the course of preparing a new edition of Psellos' funeral orations, now published in the series Bibliotheca Teubneriana. A volume containing all of these texts suggested itself naturally to us. Each of us has written the introductions to the texts that he has translated. In addition, Anthony Kaldellis wrote the first two sections of the general introduction to the volume, and Ioannis Polemis the third section. We have read and commented on each other's translations. But this is Psellos, so some passages remain baffling.

The translators thank the two reviewers for the University of Notre Dame Press, Stratis Papaioannou and an anonymous reviewer, for their useful corrections and advice, as well as Michael Jeffreys for making useful comments after reading the volume. We are also grateful to the press and our editor, Stephen Little, for continuing their support for this project.

Note on Translations. Biblical references are to the Septuagint version of the Bible (LXX). Biblical quotations in English are the authors' own translations, following the wording of Psellos, which is based on the Septuagint and the Greek New Testament. In the translations, ellipses in brackets mean that words are missing from the manuscript text or that the text has been corrupted and cannot be properly translated; ellipses without brackets are used to convey the sense of what Psellos is doing in an equivalent way in Greek, usually the deliberate introduction of a kind of caesura or syntactical break to mark a pause, stark contrast, or reformulation of his argument.

For the sake of consistency, we are naming all three orations Funeral Orations, even though the first two (for Keroullarios and Leichoudes) are called Encomia (i.e., orations of praise) in the original manuscript. In substance, they are encomia and so can be referred to in either way. But for their formal titles we have opted for Funeral Oration.

Psellos and the Patriarchs

General Introduction

Translated in this volume are the long funeral orations that Michael Psellos, the leading intellectual of eleventh-century Byzantium, wrote for three successive ecumenical patriarchs of Constantinople, who governed the Orthodox Church in Byzantium for a total of more than thirty years: Michael I Keroullarios (1043–1058); Konstantinos III Leichoudes (1059–1063); and Ioannes VIII Xiphilinos (1064–1075). Also translated are several letters that Psellos addressed to two of them. These works are worthy of study for many reasons. First, they are important sources for both the secular and the ecclesiastical careers of these three men, which are not otherwise well documented. They are, in other words, important historical sources for a variety of events and topics, including the relations between emperors and patriarchs during a period when the Byzantine empire went from being the leading power in Europe and the Near East to a state on the verge of collapse, and when the Orthodox and Catholic Churches deepened their ongoing rift, especially with the events of 1054.

Second, these speeches are important specimens of Byzantine panegyrical rhetoric. Modern textbooks of Byzantine rhetoric (and Byzantine literature in general) give the impression that panegyrics of emperors were performed without break at the Byzantine court from late antiquity to the end of the empire in 1453, but this is a misleading picture. In fact, few such texts survive from between the seventh and the mid-eleventh century, and there is reason to think that it was Psellos who revived and institutionalized the *performance* (and not just composition) of such speeches at the court.[1] He stands at the

---

1. See the speeches in Psellos, *Orationes Panegyricae*.

1

origin of an explosive production of panegyrics that marked the Komnenian and Palaiologan courts in late centuries. Moreover, his are also the first funeral encomia of patriarchs that we have—that is, for patriarchs who were not also saints, because those received hagiographical treatments. The three orations translated here stand behind the later *routinization* of patriarchal encomia in Constantinople.

Third, the three patriarchal orations (and associated letters) are important sources for the thought of Michael Psellos and the challenges faced by his project to revive and institutionalize the study of ancient philosophy at the heart of the Orthodox Christian empire of Romanía. Two of the patriarchs (Keroullarios and Xiphilinos) had at one time or another questioned Psellos' personal commitment to the Christian faith and sought, in different ways, to discipline his intellectual explorations. Psellos seized the opportunity provided by the genre of the funeral oration to have the last word in his debates with them and to reframe these debates in more advantageous ways; and he used the funeral oration for Leichoudes to paint the portrait of an ideal patriarch as Psellos would have it.

Each speech is structured loosely around the career of each man and has two "movements," a secular one followed by a fall, and then an ecclesiastical one; the rises and falls of Leichoudes are the smoothest, those of Keroullarios are the most violent and extreme, and those of Xiphilinos are in the middle. However, the speeches focus less on facts and data and more on abstract definitions of different virtues and states of being. They are, in short, brief ethical treatises by Psellos and reflect his idiosyncratic Platonic philosophy. They were not written to be spoken aloud at the patriarchs' funerals, despite their occasional affectation of such a dramatic setting (the speech for Leichoudes was written at least twelve years after his death, that for Keroullarios at least one year later). If they were in fact delivered orally, it was probably in shorter versions that were less philosophically embellished. They are ethical character-portraits, including analyses of the virtues shown by the man in question.

This is not the place to offer detailed analysis of the rhetorical qualities and theory behind these speeches.[2] In addition to the "movements" at the level of overall structure and the ongoing development of ethical theory (a progressive improvement from Keroullarios to Xiphilinos and, finally, Leichoudes), readers should watch for the moments when patriarchs and emperors interact, often in

---

2. Readers interested in these aspects should consult the magisterial recent study of Psellos' rhetoric by Papaioannou (2013).

confrontation, because these moments serve to define the character of the man in question. The emperors are in many ways the "mirrors" in which the patriarchs are reflected. Finally, readers will notice Psellos' resort to spatial-geometrical imagery and apparent paradoxes to explain ethical concepts: opposites thereby become complementary; setbacks contain the seeds for future progress; ascent is in fact descent, and vice versa; things change (on the surface) but really remain the same (underneath); beginnings and endings meet; and virtues are described in terms of figures and diagrams, peaks, circles, and oscillations. These figures make Psellos fun to read but also frustratingly opaque at times.

The present introduction consists of three sections, the first two by Anthony Kaldellis: a brief biography of Psellos (reused from the first volume in the series, *Mothers and Sons, Fathers and Daughters: The Byzantine Family of Michael Psellos*, but revised and updated); a historical and interpretive essay on Psellos' relationships with the patriarchs; and, by Ioannis Polemis, an interpretation of the funeral orations for Keroullarios and Xiphilinos.

A Brief, Revised Biography of Michael Psellos

No biography of Michael Psellos exists in any language, though the pieces are slowly falling into place and past errors are being cleared up.[3] A brief statement of what is known will provide the necessary context against which to discuss his relations with the three patriarchs Keroullarios, Leichoudes, and Xiphilinos.

Konstantinos Psellos—the baptismal name of the later monk Michael—was born in 1018, during the reign of Basileios II (976–1025) and the apogee of Byzantine power, to a "middle-class" family in Constantinople. Early on, his mother Theodote perceived that he was clever and encouraged his studies with an eye to a career in the imperial administration. It seems that he studied at the school housed in the local monastery of *ta Narsou*, with which Psellos maintained a lifelong connection. He later boasted that school lessons were child's play for him and that by the age of ten he could recite and expound the entire *Iliad*.[4] He was also a purely urban creature, sixteen years old before

3. See Riedinger (2010); see Papaioannou (2013) 4–13 for another short account of his life (with more documentation).
4. Psellos, *Encomium for His Mother* 5–6. In the *Chronographia* 4.4 he implies that he started to study Homer when he was sixteen, but this is too late. For *ta Narsou*, see Hondridou (2002) 159–160, citing previous scholarship.

he even set eyes on the fields outside the walls, or so he claimed (probably only in Constantinople could this happen in all of Christendom). By that age he had begun to study rhetoric and joined the staff of a provincial judge, but this internship was, he implies, cut short by the death of his beloved sister.[5] Psellos' instructors in rhetoric were Ioannes Mauropous, who was famous as a teacher but would not make his mark as a writer until after Psellos' rise at the court, and Niketas, who would later serve under Psellos in the reformed educational system.[6] As far as philosophy was concerned, Psellos claimed to have studied it largely on his own: whereas he was "a perfect philosopher," his friends were only "lovers of philosophy."[7]

In 1042 Psellos appears as a secretary under Michael V Kalaphates (1041–1042), and his career had clearly begun under that emperor's uncle and predecessor, Michael IV the Paphlagonian (1034–1041). Though only twenty, he already displayed a knack for making friends in high places, including Alousianos, son of the last Bulgarian tsar (Ivan Vladislav), who joined Deljan's revolt against the empire, deposed its leader, and betrayed it to Michael IV in exchange for titles; and the captain of the guard sent against Michael V in the popular riot of 1042, an event of which Psellos later wrote a dramatic first-hand account.[8] His standing at the court rose dramatically under Konstantinos IX Monomachos (1042–1055), a charming if frivolous patron of the arts and of education, whose expenditures and neglect of the army were topics of controversy. Psellos became one of his intimate advisors and secretaries, a position earned largely by "the grace of my language. . . . For I am told that my speech is beautiful, even when making routine statements." He also acted as the emperor's spokesman, writing eloquent speeches in his praise and in support of his policies (regardless of whether he agreed with them).[9] He had by then befriended Konstantinos Leichoudes, Monomachos' "prime minister" and later a patriarch (1059–1063), whom Psellos admired for his urbane, philosophical, and flexible statesmanship, and had facilitated the intro-

5. Psellos, *Encomium for His Mother* 15.

6. For Psellos and Mauropous, see Karpozilos (1982) 26–28; and Ljubarskij (2004) 70–83; for Niketas, see Psellos, *Funeral Oration for Niketas* 3–6.

7. Psellos, *Chronographia* 6.192.

8. Psellos, *Chronographia* 4.47, 5.39.

9. Psellos, *Chronographia* 6.14, 6.44–45, 7A.7. For Psellos' misgivings and his use of rhetoric at the court, see Kaldellis (1999) chs. 19–21. The orations are *Orationes Panegyricae* 1–10.

duction to the court of his teacher Mauropous (later the bishop of Euchaïta in Asia Minor) and his friend Ioannes Xiphilinos, another future patriarch (1064–1075), alongside whom he continued to teach privately. Xiphilinos took on students interested in the law and Psellos those who wanted to study philosophy and rhetoric. When a dispute broke out (around 1045–1047) among their students, the emperor intervened and granted official recognition to both schools. Psellos assumed the lofty title of Consul of the Philosophers and seems to have exercised some supervision over higher education in the capital, although the institutional aspects of his position are unclear. Meanwhile, Xiphilinos was made "Guardian of the Laws" (*nomophylax*) in charge of the new law school, whose foundation was chartered in an imperial edict probably authored by Mauropous (it is not clear how long Xiphilinos held this position, which quickly became controversial). Discussing these new foundations thirty years later, the historian Michael Attaleiates claims that Psellos "surpassed all of our contemporaries in knowledge." The late 1040s has been called the government of the philosophers at Monomachos' court.[10]

In those years Psellos laid the foundations of his philosophical revolution. He delivered hundreds of lectures on philosophical, theological, scientific, and exegetical topics, taking charge of the education of many who would go on to serve in the state administration and the Church. He boasted of the diverse origin of the students who attended his classes: "I have made Celts and Arabs yield to me and on account of my fame they come here . . . while the Nile irrigates the land of the Egyptians, my speech irrigates their souls. If you ask a Persian or an Ethiopian they will say that they have known me and admired me and sought me out."[11] Psellos projected an ideal of vast polymathy subordinated to the queen of sciences, philosophy, and often barely discriminated between pagan and Christian wisdom; at the same time he presented himself as a restorer of higher learning, claiming to have single-handedly dispelled a dark age of philosophy. He also began to wield influence at the court, contracting an advantageous marriage and amassing patrons, clients, titles, a fine town house, and enemies against whom he wrote defensive tracts. The regime of the philosophers began to unravel around 1050, under pressure by forces

10. Various opinions have been expressed regarding the foundation of the schools: Wolska-Connus (1976); Lemerle (1977), for the phrase "government of the philosophers"; Agapitos (1998); and Hondridou (2002) 155–253; cf. Attaleiates, *History* 21.

11. Psellos, *Letter to Keroullarios* 3. For the truth behind this boast, see Wilson (1983) 164–165; Volk (1990) 15–20. For Psellos' teaching position, see Kaldellis (2005).

that we cannot precisely identify: Leichoudes was replaced; Mauropous was sent off against his will to serve as bishop of Euchaïta in north-central Asia Minor; Xiphilinos became a monk on Mt. Olympos in Bithynia; and Psellos clung to the court, but came under increasing fire and suspicion for his beliefs. He was even investigated by the Holy Synod, and his treatises were scrutinized for hidden meanings (see the following section for his relations with Keroullarios). In late 1054, Psellos was tonsured and took the name Michael. This was soon before Monomachos' death in early 1055, which raised further suspicions: had Psellos predicted his death through astrology?[12]

Psellos disliked both the false premises and hypocritical practice of Christian asceticism, and so it is no surprise that his brief stay on Mt. Olympos (1055–1056) was unhappy. He had previously composed a witty parody of the liturgy that exposed one of the holy mountain's heavy drinkers. While in residence there, he composed a philosophical funeral oration for his monastery's recently deceased founder and a eulogy of the mountain itself, praising its natural beauties and defensively noting in the first few lines that the many stars of its night sky were only lifeless bodies. Unlike Xiphilinos, however, Psellos was not sincere in following his new vocation, and he quickly returned to the capital under the empress Theodora (1055–1056). For years afterward he exchanged hostile letters and poems with some of the monks on Olympos. "Father Zeus," wrote a wit among the latter, "you could not endure Olympos even briefly, your goddesses weren't there with you," to which Psellos responded with a torrent of abuse.[13] His friendship with Xiphilinos also seems to have been damaged during his stay, owing to their philosophical disagreement on the value of Plato and of a personal commitment to monasticism (see the following section for their relationship).

Psellos' return led to years of intrigue for him. Mistrusted at the court of Theodora, which was dominated by his enemies, he was appointed by Mi-

12. On Psellos' house: Psellos, *Chronographia* 7A.7; on clients: Ljubarskij (2004) 49–51; on defensive tracts: *Oratoria Minora* 6–10 (the chronology of these works is not secure); on Mauropous: Karpozilos (1982) 33–40. For a cryptic account of his departure from the court, see *Chronographia* 6.191–200 (and below); on astrology: *Chronographia* 6A.10–12.

13. For Olympos, see Psellos, *Funeral Oration for Xiphilinos* (in this volume); cf. Gautier (1974) 15–21. On parody: Psellos, *Poem* 22. See also his *Funeral Oration for Nikolaos, Abbot of the Monastery of the Beautiful Source on Olympos* (*Orationes Funebres I*, 10), and *Regarding Olympos* (*Oratoria Minora* 36), on which see, in general, Weiss (1977) 283–291. For the bitter exchanges, see *Poem* 21 and *Letters S* 35, 166–167, and 185, with de Vries-van der Velden (1996) 119.

chael VI (a Bringas, known as Stratiotikos or as the Old) (1056–1057) to head an embassy to the rebel Isaakios Komnenos, who had just defeated the imperial armies. After two trips to Nikomedeia, Psellos finally negotiated an agreement, but meanwhile a faction in the capital, including the ambitious patriarch Michael Keroullarios and a large number of the City's population, deposed the weak emperor. After this event was announced, Psellos spent the night in terror at the rebel camp, but the next day Isaakios made him one of his advisors and appointed him a President of the Senate before they entered the City together in triumph. Some, of course, suspected that Psellos had simply betrayed Michael VI and joined forces with Isaakios.[14]

The first Komnenos to rule Byzantium tried desperately to restore the imperial army and finances. What endeared him to Psellos was his confiscation of monastic wealth and, above all, his deposition in 1058 of Keroullarios, in Psellos' view an arrogant, contentious, and bigoted prelate—in fact, a failed claimant to the throne in 1040. According to a traditional scholarly narrative, Keroullarios had wrecked the empire's relations with the West in 1054, despite his alleged ignorance of religious matters. Now, under Isaakios, he was encroaching on imperial authority. Keroullarios was almost certainly among those who had undermined Monomachos' cabinet of intellectuals in the early 1050s and had humiliated Psellos by forcing him to produce a confession of faith.[15] Philosophy now went on the offensive. In a heavily sarcastic letter Psellos cast Keroullarios as the embodiment of "angelic" obscurantism, inflexibility, and boorishness, which he associated with Christian asceticism. Isaakios appointed Psellos to direct the prosecution of the recalcitrant patriarch, who, however, died after his arrest and before the trial could begin. Psellos went on to write a long prosecution speech anyway. Keroullarios was replaced by Leichoudes, Psellos' old friend and ally.[16]

In 1059, Isaakios fell ill and abdicated under mysterious circumstances. As a member of his court, Psellos encouraged this decision against the wishes of

14. Psellos, *Chronographia* 7.15–42; Skylitzes, *Synopsis*, p. 497. See Kaldellis (1999) 150–154, 167–168, for Psellos' long and self-serving account of the embassy.

15. On monastic wealth: Psellos, *Chronographia* 7.59–60; cf. Attaleiates, *History* 61–62. For Keroullarios in general, see Tinnefeld (1989); for his limitations, Kolbaba (2000) 33, 36, 94, 134; for his imperial pretensions, Dagron (2003) 235–247. On the Confession of Faith: Psellos, *Theologica Minora II* 35, with Garzya (1967); Hondridou (2002) 238–239; and see the following section of this introduction.

16. Psellos, *Letter to Keroullarios*. On the latter's death and Leichoudes: *Chronographia* 7.65–66, with Kaldellis (1999) 174–175. See also the extravant *Accusation of the Archpriest before the Synod* (*Orationes Forenses* 1).

the emperor's wife and, likely exaggerating his role in the whole process, claims that he personally invested his successor, Konstantinos X Doukas (1059–1067), before Isaakios had fully made up his mind; it was Psellos who then wrote the proclamation of the new emperor that was distributed to the provinces. Psellos was a close friend of the Doukai, especially the emperor's brother, the *kaisar* Ioannes Doukas.[17] The good-natured, deeply pious, but unwarlike new emperor did little to halt the empire's rapid decline as the Seljuks raided Asia Minor and sacked major cities. Psellos, now in his forties, spent the 1060s as an honored member of the imperial family, wielding some influence behind the throne. He was appointed tutor of Doukas' son and heir, Michael, for whom he composed a number of didactic and relatively superficial works on legal, historical, and scientific topics, sometimes rededicating to him works originally presented to Konstantinos IX Monomachos. We can detect his hand at work in the choice of Xiphilinos to replace Leichoudes as patriarch in 1064. In the early years of the reign he also completed the first edition of his *Chronographia*, covering the emperors from Basileios II to Isaakios (i.e., 976–1059). Beyond its ambitious philosophical message, this text employs masterful and virtually unprecedented literary techniques to demythologize the imperial position and expose the all-too-human qualities of God's anointed. This by itself implies a political theory because Psellos did not believe that "ideal" emperors were possible: all emperors were both good and bad in different respects, and those with the most good-natured character were often the worse rulers. But there is also a more subversive theme running through the work: the empire must be governed by soldiers in these times, not civilians, and its resources should be used to support the army, not so much the civilian administration, the Church, or the monasteries.[18]

Konstantinos' death in 1067 precipitated a crisis in the Doukas regime. His widow, Eudokia Makrembolitissa, a niece of Keroullarios, broke her oath to her husband by marrying and elevating to the throne the handsome general and former rebel Romanos Diogenes (1068–1071). The degree to which Eudokia formed a faction at the court, separate from that of Ioannes Doukas

17. For Psellos' medical knowledge and practice, see Volk (1990). Isaakios' wife, Aikaterine, was the sister of Psellos' friend Alousianos. On the proclamation: *Oratoria Minora* 5. For Ioannes Doukas, see Polemis (1968) 34–41; Ljubarskij (2004) 111–119.

18. The literary qualities of the *Chronographia* are slowly gaining attention. On the mixture of qualities: Psellos, *Chronographia* 6.25–28. On political theory: Kaldellis (1999) chs. 5–6, 9, 24.

and Psellos, remains to be studied. Romanos tried to restore the military situation by conducting long and determined, albeit inconclusive, campaigns against the Seljuks. Ioannes Doukas was forced to the sidelines, and Psellos himself was distrusted, despite the fact that he continued, as always, to praise the emperor in public orations and draft his pronouncements. Psellos even accompanied the emperor's expedition of 1069, at least for a while, joining Michael Attaleiates in the emperor's council of advisors. Psellos would later claim that he disagreed with Romanos' strategy and tactics and proffered his own, based on his superior understanding of the "science" of war.[19] But it was intrigue that restored the Doukai and sealed the fate of Byzantine Anatolia. It was suspected that Ioannes' son Andronikos betrayed Romanos at the battle of Manzikert in 1071 (though there were additional reasons for the defeat). Psellos and Ioannes promptly deposed Eudokia, elevated her son Michael VII Doukas (1071–1078) to the throne, and declared Romanos an outlaw, refusing to recognize his surprisingly favorable agreement with Alp Arslan. A civil war conducted by the Doukai resulted in the surrender, tonsure, and brutal— in fact, fatal—blinding of Romanos. In the brief supplement to the *Chronographia* that he wrote around 1075, whose purpose seems to have been to expose the frivolity of his patrons the Doukai through sarcastic praise, Psellos boasted of the power that he personally wielded at the court in those critical days.[20] A moving letter of consolation from Psellos to the blinded Romanos— which referred to God as the "Sleepless Eye that watches over all," encouraged him to find his "inner sight," and was written soon after a bombastic congratulatory letter to his conqueror Andronikos—cannot divert our attention from the damage done to the empire by the new Doukas regime, nor does Psellos' devastating sarcasm regarding his patrons mitigate his role in those events.[21]

19. Psellos, *Chronographia* 7B.12–16. On the panegyrics for Romanos: *Orationes Panegyricae* 18–21. For philosophers as armchair generals, see *When He Resigned from the Rank of* protasekretis 33 ff. (*Oratoria Minora* 8); see also his *On Military Formation* (*De oper. daem.*, pp. 120–124). For an anguished letter that Psellos wrote during the campaign of 1069, see Snipes (1981). De Vries-van der Velden (1997) has a different view of the relationship between Psellos and Romanos; the matter certainly requires further study: Ljubarskij (2004) 55–56.

20. Psellos, *Chronographia* 7B.27–30. For Andronikos and Mantzikert, see Polemis (1968) 55–59.

21. Psellos, *Letters S* 82 and 145, respectively. Cf. Skylitzes Continuatus p. 152, based in part on Psellos' own admissions.

Michael VII was utterly incompetent as a ruler. Attaleiates said that he was fit only to be a bishop! Psellos continued to write various treatises for Michael's education and edification and draft his diplomatic correspondence, but little seems to have been done by the regime to halt the decline of imperial authority. Certainly, we do not know what kind of influence Psellos had at this time; the court politics of the period remain obscure. Yet contemporaries did complain that the emperor was spending all his time "on the vain and useless study of letters, trying constantly to compose iambic and anapestic verses . . . deceived in this by the Consul of the Philosophers."[22] To this ignoble end Psellos, charmed by the mystique of the palace, had led a career that had promised so much for the philosophical renewal under Monomachos, ultimately betraying his own astute analysis of the empire's practical needs. The emperor's favor was now held by a capable but allegedly corrupt eunuch named Nikephoritzes, who seems to have been on good terms with Psellos but who led the empire to the nadir of its fortunes. The position of Consul of the Philosophers was eventually given to Psellos' student Ioannes Italos. Psellos himself is possibly not heard from again after 1075–1076, when he left off writing his sarcastic account of the Doukas regime, composed a funeral oration for Xiphilinos, and welcomed back to the capital his old teacher Mauropous (though some letters may be dated even later, extending his life).[23] In two of his letters, he had indicated a wish to be buried at the monastery of the Beautiful Spring (*Horaia Pege*), possibly property that he owned on Bithynian Olympos.[24]

Psellos and the Patriarchs: A Historical and Interpretive Essay

This section will survey Psellos' relationships with the three patriarchs and interpret some of the key texts that he addressed to each, focusing on the fu-

---

22. Attaleiates, *History* 303. On complaints: Skylitzes Continuatus p. 171. Cf. Psellos, *Chronographia* 7C.4, for Michael's intellectual interests, including iambic verses. For Psellos' writings associated with Michael VII, see Polemis (1968) 44–45.

23. On Italos: Anna Komnene, *Alexiad* 5.8.5. The latest discussions of Psellos' death are Kaldellis (2011); and Papaioannou (2013) 11–12 n. 36. On Mauropous' return: Karpozilos (1982) 46. Various pieces of evidence have been put forward to show that Psellos lived past 1080, e.g., by Ljubarskij (2004) 58–63, but all are dubious and none may be accepted at this time.

24. Psellos, *Letters KD* 177, 228; I thank M. Jeffreys for the identification (personal communication).

neral orations (which are all also encomia) and select letters. It follows the order in which the orations were likely composed (Keroullarios, Xiphilinos, Leichoudes), which does not correspond to the order of their tenures in office and death.

Psellos and Keroullarios

In the *Chronographia*, Psellos bluntly calls the announcement of Keroullarios' death an εὐαγγελία (*euangelia*), a piece of "good news" that promised a future more free of cares (7.65.11–12). *Euangelion* in Greek is the word for Gospel, a joyous message of salvation, and in other contexts it could refer to one's recovery from sickness—perhaps not for Keroullarios himself in this case, but certainly for the emperor and his court philosopher. Keroullarios was an abrasive patriarch who had behaved imperiously toward all the emperors under whom he had served. The last of them, Isaakios I Komnenos (1057–1059), had reached the limit of his patience when he ordered the patriarch arrested and sent off to exile, toward the end of 1058.[25] Keroullarios refused to be helpful by abdicating, which forced the emperor to set up a puppet court to formally depose him. This process could not go well. The verdict was not in doubt, but the patriarch enjoyed some support among the people of Constantinople. These were the cares from which Keroullarios' sudden death, after a brief illness, saved the emperor. But the court philosopher had begun to draw up an indictment, which he probably continued to work on even after the patriarch's death, until it reached its present length; it vehemently accuses Keroullarios of heresy, paganism, political sedition, murder, sacrilege, and conduct unbecoming a hierarch. When Psellos later took on the task of writing a panegyrical funeral oration for Keroullarios (in the early 1060s, around the same time that he was finishing the first edition of the *Chronographia*), there was considerable bad blood between him and his subject.

It is difficult to trace the history of Psellos' relationship to Keroullarios, primarily because his letters to the patriarch, which form the bulk of our evidence, cannot be precisely dated. Their relationship had not always been a bad one. Around the mid-1040s, Keroullarios had sent his fatherless nephews, Nikephoros and Konstantinos, to study under Psellos, and the latter had apparently

---

25. For Keroullarios' career in general, see Tinnefeld (1989).

formed a lasting friendship with them, especially Konstantinos, judging from the intimate nature of their correspondence, which continued into the 1070s to Psellos' death.[26] Konstantinos, as we will see, became an intermediary between the philosopher and the patriarch when things began to sour. And it was these nephews who were the intended audience of the funeral oration; Psellos probably wrote it for their benefit, which also explains why he discusses their father, Keroullarios' brother, at such length toward the beginning (section nos. 7–15). The nephews themselves are mentioned prominently in the text (41), especially at the end, where one of them has a vision of Keroullarios enthroned next to an angel (61).

Referring to the initial stages of their relationship, Psellos claims in the funeral oration that Keroullarios regarded him as his "closest friend" and that he had confessed to him that he had erotic dreams (26). Not much weight can be put on this expression of "friendship," especially in a work such as this.[27] It seems also that Keroullarios consulted Psellos on difficult and esoteric intellectual matters (30, 43–44), and the two exchanged conventional letters and gifts.[28] In a brief letter, whose context is unfortunately irrecoverable, Psellos praises the patriarch for setting aside strict justice in order to show compassion; this related to a third party, but Psellos also thanks him for a favor to himself (*Letter KD* 71). The phrasing of this praise, as we will see, would resonate in later writings. In a sign of growing estrangement, Psellos protests in another letter that the patriarch has excluded him and cut him off from access to his person: his attempts to make contact were being viewed with suspicion and hostility (*Letter S* 159). In a follow-up letter, Psellos admits that he now has slightly more access, but only through the patriarch's nephew Konstantinos, which was not good enough (*Letter S* 160). The background and the causes of his complaints are impossible to tease out.

Another letter reveals a dramatic escalation of tension and even hostilities (*Letter S* 139). The patriarch, according to Psellos, has sent repeated storms and waves to buffet him, almost drowning him. His goons (to whom Psellos gives nicknames, such as "the bearded comet") have attacked him mercilessly; priestly hands have dragged him from the sanctuary and torn him to pieces;

26. The letters are listed in Papaioannou (1998) 101. One of them is translated by Papaioannou in Kaldellis (2006) 173–175. The nephews' study under Psellos is mentioned at the end of the *Funeral Oration for Keroullarios* 41.

27. Cf. Tinnefeld (1973).

28. Psellos, *Letters S* 56–59, 162, 164.

and an ecclesiastical synod is now heaping charges on him, accusing him not of a private fault but a public crime. Psellos begs the patriarch to put an end to this persecution and save him. We do not know whether this situation was related to the alienation between the two mentioned in the letters discussed above, but it fits the context of the last year of the emperor Konstantinos IX Monomachos (i.e., 1054). Psellos' friends and allies (Mauropous, Leichoudes, and Xiphilinos) had all left the court by then, and the emperor was weak. According to a traditional narrative, the patriarch had just subverted the emperor's negotiations with the Latins, even using the threat of popular unrest to force Monomachos' hand (this narrative is problematic on many levels, but here is not the place to revisit it). Psellos in fact had been employed by the emperor in those negotiations, at least at the minimal level of delivering documents back and forth.[29] We know from other texts that this period was a dangerous one for Psellos. He sought desperately to flee from the court and the ailing and unsteady monarch, eventually by becoming a monk and going to Mt. Olympos in Bithynia to join Xiphilinos.[30]

Why was the Synod investigating Psellos? All the evidence that we have indicates that he was being accused of some combination of occult paganism that stemmed from his intellectual interests. In the *Chronographia*, he says (without reference to a Church synod) that before Monomachos' death many suspected that he had such powers, and he proceeds to give a long but ambiguous defense of his intellectual interests as not being necessarily unChristian.[31] His funeral oration for his mother, which was actually written in the final days of Monomachos, also concludes (27–30) with a long account and justification of Psellos' pagan and occult interests. The purpose of this text is to show that his philosophy was really inspired by the ascetic and pious example of his mother, which also now led him to the monastic life and away from Monomachos' court! Psellos' preoccupation with his intellectual integrity seems, then, to have been quite intense in the year 1054/1055, and it is the only time when we can date a formal, and hostile, investigation by the Synod under Keroullarios. This is also the likely context for the "Exposition of the Faith," in form a personal confession, "delivered to the emperor Monomachos in order to refute those who were slandering him."[32] Psellos is still called Konstantinos

29. See the Synodal Decree of 1054 in Will (1861) 166.
30. E.g., Psellos, *Chronographia* 6.191–203; and see below.
31. Psellos, *Chronographia* 6A.10–12; see Kaldellis (1999) 119–127 and passim.
32. Psellos, *Theologica II* 35 (pp. 133–136).

(not Michael) in this exposition, so its delivery took place before he went to Bithynia.[33] But it is not clear that Keroullarios himself was necessarily the motive force behind the persecution.

This background can cast a sinister light on something that Psellos reports neutrally in the *Funeral Oration for Keroullarios* (43), namely, that Keroullarios so loved Psellos' compositions on esoteric and metaphysical matters that he would listen to him during his visits and interrogate him closely on Scripture: the patriarch had even studied the standard commentaries in advance to be able to test the philosopher properly. This sounds almost like an inquiry. And in the following section of the oration (44), Psellos refers to a falling-out between himself and the patriarch, but this does not seem to refer to the context of his *Indictment against Keroullarios* (completed in 1058); rather, some "people who envied me managed to estrange him from me." This seems to refer to the turbulent events of 1054. Monomachos died in early January 1055, and we cannot date exactly when Psellos departed for his monastic retreat. Another letter (*Letter M* 16) reveals that the persecution continued under Theodora (1055–1056), although we do not know whether this was before or after the Bithynian sojourn (or even during Monomachos' final illness). In this letter, Psellos again complains to the patriarch that their relationship was being poisoned and that he was being besieged. He had defended himself, but the persecution would not stop. He had been on good terms with the patriarch previously, but now he felt that he was being treated badly and inconsistently. A brief reconciliation had given way to a more violent storm. Psellos had not turned to the empress for help, though she was willing to listen. There was another reconciliation, and another turn for the worse. People now suspected his career, his chair, and his customary frankness of speech. The patriarch jabbed at him from the side. Psellos states that his profession of faith was being regarded as insincere. He brought his writings to be scrutinized, and yet Keroullarios was on the lookout for "hidden meanings beneath the surface statements." We know from many of his writings that Psellos was both a close student of the rhetorical techniques of dissimulation and a likely practitioner of them.[34] The matter was, again, primarily about his religion.

The reign of Isaakios I Komnenos (1057–1059) gave Psellos the opportunity to strike back, politically, rhetorically, and philosophically. In the *Chrono-*

---

33. Garzya (1967) 42.
34. Kaldellis (1999) passim and (2007) 205–209.

graphia, Psellos presents the new emperor as sympathetic to his philosophical agenda, the elimination of the arrogant Keroullarios being one pillar of that project.[35] The next relevant text is Psellos' long *Letter to Keroullarios* (chapter 1 in this volume). It is impossible to offer conclusive arguments about tone, especially in such an allusive writer operating on multiple levels. Still, this text appears to be largely polemical and draws a biting contrast between the two lives of Psellos and Keroullarios. It is possible to link it to the context of the arrest of Keroullarios by Isaakios' agents, a move that Psellos openly supported. At the end of the letter, Psellos alludes to an account of the patriarch's life that he is about to write, which may be the indictment. This is confirmed by the reference to Keroullarios' adoption of imperial regalia, which was one of the causes, or pretexts, of his downfall (6).[36]

The *Letter to Keroullarios* is, moreover, a philosophically significant document in its own right, being a declaration of war on ontological, ethical, and epistemological grounds. Psellos distinguishes between two opposing philosophical stances that are exemplified by himself and Keroullarios. Psellos is one who recognizes and accepts that he is a composite of material and spiritual elements, which cannot and should not be separated while we live in the flesh; nor should the flesh be entirely denied, though Psellos playfully refuses to state the ways in which he yields to it (2). This was not merely a strategic approach taken in this letter. In many texts and in explicit terms, Psellos developed a theory that rehabilitated the body from its disparagement by certain philosophical and religious traditions, arguing that human beings are both material and spiritual and should not deny one half of their nature; otherwise put, human beings are not angels and should not be held accountable to angelic standards. Yet this is what some schools of thought seemed to do, which in this instance are exemplified by Keroullarios.[37] Keroullarios, by contrast, has taken a stand in a superior metaphysical realm, from which he looks down upon mere mortals and treats them in an inflexible and inhuman way. Of course, the letter is sarcastic: the patriarch only *imagines* that he is such a Being, but in fact it is all a delusion. Psellos uses the terms of mysticism, religious initiation, and divine inspiration to define the sources of his delusion, whereas he specifies that his own sources of knowledge are books and a study of the natural sciences.

35. Kaldellis (1999) 167–178.
36. Dagron (2003) 237–247.
37. In general, Kaldellis (1999) 80–89, 154–167; (2007) 209–219.

The ethical consequences of Keroullarios' epistemology are grave. Human beings require a more adaptive approach. Keroullarios has become contemptuous of true learning, immune to eloquence, and terrifying to other people: "You . . . 'came not to bring peace, but a sword,' and you cause division among the nations, stirring up families against each other" (6). In fact, "I love, you hate; I make peace, you detest; I appease, you drive others away; I honor by praise, you abuse" (9). Psellos goes further and hints that there is in fact no way to theologize without first acquiring a rational education, the sort of thing that he teaches, and that to theologize without it courts destruction (5). Psellos boasts that Isaakios is now a philosopher-king and will implement a new agenda (4).

Some of the allusions Psellos deploys in the letter deepen his critique of Keroullarios' commitments. He applies to the patriarch words spoken about (or by) Jesus Christ (especially the allusions to John 3:13, Ephesians 2:14, and Ephesians 1:20 and 2:6 in section 1), thereby hinting that Keroullarios had reached to rather blasphemous heights in his supernatural exaltation. An allusion with striking implications may be contained in the first line of the letter: "O most prolific and affectionate of fathers." The editor of the text, Criscuolo, detected an allusion to 4 Maccabees 15:13, the story of a mother with seven sons (which qualifies her as a πολύτεκνη, which I have rendered "prolific"). The "tyrant" Antiochos commands the woman and her sons to renounce their faith and threatens them with death if they refuse. She prefers to see her children cruelly murdered, for "she preferred to preserve her faith instead, which leads to eternal life" (15:3). The pious author repeatedly designates her decision as "affectionate." This allusion—if it is that—sets the tone for the letter, which basically argues that Keroullarios has sacrificed his feelings of humanity to his metaphysical allegiances. The lines directly before and after 4 Maccabees 15:13 are significant in this context: "the mother exhorted her children to embrace a pious death," and, "seeing each tortured and burned, her disposition was not affected in the slightest, on account of her piety." On the other hand, just because we can develop the comparison does not mean that an allusion to 4 Maccabees was intended here; the verbal similarities may be only coincidental.

The *Funeral Oration for Keroullarios* was written under Konstantinos X Doukas. Section 60 alludes to a ceremonial presence of that emperor and his wife, Eudokia, Keroullarios' niece, at the deceased patriarch's tomb. It is possible that this speech was written in connection with that ceremony, which may have been an annual event,[38] though we do not know exactly in what year. The speech was also apparently written for the benefit of Keroullarios' nephews, Konstantinos and Nikephoros, with whom Psellos was on good terms and who are mentioned prominently in the work itself. One of Psellos' letters (*Letter KD* 31) reveals that Konstantinos was placed on trial for serious charges at some point early in Doukas' reign, between 1059 and 1063, around the time when the funeral oration was composed. This trial was of sufficient importance that the emperor and empress (Eudokia), the *kaisar* Ioannes, and the patriarch Leichoudes watched it closely. Konstantinos seems to have been cleared, because his career was not interrupted. But at the time, Psellos describes the trial as quite serious. It may have been connected to a major plot to overthrow the Doukas regime in the spring of 1060, a plot described in our narrative sources as enjoying fairly widespread support among the nobility in the capital.[39] If that is the case, then the nephew's relationship to Keroullarios—a man who had been involved in three challenges to imperial authority, real or alleged, against three emperors (in 1040 against Michael IV, in 1057 against Michael VI, and in 1058 against Isaakios I)—cannot have helped Konstantinos' image at the time of his trial. It is possible that the funeral oration was written against the backdrop of that event, or soon after, to clear the family name. It specifically tries to exculpate the patriarch, at least in part, from the stigma of sedition. After all, in 1054 Psellos had used the *Encomium for His Mother* to achieve a similar political goal in the battle over impressions at the court.

The mostly polemical themes of the long *Letter to Keroullarios* are present in the funeral oration as well. Psellos was willing to rehabilitate his old nemesis, but only up to a point, and he ensured that certain underlying tensions remained visible. The interplay between the two texts is subversive of the longer and later one (consider, for example, the discussions of Keroullarios' alleged "martyrdom" in the funeral oration in light of the sarcastic reference to it at the end of the letter). The following remarks will touch on some of the themes that Psellos wove into the oration, which sometimes appear as its subtext and which promote distinctively Psellian interests.

Consider, for instance, the argument of the introduction (1). Psellos begins the oration by countering the argument of "some" who believe that both speech and virtue are in decline. Speech is what Psellos is about to offer us,

38. M. Jeffreys (personal communication).
39. Cheynet (1990) 71.

and virtue is the virtue of his subject matter, the patriarch. But Psellos' rejection of this double dilemma is not balanced. He flat-out denies that there has been any decline in virtue. However, it does seem that there has been a decline in speech-making; Psellos admits this. Virtue has not been acknowledged, then, not because it is not still being produced but because it is not being praised properly. In fact, ancient virtue might have been exaggerated by the superior speeches that were made about it at the time. Psellos is going to restore a balance. In other words, the point of his speech will be to effect a change in the powers of speech: it is *speech* that Psellos has come to change, not virtue, which more or less remains constant among mankind. What has changed instead is the appearance of speakers such as Psellos. This, then, is the distinctive aspect of the opening argument of the oration, though it is sometimes paired with conventional disclaimers about the orator's inability to do justice to the vastness his subject.

Rhetoric for Psellos is not devoid of virtue; it is not only about the surface beauty of things. There is a form of it that philosophy itself adopts because it too points to truth and understanding (cf. 7). In all three patriarchal funeral orations, Psellos insists repeatedly that a fundamental aspect of rhetoric is its ability to make proper distinctions; in other words, both rhetoric and the practice of virtue require an ability to classify and know what is appropriate to the situation (27; cf. 30). Philosophical adaptation is done to benefit the other person; merely adapting for advantage is a trait of mere sophistry. For all that, far from hiding rhetoric's ability to distort reality, Psellos highlights it here just as he did in the first edition of the *Chronographia*, which he was writing at the same time: rhetoric can choose whether to present one and the same thing in a negative or a positive way (30, and especially 55, 60).[40] He wants us to remember this as we read a panegyrical account of Keroullarios, and alludes strongly in section 55 to his own parallel work, the *Indictment against Keroullarios*.

In the discussion of Keroullarios' parents (3–4), Psellos touches on themes that he develops more fully elsewhere. In the case of his father, Psellos makes an argument for the compatibility of virtue and public life, and how the two reinforce and even improve each other when they are lived together. Psellos is arguing here implicitly against the long-standing religious tradition that one can be most virtuous only in holy isolation, away from the city.[41] Rather, he is

---

40. Kaldellis (1999) 127–154.
41. For Psellos and monasticism, see Kaldellis (1999) 80–89.

arguing for a form of sanctified civic virtue, unique to Psellos' theory of the human soul as an essentially political being. He develops this theory further in the *Chronographia* (6A.7–9) and the *Funeral Oration for Leichoudes* (see the discussion of Leichoudes below). In the case of his mother, we have a theory of sanctified housewifery. These are people who earn the highest religious praise while going about their ordinary, secular lives. Psellos is literally domesticating religious rhetoric. Moreover, he goes out of his way to praise the mother's beauty, not so much because she was beautiful but because he wants to reject the long-standing philosophical tradition of disparaging physical beauty, a theme that is also prominent in the *Encomium for His Mother*.[42] He goes on to praise Keroullarios' physical beauty (5–6), digressing on the importance of this quality and taking a stand against the ancient philosophers who did not think highly of it. His theory is that a little spiritual beauty is superior to great bodily beauty, but between men of equal spiritual beauty the one who is better looking is superior. Psellos was the first thinker in the history of the Greek philosophical tradition to have a theory about this, that is how to factor physical beauty as a *positive* trait into a schema for generating a moral hierarchy.

But these matters, interesting though they are, are only introductory. The core of the *Funeral Oration for Keroullarios* is a discussion of ethics, and here the work veers close to the themes of the *Letter to Keroullarios*. In describing Keroullarios' separation from his brother after the suppression of the 1040 conspiracy, Psellos introduces us to the patriarch's view of philosophy.

> He was a truly philosophic soul, devoted to God and neglecting every other preoccupation. His was a god-like mind that had advanced truly to what was beyond all intellect. He did not take any care of mundane affairs, though he made an exception for his brother: he really lived for him. That seemed to be the only unphilosophical trait of that man who was otherwise devoted to philosophy. (14)

In other words, perfect philosophy according to Keroullarios would have been utter indifference to anything but metaphysical truth, and this is in accordance with the letter. In the funeral oration, however, Psellos immediately counters this with his own view, siding with the family-oriented Old Testament over the more radical New Testament:

---

42. Kaldellis (2006) 39, 43–45.

I think that complete impassibility and impartiality toward all other people is a sign of a callous, not a philosophic soul. I have not met anyone practicing such a philosophy, unless it be some people who have been cut off from all fellow-feeling since the time of their birth. Yes, we must despise our parents, brothers, sons, and even our own life, if that is possible, for the sake of God, choosing God in their place, but we should not cast off our family altogether. The nearer we come to God, the more we should take care of our kin. This is what the Ten Commandments clearly teach us. (14)

In other words, Keroullarios was a philosopher along Psellos' lines (because he loved his brother) in spite of *his own* view of philosophy, which would have him be completely impassive.

Later in the oration, Psellos describes Keroullarios' more metaphysical orientation in life, but in a way that reveals his own fundamental assumptions about what such people are like: "He was possessed by God, but that made him neither gloomy nor broody; rather, he was filled with a spiritual joy" (23). And, "I know that all those who fight against pleasure tend to sweat a lot, being very anxious; they are gloomy; their eyes are dry; they look sullen and do not like to come into contact with other people. But he, even though leading such a life, was full of grace" (26). We may suspect, of course, that the exception being made here for Keroullarios is for the purposes of this speech. Psellos has to make the patriarch be devoted to his family in particular (see 41: "bound to his family through the natural bond of love"—so he is a natural creature after all), because it is for their benefit that he was writing the speech.[43] But if we step outside its rhetorical constraints, we may find that the patriarch was not so different from other men of his otherworldly type.

After Keroullarios' elevation to the patriarchal throne, Psellos delivers a lesson in ethics. He draws the usual distinction between the contemplative and active lives and adds his own preferred "third way" that combines the two (24). Keroullarios, however, "invented a fourth path, not discovered by anyone else. This path has been followed by the angels, who are above us, since the time of their creation by God." The patriarch was allegedly able to *simultaneously* have his mind turned toward God and deal with the worldly matters pressing on his attention (also 27, 32, 43); Psellos' third way, by contrast, would have us alter-

---

43. In the *Funeral Oration for Xiphilinos* 17, Psellos states that natural affection pulled him away from Mt. Olympos (effectively, away from monasticism) and back to his family.

nate between the two. Of course, readers of the *Letter to Keroullarios* should be wary of such "angelic men." And in fact the strains of extreme asceticism and denial of nature creep into the funeral oration and take over the patriarch's image. We are told that Keroullarios "defeated human nature" and "had overcome his nature in a supernatural manner" (25, 32), and this was the sum of his "philosophy." Psellos reminds us, however, that we are composite creatures, rational and irrational, the latter desiring physical beauty for the purposes of sex. But he had thoroughly tamed the irrational part (26, 32), despising the body because he had had a vision of metaphysical reality (43). He was metaphysical even while still physical, being "beyond nature and becoming, even while still alive" (60). Death brought only perfection to the patriarch's chosen way of life (60).

In the *Chronographia* (6A.8), Psellos argued that the management of state affairs required a certain degree of flexibility: human beings cannot in practice be governed by rules as rigid as metaphysical doctrines. When he broaches this topic in the funeral oration, Psellos says that Keroullarios was adaptive: "Like all experienced orators, he took care to find the appropriate time for each act . . . he permitted himself freedom of speech as occasion served and adapted his speech to his interlocutor's character" (27; also see 29, 31–32). But he undercuts this picture already at the end of the same section, highlighting a fatal flaw in the patriarch's character that will recur throughout the speech, and suggesting that it stemmed from his metaphysical orientation: "Sometimes he went against the current, and many people believed that he abused his outspokenness. In fact, that was just an excessive application of the teachings of his higher knowledge" (27). He would often come across as inflexible and intransigent rather than adaptable (34), and many regarded him as a severe and rather angry person (35). Psellos does not counter the accusation but instead explains its cause: Keroullarios burned with a fiery passion to make everyone as Christian as possible, even by "whipping" and "terrifying" them into compliance. Psellos adds that this view was in accordance with the message of the Gospel. It was something about which Psellos could say—and *did* say, in the first sentence of the letter—that "the grounds for my *praise* here are drawn from personal experience" (my emphasis). Keroullarios' greatest virtue was his zeal for the faith, which was burning hot (39) and led to the rupture with Rome.

In the end, Keroullarios was undone by his arrogance and inflexibility. We can glimpse this verdict in the funeral oration. In the tension with Theodora's supporters, he looked only to higher things, "neglecting all other considerations" (46). And in his struggle with Isaakios he simply failed to adapt to circumstances (53). The "world" had the last word in dealing with the obstinate prelate. And Psellos too gains the last word in his struggle with Keroullarios through his funeral oration. He presents himself as superior to Keroullarios in ways that mattered most to him, in his knowledge of astronomy and rhetoric, for example (9). In their later discussions,

> if I am permitted to say so, he spoke less philosophically than I did in responding to him. I am addressing his own soul, who knows that: he is a jury that cannot be cheated. What I gave him in return for his disposition toward me was not only equal but greater than his own offering, to the same degree that this man was greater and more important than me (44).

Psellos and Xiphilinos

Keroullarios provided Psellos with the opportunity to explore the ethical consequences of metaphysical commitments; Leichoudes, discussed in the next section, provided him with a peg on which to hang an image of the ideal learned statesman; and his relationship with Xiphilinos was a case study of competing *intellectual* choices. Psellos and Xiphilinos had met during their studies; they made their first mark in the capital as educators (albeit in different fields); and they entered the court of Konstantinos IX Monomachos as part of a team of learned advisors, endowed by the emperor with prestigious positions in the revamped schools of the capital. They were friends and allies, but they differed in philosophical approach and eventually also in their attitude toward monasticism. Psellos again would have the last word: his texts dominate our view of the conversation.

When Psellos and Xiphilinos met as students, the latter was older and more advanced.[44] Still, in the *Chronographia* Psellos states openly that Xiphilinos and Mauropous were "lovers of philosophy, whereas I was a more perfect philosopher" (6.192). The grounds for tension existed from the beginning. In the *Funeral Oration for Xiphilinos*, Psellos stresses the fact that he himself was devoted to the study of higher subjects, namely, philosophy and rhetoric, while Xiphilinos was studying a manifestly inferior one, that is, law. Nevertheless, Xiphilinos intuitively studied law in a philosophical way, and later the two of them studied each other's fields as well, bringing them into mutual balance

---

44. *Funeral Oration for Xiphilinos* 5; *Funeral Oration for Leichoudes* 4. For the career of Xiphilinos, see in general Bonis (1937).

(5–6). Thus Psellos, for all that he was younger, emerges as philosophically superior. This contrast, we should note, is reminiscent of the similar claims made in the *Funeral Oration for Keroullarios* (see above). Psellos retained his advantage in being the first to secure a court appointment: he became imperial secretary, and only then was Xiphilinos appointed a judge (8–9). So far the speaker has outstripped his subject. No wonder he apologizes repeatedly in the funeral oration for talking about himself so much (5, 7, 11, 15).

There follows the notoriously convoluted and obscure description of the two "schools" that Psellos and Xiphilinos ran on the side, namely, of philosophy-rhetoric and of law, respectively, after what appears to have been a period of decline in the teaching of these disciplines. The presence of these two schools seems to have polarized the students in the capital and led to the belief that Psellos and Xiphilinos were rivals, even enemies. Next, their possibly private schools were co-opted (in a way that remains unclear) by Konstantinos IX Monomachos. The narrative in section 10 has baffled the scholars who have tried to reconstruct the background, events, and institutions behind the creation of the teaching (and administrative?) posts for our two scholars: the so-called "Consul of the Philosophers" and the "Guardian of the Laws" (*nomophylax*), respectively.[45] It seems that Monomachos kept transferring them back and forth between the palace and their teaching positions.

Intellectually and politically, Psellos presents himself as being slightly in the lead, ahead of Xiphilinos. This order is reversed, however, when he turns to their allegedly mutual decision to flee the court and become monks (12–14). Here, Xiphilinos took the lead and implemented his resolution before the situation at the court became intolerable; Psellos, by contrast, waited until the last possible moment (15–16; for the context of his departure, see the discussion of Psellos and Keroullarios above).[46] The date of Xiphilinos' departure cannot be fixed (ca. 1050–1053); we have a letter by Psellos promising to follow him ("not everyone is called to follow the path at the same time": *Letter S* 36 = *Letter KD* 273).[47] But pressured by Keroullarios' inquiries (see above) and abandoned by Monomachos, Psellos eventually left for Mt. Olympos in Bithynia

45. See the works cited in notes 43 and 45 of section 10.

46. See also Psellos, *Chronographia* 6.193–200.

47. Other letters that may refer to Psellos' imminent or recent tonsure and departure from Constantinople for Mt. Olympos include *Letters S* 114 and 115 (about going to the court after his tonsure), 101 (claiming he has been cut off from holding secular positions), 185 (defending himself from the charge of being a sophist and not a philosopher), and possibly *Letter KD* 170; see also below.

to join Xiphilinos, a meeting that he described in joyous terms (16–17). Psellos' monastic retreat, however, was a disaster: he was not cut out for asceticism, he was cut off from his family, books, and the capital, and he quickly returned, probably within the year (1055). (As mentioned earlier, he also managed, while at Olympos, to stir up an acrimonious dispute with some of the monks.)

At this point, we must pause in our discussion of the *Funeral Oration for Xiphilinos* and turn to the two letters by Psellos to Xiphilinos that are also translated in this volume, because the background exchange that they imply helps to explain the persistent references to Plato in the oration and the work's strange conclusion. Psellos and Xiphilinos continued to correspond between Psellos' departure from Bithynia in 1055 and Xiphilinos' return to Constantinople in late 1063. The long and bitter *Letter to Xiphilinos* (*Letter S* 175) is probably to be dated toward the start of that period, possibly in 1055–1057, because it refers to Psellos' recent tonsure (e.g., section 2). It was written in response to a letter sent by Xiphilinos that contained serious accusations against Psellos, which resonated powerfully with the investigations of Keroullarios one or two years earlier. We can partially reconstruct those accusations from Psellos' reply. But it also seems that Xiphilinos' letter was, in turn, a response to Psellos' earlier *Letter KD* 191, which is the first of the two letters between them that are translated in this volume (chapter 4). Xiphilinos seems to have mocked Psellos' use of geometrical theory (cf. the "lines" discussion in the long *Letter to Xiphilinos*) to define the soul and his geographical example of men from Libya and Europe. These are distinctive points of contact between the two letters. It is, however, possible that there were more exchanges between *Letter KD* 191 and the *Letter to Xiphilinos*; at any rate, they belong in a tight series.[48]

In evaluating the course of this dispute, we have to realize that there is nothing controversial in *Letter KD* 191: Psellos was writing a fairly conventional letter of friendship, drawing on classical and Christian examples to illustrate his feelings of separation from his friend, to position himself between the ideals of quiet contemplation (practiced by Xiphilinos in Bithynia) and the active life (to which Psellos has now returned), and to present himself as torn between them, while conceding the upper hand to Xiphilinos in terms of virtue. He could not have been expecting what he received. Xiphilinos had apparently had enough of his old friend's temporizing, evasiveness, possible insincerity, and incurable flirtation with pagan teaching, to say nothing of his disgraceful behavior on

---

48. Criscuolo (1975) 123 hesitates to draw them so closely together.

Mt. Olympos. Suspicions must have been building up that took Psellos by surprise. In his own letter, Xiphilinos seems to have referred dismissively to "your Plato" and accused Psellos of "abandoning God to cling to Plato and the Academy" (2) by "separating us from Christ and ranking us with Plato" (7). Underlying issues included the utility of secular learning to men who had now embraced a higher way of life (monasticism) as well as the validity of a rationalist view that asked for proof for everything to be believed (2, 4).

To understand Psellos' response in the long *Letter to Xiphilinos*, we must first identify the exact tone of its opening. This opening is often wrongly read as the triumphant claim that "Plato *is* mine!" (i.e., you have no claim to him). In fact, it is a statement of outrage: "How *dare* you say that Plato is *mine*!" (i.e., that I belong to Plato and, by extension, not to Christ). Psellos *does* eventually lay claim to Plato (see 7), but only after laying the proper foundation for such a claim. Invoking the right Church Fathers in support,[49] he argues that ancient philosophy, beyond the stylistic merits of an author such as Plato, is not only useful but perhaps also necessary for the proper understanding of Christian doctrine; moreover, one cannot claim to have grasped the essential points of disagreement between the two sides without having first studied pagan thought in detail in order to understand exactly where and how it goes wrong in comparison to Christian thought. Only then can one say that one "owns" Plato (as we say in modern English), that is, claim to have mastered him and to know both his strengths and weaknesses. Lacking such study, Plato "owns" you, which is what he now says to Xiphilinos: Plato is "yours" (2). Indiscriminate blame of Plato is equivalent to ignorance of his work, which opens the field to powerful counter-accusations: "you *Plato-hater* and *misologist*, lest I call you a *hater of philosophy*" (2). Finally, Psellos raises issues of exegesis, namely, that much of Scripture cannot (or should not) be taken literally because it figurally represents metaphysical truths that can be stated in a nonfigurative way only by using the language of Neoplatonism (see section 5 on Moses' ascent to Sinai).[50]

This argument for the importance and validity of pagan philosophy was probably the strongest that Psellos could muster under the circumstances, given the character and inclinations of his correspondent. It is more rhetorical bluster and posturing than anything. And he slips in some jabs as well, for example, his observation that Jesus was to be seen often in the marketplace, not

49. For this rhetorical strategy, see Kaldellis (2012).
50. Kaldellis (2007) 198–202.

so much in the mountains (6). At issue was whether Psellos could be regarded as a Christian thinker. Some in the Holy Synod of Constantinople had denied it in 1054; Xiphilinos was now also having doubts; an anonymous satirist denied it soon after Psellos' death;[51] and the question still remains open today. Xiphilinos seems to have been appeased, at any rate, perhaps mistaking the anger of Psellos' response as pious sincerity. Their relationship was restored, and Psellos implies in the funeral oration (18–19) that he personally arranged Xiphilinos' elevation to the patriarchal throne in 1063–1064.

Let us now return to the funeral oration, written almost twenty years after the bitter exchange of ca. 1056. We do not know whether Psellos and Xiphilinos had continued to debate the merits and flaws of ancient philosophy and of Plato in particular, but the oration, as always, allowed Psellos to have the last word. He says here that Xiphilinos "despised Plato and his doctrines, but he admired and praised him for eulogizing the method of division" (6). What is noteworthy, however, is how densely Psellos uses ideas, expressions, and images taken from the Platonic dialogues in this oration specifically, far more so than in the others (they can be tracked through the notes to the translation). He gives us a Platonizing reading of Xiphilinos. The ascent of Xiphilinos' soul while he was a monk is presented in textbook Neoplatonic terms, as if this were one of Psellos' lectures on Plotinos (18); it picks up on and continues what he had said about Moses and Sinai in the *Letter to Xiphilinos*. His elevation to the patriarchal throne is presented as a Platonic descent into the cave (19).

The oration pays perfunctory attention to Xiphilinos' moral virtues. Psellos notes that the office of patriarch enabled him to combine the contemplative and the active lives (20); he briefly discusses his continued asceticism, adornment of churches, and charity (21). But the climax of the oration, taking up a large part of the whole (22–27), is a methodical exposition of his intellectual pursuits by field and of his attainments in each. Psellos hammers the Platonism home here, too, but in a subtle and indirect way. For example, he introduces an exposition of the Neoplatonic theory of ascent, but only to explain *by way of analogy* how Xiphilinos understood the law in a superior way, that is, similar to the way in which metaphysicians reach for first principles. Psellos has again effectively intruded his own metaphysical thinking into the funeral oration without actually stating that Xiphilinos shared it with him; he uses it ostensibly only as an analogy (22). Likewise, in his discussion of rhetoric he

---

51. For Psellos in the satire *Timarion*, see also Kaldellis (2012) 148–149.

presents Xiphilinos' approach to rhetoric through the *analogy* of the Platonic Demiurge's creation of the world, basically comparing the patriarch to Plato's Creator God, for all that he adds here the obligatory rejection of Platonic metaphysics (22). The following section makes an even more audacious claim. Psellos explicitly positions Xiphilinos at the interface between the pagan and Christian philosophies (23). Unless the patriarch had radically changed his basic outlook on this question in the twenty years since Psellos' *Letter to Xiphilinos*, this does not seem to be where he thought that he stood in relation to pagan and Christian thought. He was a man who seems to have finally dispensed with secular learning altogether. The person who did stand between the two philosophies, however, was Psellos himself.

This section of the funeral speech is strikingly similar to that at the end of Psellos' *Encomium for His Mother*, which lists the author's own fields of interest. In fact, the text in sections 22–27 of the *Funeral Oration for Xiphilinos* can instill in the reader a strange sense of dislocation, as we momentarily lose sight of the fact that it is about someone else, not Psellos himself. Or is it? Has Psellos basically reproduced a list of some of *his own* preoccupations and passed it off under the name and persona of the pious patriarch through a performance of ventriloquism? I find it difficult to believe that Ioannes Xiphilinos would even recognize, much less understand, many of the technical concepts and theories in astronomy, mathematics, geometry, music, and optics that Psellos attributes to him toward the end (26). In fact, the orator has slyly introduced himself into the speech: the driving mode of his exposition is to ask, seemingly rhetorically, "Who understood these matters better than he did?" On the surface level of the rhetorical argument, we are probably meant to think "no one," but if we stop and actually think about it, we realize that these questions point to Psellos himself: it was Psellos who understood these matters better than Xiphilinos. Not only has he revealed, at the beginning of the oration, that he was more philosophically advanced than Xiphilinos, but also the topics that he presents here correspond closely to Psellos' own lectures and didactic works (see again the notes to the translation). He includes a section (23) on the symbolic-Platonic interpretation of Scripture along the same lines that he himself favored in his lectures, surveyed in the *Encomium for His Mother* and defended in the *Letter to Xiphilinos*. In short, Psellos subsumes the patriarch within his own intellectual pursuits, while implying (as he had also stated directly in the case of Keroullarios) that he was superior to Xiphilinos in this regard.

Psellos' intellectual crypto-autobiography in the *Funeral Oration for Xiphilinos* deploys the obligatory and usual Christian precautions, just as the oration for his mother does. In section 24, Psellos dismisses some of the beliefs of a hypothetical partisan of the *Chaldaean Oracles*, which then slips into a sustained critique of some of the deficiencies of Aristotle's thought. The second-person address has led some earlier readers of the text to mistake this as a direct attack on Xiphilinos and his Aristotelian affiliation.[52] There is no reason to think that the past tensions between Psellos and Xiphilinos reflected a dispute between Plato and Aristotle, although some scholars have argued that Christian thinkers generally found Aristotle easier to process, adapt, and adjust to Christianity than Plato.[53] This may be why Psellos turns on Aristotle here, not Plato. In fact, in these sections (24−25) Psellos seems to be criticizing Aristotle mainly for failing to provide the proper foundational concepts by which to do metaphysics, and seems accordingly to be hinting that the Platonic tradition provided solutions for some of the impasses of Aristotelian thought. In section 25, Psellos seems to emerge and speak openly in his own voice now about what he accepts in Aristotelian thought. We momentarily lose sight of the honoree, Xiphilinos, who returns to the speech only to die off. Psellos effectively has the last word in his debate with Xiphilinos over the appropriation of ancient philosophy.

Psellos and Leichoudes

There is less to say about this relationship, because it did not generate visible tension at any point of its history. In fact, were it not for Psellos' idealization of Leichoudes, partly in the *Chronographia* and especially in the *Funeral Oration for Leichoudes*, we would know almost nothing about the man at all, and as it stands what we have is a rather generic character portrait, not a convincing picture of a real person. What is especially interesting about this funeral oration, however, is the date of its composition: for all that Psellos pretends to be speaking at the funeral (19), it was written after the death of Xiphilinos (4), thus after August 1075, at least twelve years following the death of Leichoudes, and probably after the *Funeral Oration for Xiphilinos* was written as well. What led Psellos to retroactively write this speech? In section 4, he states

52. Anastasi (1966) 52−56.
53. For the latest version of this argument, see Siniossoglou (2011).

that he has not yet written a speech for the fourth member of his philosophical coterie of the 1030s and 1040s, that is, Ioannes Mauropous. But since we have such a speech for Mauropous,[54] it must have been written after the funeral oration for Leichoudes. It seems, then, that after the death of Xiphilinos and the composition of his funeral oration, Psellos wrote panegyrical orations for all the members of his circle, first Leichoudes and then Mauropous (who was still alive, and would outlive Psellos).[55] Psellos himself died soon thereafter, though we do not know exactly when.[56]

At critical moments in Byzantine history, Konstantinos Leichoudes held the two highest positions in the realm beneath the emperor: he was the *mesazon* (literally, "middle-man" or "intermediary") of the emperor Konstantinos IX Monomachos (a kind of prime minister in charge of the administration) from 1043 to ca. 1050 (we do not know when he was displaced by rivals at the court), during which time he patronized the "circle of philosophers" around Psellos; and then he was patriarch from 1059 to 1063—Psellos' choice, allegedly, to replace the deposed Keroullarios. And yet, whether as *mesazon* or as patriarch, he is not associated with any particular policy, initiative, or controversy (except for a crackdown on Monophysites). So he was either good at keeping things quiet (a remarkable and rare trait in politicians) or a cipher. Be that as it may, the Leichoudes of Psellos' oration is precisely a cipher, stripped of distinctive human traits and filled up with abstract formulations of Psellos' political ideals.

For Psellos, Leichoudes did not represent the antithesis of Keroullarios. Keroullarios was an extreme (of metaphysical purity and inflexibility), and the antithesis of one extreme would have to be another extreme (in the Platonic scale of things, probably one of bodily indulgence and instability). Psellos was not one for extremes. Rather, Leichoudes for him represented a harmonious mixture of all the best elements of human life, a "middle" point from which one could adapt easily to people and circumstances in all directions and deal with them in the best and most advantageous way. This approach Psellos dubbed "the political life," and it might as well have been the opposite of what Keroullarios represented. Psellos gives a theoretical exposition of the "political personality" in the *Chronographia* when he recounts how Leichoudes was appointed to replace Keroullarios on the patriarchal throne: Leichoudes

54. Psellos, *Orationes Panegyricae* 17.
55. Criscuolo (1983) 34.
56. Kaldellis (2011).

brought a "political" mentality to the priesthood (7.66; cf. also 6.177–179, 7.19).[57] This is the precisely the theoretical template that informs the *Funeral Oration for Leichoudes*. There, Psellos denies that sacerdotal offices are superior to political ones: rather, "the difference between better and worse has to do with one's choices in life and not with career-tracks. The good makes itself equally available to both careers" (13).

In a sense, therefore, Leichoudes represented a "political" takeover of the patriarchal office, a move away from rigid metaphysicians such as Keroullarios. Leichoudes

> actually imported transferable things from the political life into the sacerdotal one, namely, a profundity of judgment, the ability to divide each thing into its elements, honorable conduct, a harmony of habits, and all the other qualities that testify to his divine soul. (14)

Such a "political" man, moreover, knows what is appropriate in each case to each thing. Paradoxically, this means that a "political bishop" should be *less* involved in politics: "Above all, a high priest should not become too involved in public affairs nor display too much ambition regarding them" (14). This is a direct jab at Keroullarios and expresses fully Psellos' strong preference for a secular state free of priestly meddling.[58] A "political" patriarch is a less politicized one because he is more discreet. Unlike Keroullarios (who, in the *Letter to Keroullarios*, comes to bring a sword rather than peace), Leichoudes "belonged to the party of peace" (7). "It was a distinctive mark of his personality that it lacked harshness" (15). Leichoudes is the perfect anti-Keroullarios— for all that he is merely an idea in Psellos' repertoire of human tropes.

Leichoudes combined divine, spiritual, and bodily qualities (1). He proved to be adaptible, "adjusting himself perfectly to the attitudes of his audience" (4), but he also knew, in "the perfect mixture of his character," when to be quiet as well (6). His office of *mesazon* under Konstantinos IX was an apt characterization. He functioned as a knot onto which every branch of the state was tied "in such a way that their highest points all converged there" (6). Even as a student he harmonized the fields of rhetoric and law: "he wove together through

57. The idea has also been explored by Criscuolo in a number of publications, esp. (1981) 20–22; (1982); (1983) 15–16, 60–72. See also Ljubarski (2004) 92–95; Kaldellis (1999) 154–166.

58. Kaldellis (1999) 77–80, 167–184.

each other those arts that seemed to be distinct from each other, and he brought together fields that were generally taken to be discrete and supposed to have no part of each other" (5). "His clothing too was neither excessive nor casually shabby. It always aimed at proportion," so too his diet (8).

Psellos' praise of this idealized Leichoudes cannot be understood apart from his rejection of the inflexible, intransigent, and harsh types exemplified by Keroullarios. He makes clear that the problem originates in religious zealotry, and basically tells them to go to Hell:

> I do not praise those who have decided to overcome their nature or those whose souls are abrupt, who lack empathy and refuse to associate with friends and family. Such a person seems to me to have turned his back on our world, though he also turns to higher matters. . . . Even if he is devoted to God he will not neglect his duty toward his friends nor utterly overlook what is suitable for friends and family. So let those who fly above the air bid us farewell, and *get lost!* I join the ranks of the more empathetic and would rather accept the blame for not philosophizing in a perfect way than for being insensible and lacking feeling toward natural states. (14)

In the *Chronographia* (6A.8), Psellos says that these people should go climb upon their heights and live among the angels, that is, away from us mere mortals. Lack of basic humanity was only one horn of Psellos' two-pronged critique of contemporary monasticism. The other was hypocrisy: in the *Chronographia* he shows that behind the rhetoric of self-denial there often lived gluttonous souls.[59] This critique emerges in the *Funeral Oration for Leichoudes* as well, when he praises Leichoudes for making the monastery that he founded

> a place not for luxury but asceticism. It sufficed for him to give those who chose to philosophize there only as much as sufficed for their necessities, such that they would not want to have anything redundant or even be able to obtain it if they wanted it. (17)

In fact, he claims that Leichoudes was tempted to shutter the whole operation, sell its assets, and distribute them to the needy, and that he was disuaded

---

59. Kaldellis (1999) 80–89.

from doing this by none other than Psellos himself, who convinced him to follow a more moderate path.

In short, the Leichoudes of the oration is a cipher for Psellos' own values and his repudiation of religious zealotry. There are even indications that, in his eternal pursuit of disguised autobiography, Psellos modeled aspects of his old friend on himself. He has been accused of doing this in a number of texts, most amusingly in his *Life of Saint Auxentios*.[60] When he comments, for instance, on Leichoudes' near-infinite versatility—"his nature was suitable for everything" (5)—we gain a glimpse of Psellos' self-presentations in other texts. When he says that Leichoudes "wanted to philosophize in the study of all fields" (7), this resonates with Psellos own much-vaunted polymathy (see *Chronographia* 6.35–43, esp. 6.40). Psellos then implausibly includes in Leichoudes' studies the technical works of the ancient scientists Archimedes, Hipparchos, and Heron (7), on which we know that Psellos lectured and gave demonstrations.[61] Just as he did in the *Funeral Oration for Xiphilinos*, Psellos here too has poured something of himself into his subject. No one wrote a funeral oration or encomium for Psellos when he died. But he had already done so himself, for himself, in so many ways.

Reading between the Lines in the Funeral Orations

Psellos composed funeral orations for two strong personalities, Keroullarios and Xiphilinos, with whom he had rather turbulent relations. It was well known even at the time of these orations that Psellos had also composed the indictment against Keroullarios. Unable to conceal this fact, he tries to refute any accusations that could be leveled against him, in a rather curious manner. In section 55 of the *Funeral Oration for Keroullarios*, he argues that no one can accuse the accusers of the patriarch, since each subject can be judged in two ways, and orators are in a position to present a matter from both perspectives, positive and negative. This is a typical sophistic evaluation of reality. But it is not the only case of such an evaluation by Psellos. In section 40, praising Keroullarios' doctrinal knowledge, Psellos offers an example of his

60. Kazhdan (1983).

61. Cf. Psellos, *Oratoria Minora* 8.168–175 (p. 35); they are mentioned in other places in his works and lectures.

versatility in such matters and of his piety: the patriarch once expressed the view that Judas the Iscariot betrayed our Lord but at the same time became the cause of our salvation. Why did Psellos choose this particular example? The meaning of the passage is obscure, unless one combines it with the passage in section 55. The two passages seem to have the same meaning: even the most detestable act can be judged in a positive manner, depending on the ability of the one who judges it. Rather similar is Psellos' attitude toward the collaborators of the empress Theodora who rushed to proclaim Michael VI Stratiotikos emperor in spite of his inability to govern the state. In section 48 he expresses the view that no one can be considered innocent of his deeds, in spite of the fact that everything is preordained by divine providence. However, immediately afterward he expresses a second thought: we may consider all people innocent, even those who did not hesitate to proclaim an incompetent old man as emperor. It is noteworthy that Psellos does not rush to castigate the persecutors of Keroullarios, the emperors Michael IV and Isaakios I; on the contrary, Psellos points out that both emperors were able administrators and virtuous persons.

In the *Funeral Oration for Keroullarios*, therefore, Psellos' hints concerning the relativity of human acts constitute, so to speak, a theoretical system: men cannot be judged severely; everything is ordained by God; and men are mere executors of his will. In this way, Psellos seeks to exonerate himself for his behavior during the deposition and trial of Keroullarios. Is Psellos to be compared with Judas? In a sense, yes, although he refrains from stating this explicitly. The *Funeral Oration for Keroullarios* is in a way his apology for the *Indictment against Keroullarios* that he had composed earlier. The oration was possibly delivered before or presented to the emperor Konstantinos X and the empress Eudokia, Keroullarios' niece. By comparing himself to Judas, albeit tangentially, Psellos appears to be seeking the dead patriarch's pardon. But the way he presents these hints helps him to avoid a public humiliation. More importantly, he denies the absolute value of human judgments, thus opening the way for a radical reevaluation of the complex system of Byzantine moral values. Psellos is careful enough not to press his point further, but this was a necessary consequence of his views. At the same time, Psellos tries to undermine Keroullarios' moral integrity by referring frequently to the criticisms of his opponents: he does not hide the fact that Keroullarios was accused of arrogance and intolerant behavior toward his fellows. In spite of not adopting those accusations, the fact that he records them is significant.

The relations of Psellos with Xiphilinos were also troubled. Although Xiphilinos and Psellos were initially friends, a certain alienation between them arose, as Xiphilinos gradually adopted more conservative positions concerning the value of the Hellenic heritage so highly esteemed by Psellos. In the *Funeral Oration for Xiphilinos*, Psellos is anxious to compare himself to Xiphilinos. This is done in such a manner as to prove his own superiority: Psellos studied rhetoric and philosophy first, while Xiphilinos devoted himself to the study of law, turning to the liberal arts later on. Seemingly, Psellos praises Xiphilinos for his knowledge of the law, but one should not forget that in his other works, Psellos speaks with contempt for all those who prefer to study law instead of philosophy.[62] Therefore, this part of Psellos' oration, if attentively read, seems to downgrade Xiphilinos. Psellos took his exams first and was appointed secretary in the palace, while Xiphilinos took the same position afterward due to Psellos' intercessions. Psellos was also responsible for the appointment of Xiphilinos as the new patriarch after the death of Leichoudes. In spite of his frequent protests that he has no intention to highlight his own achievements, in fact, Psellos presents himself as the main protagonist of all the events of Xiphilinos' life.

Even more interesting is Psellos' evaluation of the ascetic life. On the surface, both Psellos and Xiphilinos consider the ascetic life the noblest human ideal and are eager to become monks. After initial difficulties, Xiphilinos becomes a monk, while Psellos remains in Constantinople unable to make a decision. Only after the death of the emperor Konstantinos IX Monomachos does Psellos overcome his initial doubts and go to Mt. Olympos to join his friend. After describing Olympos in lyrical terms and giving a moving account of his encounter with Xiphilinos (16–17), he concludes this section of the oration in a rather unexpected way: after all his lyric hymns to the contemplative life of the monks, Psellos does not join the community of Xiphilinos but returns to Constantinople! He does not omit to say that his decision to leave the company of Xiphilinos was painful to him (βοῶν καὶ κοπτόμενος), but he does not bother to give an explanation for it. A long chapter is then inserted (18), in which Psellos, after praising the contemplative life once more, rushes to point out that man is not responsible for his acts but that God preordains everything, and God decided to elevate Xiphilinos to the great dignity of the patriarchate. Xiphilinos is reluctant to accept the offer of that dignity; in sec-

---

62. Psellos, *Philosophica Minora* I 2.2–11 (p. 1).

tion 19 he considers his elevation to the patriarchal dignity as a κατάβασις (descent). In all probability, this is a reminiscence of Plato, *Republic* 539e. In any case, this attitude of Xiphilinos is in agreement with the position of Psellos, as expounded so far: nothing is nobler than the contemplative life. What surprises us is the answer that Psellos gives to the objections of his friend: namely, this elevation is not a descent but rather an ascent, since the patriarchal dignity will give him the opportunity to teach the people, initiating disciples into the mysteries of God. Teaching is nobler than being taught! But then the discussion between the two friends is interrupted by the emperor.

How can this discrepancy be explained? By arguing that the abandonment of the monastic life by Xiphilinos is not a descent but an ascent, Psellos in fact denies the absolute value of the *vita contemplativa* as understood by the Byzantine monks.[63] One may object that we overestimate the importance of this slight inconsistency in the text of Psellos. However, such loopholes and contradictions in the work of a medieval author are not devoid of significance, as Leo Strauss has pointed out; in most cases they may be intentional. To quote a characteristic remark of Strauss in one of his most important essays: "The real opinion of an author is not necessarily identical with that which he expresses in the largest number of passages."[64] Psellos is an author whose ability to conceal his real views has been frequently noted. One should consider the possibility that by denying in a discreet way the absolute value of the monastic life in his *Funeral Oration for Xiphilinos*, Psellos wants to justify his own reluctance to become a monk and his decision to abandon the spiritual pleasures of the monastic life for the more mundane pleasures of the *vita activa*. Psellos was a great teacher himself, and he was proud of being in a position to combine the contemplative life of the scholar with the practical life of the politician.[65] The *Funeral Oration for Xiphilinos*, while seemingly praising his friend, is in a fact an apology for himself and his own life and career.

---

63. On Psellos's rejection of extreme spirituality, see Kaldellis (1999) 160–162.

64. Strauss (1952) 30. See also the remark of Kaldellis (1999) 149: "apparent contradictions may point toward hidden or implied teachings."

65. See, for example, Psellos, *Oratoria Minora* 10.39–45 (p. 41). The term *katabasis* is employed in this passage, too. Psellos employs the same verb *(katabethi)* in his *Letter S* 37 (p. 270) to Xiphilinos in a similar context.

1   *Letter to the Patriarch Kyr Michael Keroullarios*

Anthony Kaldellis

Introduction

For a discussion of this polemical and sarcastic letter to Keroullarios in the context of Psellos' relationship with the patriarch, see the general introduction. The letter was first published as *Letter S* 207 (in *Letters S*, ed. Sathas, vol. 5, pp. 505–513), and then reedited, with an Italian translation and commentary, by Criscuolo (in *Michele Psello: Epistola a Michele Cerulario*, originally appearing in 1973, reissued in a second edition in 1990). Criscuolo's apparatus cites numerous ancient and Byzantine texts that contain expressions similar to those used here by Psellos, without implying that he was alluding to them in all cases. The reader should consult that apparatus to find more parallels than I have chosen to cite here. When I have cited parallels that Criscuolo does not, it is (in almost all cases) because I suspect that Psellos *was* alluding to them. See also the general introduction for a discussion of some of those allusions. The present translation is based on Criscuolo's revised edition. The bold numbers in the translation correspond to section numbers in that edition.

Letter to the Patriarch Kyr Michael Keroullarios

1. You perhaps, O most prolific and affectionate of fathers[1]—the grounds for my praise here are drawn from personal experience[2]—you mystic initiate and contemplator of all that is past and present, that is unspeakable and secret—for many reports celebrate that fact and also no one at all is ignorant of it, unless he has been struck dumb—you, then, just as has been said, left the earth and ascended into the air, from where you had come back down to us,[3] and, associating with the Powers that exist up there and having become similar to them to the best of your ability, you are attempting to lead human life too toward that same form [of being]. But that is unenviable and inimitable. For, as they say, "the boundaries of Phrygians and Mysians are kept separate from one another."[4] And yet you are now situated between the boundaries of the two natures, as it were, resembling our species in form and shape, but with respect to your active operations and your most sharp motions you conform directly to the entities that exist above us. Who then would emulate or imitate you, unless he wanted to fight openly against shadows?

Do not be angry then, you most mild and peaceful man, you who joined together things that were divided and removed the barrier that stood between them,[5] if I have recoiled away from your kind of life and chosen one diametrically opposed to it.[6] For you are a heavenly angel, as Paul's saying

1. Cf. 4 Maccabees 15:13, and see the general introduction for a discussion.
2. At *Chronographia* 4.16.4–5, Psellos uses an almost identical phrase to describe the well-founded suspicions of adultery that Michael IV Paphlagon entertained against the empress Zoe.
3. In John 3:13 Jesus says, "No one has gone up to heaven except for the one who came down from heaven, the Son of Man."
4. A Byzantine proverb indicating the incompatibility of two things.
5. Cf. Ephesians 2:14, on how Jesus brought Gentiles and Jews together by abolishing the wall that stood between them, namely, the Law.
6. Cf. Lucian, *The Downward Journey or The Tyrant* 14, for the expression.

has it,[7] but that thing which I am, a logical nature with a body, I neither could [alter or renounce] even if I wanted to, nor would I want to, even if I could do so,[8] or rather, I am deprived of both ability and desire. But with you, your strength is bestowed by God and your will inspired by divinity. I hope that you do not become enraged at me for not sharing or participating in your frenzy, but rather show leniency to me, who am living the life that has been given to me, or else indicate who of all men has the power to imitate you, or even the will itself to do so. If, however, you have always been some kind of wondrous portent, as every tongue attests, why then are you trying to work similar wonders upon a person who was neither born for such a life nor has any inclination to pursue your art?

2. I confess that I am a man, an animal subject to change and alteration,[9] a logical soul making use of a material body, a novel compound[10] of discordant components. Sometimes, when I can, I lighten the burden on the better part of my being by removing the burdensome weight of the nature conjoined with it (to a reasonable extent), while on other occasions . . . But I am not about to slander myself![11] You alone, however, are of all people unchangeable and unmovable, as though some nature, different from our regular human one, had taken its stand upon itself and become utterly inflexible,[12] indifferent to anyone making peaceful overtures or atoning with tears! Who would emulate you for that?

But so as not to examine the lion too closely,[13] that great beast of prey whose mane flows in waves over the entire earth, I will make a summary, drawn from primary elements and arranged in general headings,[14] of your unenviable nature and your inimitable actions, lest you should frown at me when I am

7. In Ephesians 1:20 and 2:6, God raises up Christ and enthrones him in the heavens.

8. Cf. Synesios, *Letter* 95 (p. 160.10–11), who uses the same phrase to deny that he wants to take vengeance on a bitter enemy; see also his *Dion* 5.

9. Cf. Plutarch, *Placita philosophorum* 1.9 (*Moralia* 882C); according to Thales, Pythagoras, and the Stoics, this is true of matter.

10. Cf. Plutarch, *The Reply to Kolotes* 21 (*Moralia* 1119A); cf. also Clement of Alexandria, *Paidagogos* 2.2 (*PG* 8.412a).

11. Cf. Psellos, *Letter KD* 160 (p. 187.12–14): "for I am a man, a soul attached to a body. Therefore I take pleasure in both concepts and sensations."

12. Cf. Synesios, *Dion* 8: "For I know that I am a man, and not a God, that I should be inflexible toward every pleasure."

13. Cf. Plutarch, *On the Obsolescence of Oracles* 3 (*Moralia* 410C); this was an expression used to expose an exaggerated importance, conclusion, or quality.

14. Cf. Plato, *Timaeus* 26c.

unable to imitate you. From the outset I gathered up knowledge and collected it together over time in small increments; it is, so to speak, of the same age as myself. For I often hold converse with books, and discover some of their contents by inquiring and drawing conclusions on the basis of commonly accepted principles, while the rest, as though I had engaged with the material myself,[15] is conveyed to me by someone who is an expert, who possesses the educative art. Hence I thoroughly mastered some areas of philosophy; I purified my speech[16] through the sophistic arts; I taught my students geometry, and was the first to institute it as a subject; I also discovered some of the principles of musical theory; I set straight not a few accounts of the motions that surround the sphere;[17] I also made the science of our beliefs [Christianity] far more accurate; I expounded the teachings of theology; I disclosed the depth of allegory; and finally—though may the bolt of malicious envy not strike me![18]— I made every science exact.

But for you, wisdom and theology proceed from different first principles, of which we know nothing, nor are we even acquainted with them, unless of course you are referring to the "tablets of Zeus."[19] For you have neither philosophized, nor learned stereometry,[20] nor ever studied books. Neither have you come across any wise men, whether Greeks or barbarians, nor any others,[21] and to us you have plainly appeared to be, as you would say, absolute science-in-itself and wisdom-in-itself.[22] You are not formed of heart and liver, as some physiologists have ascertained about our nature, but of the head, or all at once, like Nature, like the Idea, like the Soul, like the highly-honored Mind. Do you see by how many great mountains, seas, and continents we stand separated directly from one another? Neither could you imitate me, nor would I want or be willing to imitate you.

3. Now see the rest of the picture. Your family is illustrious, on both sides. For both your grandfather and your great-grandfather were, if anyone ever

---

15. This clause is unclear.
16. Cf. Synesios, *Letter* 154 (p. 272.5–6).
17. I.e., the motions of the heavenly bodies.
18. Cf. Homer, *Odyssey* 9.495.
19. Cf. Lucian, *On Salaried Posts in Great Houses* 12.
20. I.e., three-dimensional geometry.
21. What others, if the world is divided between Greeks and barbarians? Old Testament or Christian figures?
22. In Christian authors, *autosophia* designates the absolute wisdom of God.

was, renowned, and their names "lay upon the lips of all men."[23] And on account of this more than anything else you exalt the pinnacle of the sacerdotal career. But for me and for Phokion,[24] lest I also mention some of the Prophets, our ancestry is not highly illustrious, or perhaps it is illustrious, but I will be silent about it. For I want to be characterized not by a rotten conceit, but by my vigorous eloquence. And your dress has had a fine purple border since birth [. . .], as though you held a consular position, its characteristic marks being the twelve axes and the rod-bearers, the symbols of, and first steps toward, the chief-priesthood. I, however, did not need whip-bearing attendants[25] when I was acquiring the rudiments of my learning, and my mantle seemed fit for a self-made philosopher.[26] How, then, can we ever come to an agreement, given that we are so separated in our lives and family origins and characters? For, as though decreed by astral configurations, everything has been done for you in a royal fashion right from the beginning, but for me everything is painfully rough and philosophical; your life has an appearance of novelty and marvel, whereas mine is ordinary and bearable.

For these reasons you shun my company and companionship, you disparage eloquence [or reason] and scorn true culture, and no quality of mine is capable of charming you,[27] neither the language of my improvised speeches, nor my words patterned in beautiful rhythms, nor my mild disposition, nor my philosophical ethos, nor my prosaic and supine character.[28] But I have made Celts and Arabs yield to me,[29] and on account of my fame they regularly come down here to study even from the other continent;[30] and while the Nile

---

23. Cf. Theognis, *Elegies* 1.239: "of many men." Cf. *Greek Anthology* 9.62 (Euenos of Askalon): "of all the Greeks."

24. Cf. Plutarch, *Phokion* 4.1–2.

25. Cf. Plutarch, *On the Delays of Divine Vengeance* 7 (*Moralia* 553A).

26. Cf. Dion Chrysostomos, *Or.* 1.9, who describes himself in this way by emphasizing his sufferings and labors during his exile.

27. According to his self-portrayal in the *Chronographia*, Psellos worked his way up the social and political ladder by deploying his considerable charm on emperors and other powerful men.

28. Cf. Synesios, *On Kingship* 10 (10d–11a). "An ironic self-description if ever there was one": Wilson (1971) 80.

29. A reference to Psellos' foreign students. For a possible Arab student, see Volk (1990) 15–16.

30. I.e., Africa.

irrigates the land of the Egyptians, my speech irrigates their souls.[31] And if you ask a Persian or an Ethiopian, they will say that they have known me and admired me and sought me out. And now someone from across the boundary of Babylon[32] has come to drink from my springs[33] through an insatiable desire of his. One of the nations calls me "a lamp of wisdom," another gives me the name "luminary," while others distinguish me in other ways, with the most beautiful names. You alone have not listened to my lyre, or rather you have heard it, but an oak tree is not fit to hear the Orphic harmony.[34] I want to say nothing more, so greatly excessive is the firmness of your character and the inflexibility of your soul, lest I say also the contempt resulting from the manner of your education.[35]

4. I do not say these things to ridicule you, but rather in admiration of your resistance to all charms. Such a species of man [as yourself] also takes full part in the management of public affairs, and you would never be able to charm it by elegantly adjusting the harmony and concord of the notes. Thus I am in all ways turned against your nature and, even though you have sprung with me from the same source[36] and have been produced from the same furrow, I do not know whether you grew straight up or shot out sideways and thus the family resemblance has became alienated for me. But the most divine and philosophical emperor,[37] upon whom the crown was fitted not because of human favor nor through human action, but, suitably, from above; that most beautiful sapling which sprouted afresh from the other side,[38] has partaken of my quality and nature of existence. Look at the actual mentality of the man. He joins together the philosopher's threadbare cloak with the purple robe, and is now attempting to reintroduce philosophy into imperial affairs, just as once Caesar and Augustus did, and, indeed, anyone else who valued the flower of

31. Cf. Pseudo-Lucian, *Erotes* 45.

32. Probably a reference to Baghdad.

33. For the significance of Psellos' use of this word in the *Chronographia*, see Kaldellis (1999) 15–16.

34. For Psellos *not* being made of oak or rocks, see *Letter S* 7 (p. 308).

35. Or, possibly, "your contempt for learning."

36. Cf. Hesiod, *Works and Days* 108: "gods and mortal men sprang from the same source."

37. I.e., Isaakios I Komnenos (1057–1059).

38. It is not clear what this means; from Asia, where Isaakios' revolt began? Or possibly that Isaakios had a military background, as opposed to the civilian ones of Psellos and his associates.

eloquence. One chose Arrian, another Rusticus,[39] a third someone else still, and appointed them as advisors, counselors, and governors of nations, thus tailoring their political philosophy to their subjects.

But this is nothing new. For you have become utterly self-sufficient within yourself, issuing from that source,[40] and have no need for eloquence or even for wisdom itself,[41] but at the same time you sacrifice the divine Lamb,[42] consecrate your hands with the victim,[43] and dexterously accommodate everything. Each of us is born as a small part of nature and, just as the parts of the body need one another in order to stay together, so too the partial entities that compose whole beings require each other's agreement. See also your colleagues at the pulpit: one of them was assigned to the east,[44] another to Alexandria, while another obtained Palestine,[45] and one more Elder Rome. Well, their [episcopal] thrones snatched them away from us, but reason itself again submits them to us.

5. Now perhaps you have knowledge of ineffable and mystical wisdom, but you are ignorant of that which proceeds from reason and the appropriate theory.[46] I also have a throne here, raised up high and sublime,[47] in no way inferior to yours, lest I say far more self-sufficient, and you will neither theologize, nor expound the canons, nor perform any other divine service, without employing my eloquence. For I am the yardstick and ruler by which these things are measured.[48] But if you set sail across the great and deep ocean of

39. Arrian was the famous author and student of Epiktetos, associated with the emperors Trajan and Hadrian. Rusticus was one of the Stoic teachers of Marcus Aurelius (cf. *Meditations* 1.7, 1.17.4). Psellos draws his list from the orations of the fourth-century philosopher and statesman Themistios (*Or.* 34.8), whose attempt to influence political power in the direction of philosophy through the exercise of rhetoric Psellos clearly aspired to revive.

40. Presumably a divine source.

41. This statement, of course, contradicts the (sarcastic) claim made above that Keroullarios *was* wisdom itself (*autosophia*).

42. Cf. John 1:29, 1:36, etc.

43. Cf. Exodus 29:10, on the procedure to be followed in sacrificing a bull.

44. I.e., the patriarchal see of Antioch.

45. I.e., the patriarchal see of Jerusalem.

46. Possibly referring to rhetorical theory.

47. Cf. Isaiah 6:1: "I saw the Lord seated upon a high and lofty throne."

48. Cf. Aristotle, *Nicomachean Ethics* 1113a33: "For each state of character has its own ideas of the noble and the pleasant, and perhaps the good man differs from others most by seeing the truth in each class of things, being, as it were, the norm and measure of them."

theology upon your raft, I will say to you allusively that "you will hit upon jutting rocks"[49] and arrive at "harborless shores."[50]

But from where do my words flow? It concerns the incongruence and incommunicability that exist between us. I was a lover of philosophy[51] right from the start, while you were mystically involved with those lofty matters that are above us, through which, as you yourself would say, you made your way upon the path of martyrdom, were proclaimed as the winner of the crown,[52] and were judged the chief of the good and sacred company.[53] You succumbed to the better arguments of Scripture[54] [...], through which[55] you obtained the more divine state. [But I ...] except to the extent that I researched homonyms and synonyms, distinguishing individually between them and establishing their nature, investigated the Idea, researched nature, inquired into the causes of number, and specified precisely the nature of philosophical terminology and of logical discourse, and how the two are in accordance and also divided from one another. *You* would call these pursuits nonsensical and vain, but to me they are quite attainable.[56]

6. Let him wear the golden sandal to whom it is destined.[57] But I am so old-fashioned and ignorant that I have not risen above my lot, but rather I must deal with slaves as though they have political rights equal to my own. So then, if I am not invited as a guest to someone's house and share his hearth, I sit at the common table and drink from that same cup. And should someone think less of me, I do not get very angry; should he laugh at me when I slip and fall, I do not cause trouble; should he offend me, I consider the

---

49. Cf. Homer, *Iliad* 16.407.

50. Cf. Euripides, *Helen* 1211 and Homer, *Odyssey* 5.405.

51. Cf. Psellos, *Chronographia* 7.58.1, said of Isaakios I Komnenos.

52. Cf. 2 Timothy 4:7–8.

53. Cf. Psellos, *Chronographia* 7.36.16, where similar words describe Keroullarios as the leader of the plot against Michael VI in 1057.

54. It is possible that γραφῶν here means the legal indictment against Keroullarios, not Scripture.

55. Not the arguments of Scripture; the antecedent is missing.

56. Cf. 1 Corinthians 3:19: "the wisdom of the world is folly to God"; Psalm 93:11: "the Lord knows the reasonings of men that they are vain," quoted approvingly in 1 Corinthians 3:20.

57. I.e., the emperor, as opposed to the patriarch, who was affecting imperial status by wearing purple sandals.

offense to be no more than a childish jest. But in *you* everything is supremely perfect and beyond the very boundaries of our nature! People are more afraid of you than of the conflagration the Chaldaeans talk about.[58] If you speak, they are horrified; if you look at them, they freeze; if you draw your eyebrows together,[59] they die, whence if they have dared to oppose you in some matter, even if they are alive, they are counted as if among the dead. My hand is not accustomed to the twig and the rod,[60] but if it should happen that I see someone being struck by another, I immediately close my eyes and shun the place as though it were a prison. You, by contrast, "came not to bring peace, but a sword,"[61] and you cause division among the nations,[62] stirring up families against each other. These things have been attested and fulfilled by you alone of all the people of our time. And why should I also not speak of the greater and more sublime things?

7. I will briefly use the words of the Apostle. Now, I am not a philosopher or a "teacher,"[63] nor did I take up the yoke of the Lord voluntarily, nor do I "carry around the death of Jesus,"[64] but I have feared the fire of the "divine tribunal"[65]—how else may I put it? I have stood among the catechumens, albeit from afar, and my eye has never looked fixedly upon the sacrificial victim that is carved up on our behalf. But you alone of all men boldly enter into the inner sanctuary[66] with a cheerful soul and smiling lips, and, casually pulling aside the curtain, you circle around the altar[67] and make use of the

58. In Neoplatonic and Byzantine thought, the "Chaldaeans" referred to the mystical doctrines contained (or read into) a set of oracles produced in the second century AD. A conflagration of the world is one idea hinted at in those mysterious verses, which survive only in fragments and quotations today.

59. Cf. Aristophanes, *Clouds* 582, on the power of the Clouds to cause havoc.

60. I.e., to instruments of punishment.

61. Cf. Matthew 10:34.

62. An allusion to the schism of 1054?

63. Cf. 1 Corinthians 12:28. "Philosopher" in this context probably means "monk."

64. Cf. 2 Corinthians 4:10. This sentence can be recast as a question, which changes its meaning: "Am I not a philosopher or a teacher, did I not take up the yoke of the Lord voluntarily, do I not carry around the death of Jesus?"

65. Cf. Romans 14.10.

66. The same expression is used at *Chronographia* 7.36.14–15 to describe the conspirators against Michael VI, who entered Hagia Sophia in order to draw the patriarch to their side.

67. Cf. Psalm 25:6.

incomprehensible and unintelligible Logos [i.e., Christ].[68] For you have approached near to that very "First Light,"[69] and so to you everything else is shadows, dreams, and childish games. For this reason you belittle emperors and rise up against every authority. It was fitting for us to have such an archpriest,[70] who, fighting in the front ranks on our behalf, only not with the sword and lance but through speech and command, has demonstrated just how much power the full-length purple robe and the crown-headband really have. These privileges of yours have been announced from above.[71] Or do you not remember them, you most divine and energetic of archpriests?

But perhaps you do remember and prefer to stay silent, and you may not take pride in the account; yet its amazing quality will make the narrative seem all the better to me. For as soon as you obtained the archpriesthood, God signified all that was to happen. A crashing stroke of lightning[72] immediately smashed the holy ground,[73] and part of it was consumed by flames while the rest of it was girded, as it were, by bands of a silver-gray color, upon which was impressed the design of a fiery dove. Being a man with great respect for divine things, you reverently consecrated it, bounding it all around with bronze and honoring it as much as was reasonable. Now, does the oracle concern us? Or rather . . .—But may it be averted from me! Pacify, propitiate, and thus "may the destruction cease."[74] Otherwise . . .[75]—But you, my most divine emperor, "strap your sword at your side, in beauty and majesty,"[76] and become, for my sake, an extinguisher of this divine and non-material conflagration!

8. My discourse must now be called back to its proper sequence.[77] I have neither offended nor hated a single person, so uncontroversial am I. But you, as though you possessed some other nature alongside the familiar one, believe

68. Cf. Plutarch, *The Reply to Kolotes* 20 (*Moralia* 1118D).

69. Cf. Pseudo-Dionysios, *The Ecclesiastical Hierarchy* 3.1.

70. Cf. Hebrews 7:26.

71. A reference to the stroke of lightning about to be discussed.

72. Cf. Aischylos, *Prometheus* 361: the bolt sent by Zeus to destroy the monster Typhon.

73. I.e., a church.

74. Cf. Psalm 105:30. In this sentence Psellos mixes second- and third-person imperatives.

75. It is not clear what the implication of this (deliberately) incomplete sentence is supposed to be.

76. Cf. Psalm 44:4 (LXX). Psellos is calling upon the emperor to protect him from the patriarch.

77. Cf. Psellos, *Chronographia* 6.46.12.

that our species is a foreign one, and you reveal the disgraces of some men while generating grounds for censure against the rest. You frown at everyone, perhaps educating them in moderation, therefore I have inquired about you, as though to the Pythia, whether I should call you a God or a man,[78] or neither, but rather the midpoint between the two. And you, a populist, cannot endure monarchy, but I often proclaim the old Homeric saying, which in turn became an Aristotelian teaching: "let there be one ruler, one king."[79] For long ago it was one and the same man who stood forth on behalf of humankind as both a propitiator and a defender, but now the compound is divided into two parts: the function of the one [the emperor] is to rule, of the other [the patriarch] it is to conduct sacerdotal matters. Come, then! "Raise beseeching hands toward God"[80] and make your peace with men and God, but political affairs will be governed by those to whom they are assigned.[81] Up to what point will you choose, with all your strength,[82] the alliance made on our behalf?[83] You stripped down brilliantly for "the race, kept the faith, and ran the course," so now accept the contest's "crown,"[84] which is a leisure from cares! May you neither rule nor reign over us, for you are too vast to be comprehensible, at least to the majority.

9. Do you see that even I have neither understood you nor accepted your hegemony? I love, you hate; I make peace, you detest; I appease, you drive others away; I honor by praise, you abuse; I endured an entire age of tyranny, but you, however, as though you had just now begun to rule, are eagerly contending to surpass the past with the present.[85] I have experienced Paul's struggles,[86] "in danger from false brothers,"[87] "abounding in griefs,"[88] slandered, the victim of tyranny, enduring every kind of unjust plot, which I neither resisted nor

---

78. In Xenophon's *Apology* (15), Socrates says this of the Spartan lawgiver Lykourgos, but within the context of his own Delphic revelation, according to which Socrates was the most free, the most just, and the most moderate man.

79. Cf. Homer, *Iliad* 2.204; Aristotle, *Metaphysics* 1076a4.

80. Cf. Deuteronomy 32:40; Synesios, *Letter* 11.

81. I.e., leave the governance of secular matters to the emperor.

82. Cf. Sophokles, *Ajax* 408.

83. The meaning is obscure.

84. Cf. 2 Timothy 4:7, which speaks of the "good race" and the "crown of justice."

85. This is obscure.

86. Cf. 2 Timothy 4:7.

87. Cf. 2 Corinthians 11:26.

88. Cf. 2 Corinthians 8:13–14.

countered with plots of my own, speaking the truth, never slandering. This alone has been a consolation in my misfortunes: with Paul I have surrendered myself "to the deep";[89] with Peter I have been crucified, or will be crucified; I incur danger along with the rest of mankind; I die with Phokion.[90] But hold back the blow of my chastisement. "The day will come . . ." and all that comes after that, according to those verses.[91] Then I too will lie with my fatherland, I will be delivered to you with my compatriots, and from Greece I will arrive at a barbarian land. But my "time has not yet come,"[92] and you will be satiated with my blood then,[93] if indeed I am turned over to you. Above or below:[94] I do not know which option to call better!

10. But once again I seem to be an old-fashioned and simple man! Desiring to compose a history of your life, I have gathered your actions together in chapters, having discovered some of them myself and learning the rest from others who know them. Many people gathered the sources for my narrations. Under each heading, organized around the appropriate concept, I will flowerily adorn the composition with rhythmical and supremely beautiful words, sowing my language with flatteries and graces[95] and all the elements of euphony, so that when someone holds my book in hand he must simultaneously both admire the deed and applaud the word. And the man who was previously hidden even from us, well, Egypt too will know him in the future, as will the spice-bearing land [Arabia Felix] and the Ocean that lies to the west, to which places my text will travel.[96]

89. Cf. 2 Corinthians 11:25.

90. Cf. Plutarch, *Phokion* 34–37. This is the second time in the letter that Psellos compares himself to Phokion.

91. Cf. Homer, *Iliad* 4.164: "when sacred Ilion will perish."

92. Cf. John 7:30.

93. Cf. Homer, *Iliad* 22.267.

94. Cf. Sophokles, *Philoktetes* 28.

95. Cf. Plutarch, *Numa* 8.10.

96. Possibly a reference to Psellos' *Indictment against Keroullarios*.

2 Funeral Oration for the Most Blessed Patriarch Kyr Michael Keroullarios

Ioannis Polemis

Introduction

The Life of Keroullarios.   Michael Keroullarios was born between 1005 and 1010 to an aristocratic family of Constantinople.[1] His father (we do not know his name) was a treasury official. We have little information about Keroullarios' early career. In 1040, after being involved in a conspiracy against the emperor Michael IV Paphlagon (1034–1041), he was arrested and banished from Constantinople together with his brother. The emperor forced him to become a monk. Only about one year later, however, Michael V Kalaphates (1041–1042) recalled him to Constantinople. The following year, Keroullarios befriended the next emperor, Konstantinos IX Monomachos (1042–1055), who arranged for his election as patriarch of Constantinople in 1043, when the incumbent, Alexios Stoudites, died. Although he owed his position to the emperor's favor, Keroullarios proved to be an independent and strong-willed patriarch, and is seen by historians as not always amenable to the emperor's wishes. According to traditional narratives, this is reflected in his handling of the negotiations with the Roman Church in 1054. Before 1054, Keroullarios had written a number of letters to fellow bishops that sharpened the perceived differences between the two Churches. He effectively began the genre of drawing up lists of

---

1. The basic facts of Keroullarios' life are laid out in Tinnefeld (1989).

the errors of the Roman Church.[2] (Some theological works, such as the so-called *Panoplia*, are attributed to him, though this attribution is far from certain.) In 1054, Keroullarios allegedly angered the papal delegates so much that Cardinal Humbert of Silva Candida excommunicated him. Keroullarios responded by excommunicating Humbert in turn, though the degree to which he was acting outside of imperial instructions here remains unclear. This exacerbated the growing rupture between the two Churches, Orthodox and Catholic.

Yet Keroullarios' influence grew stronger, probably due to his handling of the negotiations with the Latins. The *Funeral Oration for Keroullarios* does not hide his imperious attitude toward Konstantinos IX, Theodora (1055–1056)—Keroullarios insisted to her that the state needed a *man* at the helm—and Michael VI (1056–1057). In 1057, after the rebel army of the usurper Isaakios Komnenos defeated the loyalist army of Michael VI, Keroullarios, taking advantage of the uprising of the people of Constantinople, persuaded Michael to abdicate in favor of the rebel, who now became Isaakios I. Considering the new emperor his puppet, Keroullarios bossed him around and did not refrain from insulting him even in public. It seems that he took to wearing some imperial regalia as well.[3] In late 1058, Isaakios accused Keroullarios of conspiring against him, deposed him, and banned him to Prokonnesos and then to Imbros. Before he was put on trial, the patriarch, who had refused to abdicate, died. Some people considered him a saint, but others, in the political class, were troubled by the patriarch's imperial pretensions. His public humiliation possibly contributed to Isaakios' own fall from power the following year (1059). Isaakios was replaced by Konstantinos X Doukas, one of his supporters, who was married to the patriarch's niece, Eudokia Makrembolitissa.

The Funeral Oration for Keroullarios.   Psellos composed the funeral oration under Konstantinos X Doukas (1059–1067) and the empress Eudokia Makrembolitissa (ch. 60), at least one year after Keroullarios' death and possibly even later. Sideras dates it to 1063,[4] without offering any arguments for this dating, while Tinnefeld thinks that it can be dated even earlier.[5] For more on Psellos and Keroullarios, see the general introduction.

2. Kolbaba (2000).
3. Dagron (2003) 237–247.
4. Sideras (1994) 134.
5. Tinnefeld (1989) 117 n. 128.

The oration has a clear, cyclical structure. After Psellos dwells on the early life of Keroullarios, dealing with the obligatory parts of a funeral oration (place of origin, parents, and early life), he proceeds to an account of an early trial of Keroullarios concerning his involvement in the conspiracy against Michael IV. Then Psellos describes his rehabilation under the emperors Michael V and Konstantinos IX and his accession to the patriarchal throne. After dealing with various incidents that took place during his patriarchate, he comes to the second major trial of the patriarch: his dethronement by the emperor Isaakios I. Thus, the entire narrative is framed by the narrative of his two exiles, or rather "martyrdoms," as Psellos presents them. The text begins with a trial and ends with a trial. Psellos' purpose is to emphasize Keroullarios' qualities as a martyr.

Psellos employs another motif in his text: that of the Platonic descent-ascent. The patriarch's retirement from the world is presented as an ascent to God. Keroullarios himself considers his ascent to the patriarchal throne as a descent: like the Platonic philosopher, he is not willing to return to the cave to lead his fellow men to a better life, but prefers to go on living an ascetic life (chs. 20 and 22). Yet Psellos is careful to point out that Keroullarios managed to combine both lifestyles: his monastic way of life was not an impediment to the execution of his patriarchal duties. Keroullarios was able to live as a monk, while serving as ecumenical patriarch (ch. 43). That motif also appears in Psellos' *Funeral Oration for Xiphilinos*.

The *Funeral Oration for Keroullarios* was first published by Konstantinos Sathas in 1874 on the basis of MS Parisinus gr. 1182.[6] This is the unique manuscript preserving the work. The present translation is based on the new edition of the speech I prepared for the series Bibliotheca Teubneriana (*Orationes Funebres I*, ed. Polemis, pp. 1–81). Although my edition is necessarily based on the same MS, its text is not identical to that of Sathas' edition. No translations of this funeral oration have been published before. The bold numbers in the translation correspond to section numbers in my edition; the bold numbers in square brackets, such as "[1P]," correspond to the page numbers.

6. Sathas (1874) 421–462.

Funeral Oration for the Most Blessed Patriarch Kyr Michael Keroullarios

1. [1P] Most people, even some of the highly learned, believe that both power-ful virtue and persuasive speech have abandoned our era as if by chance. They cite the testimony of what they see, or rather that of their own biases. But I would never argue that virtue has ceased to flourish within the souls of those who decide to live according to it, though I do tend to agree that most people neglect to cultivate their powers of speech. Moreover, I do not attribute prog-ress or deficiency in this regard to mere chance, but to the willful disposition of each person's mind and the inclinations of his soul, whether for good or bad. Of course, those who believe that we depend on the movements of heavenly bodies deny the existence of the most important characteristic of human na-ture, I mean the free will of the soul to move and act as it wishes. Thus, they do not reward with crowns those who struggle and do not castigate those who have no regard for any noble ideals. But all who believe that the soul is able to make a choice between what is good and what is bad, agreeing in this with our sacred texts,[7] and present it as something vacillating between good and bad, both confirm the power of speech and preserve secure and intact the doctrine concerning free will. Consequently, past eras have no preferential claims as far as goodness is concerned. Our own time is not the boundary enclosing all that is bad. Either in the past or the present, or rather at all times, men keep the seeds of virtue inside their souls, and they bring forward its various fruits in direct proportion to their preparedness to be virtuous or not.

In the past, moreover, there were many powerful orators, and with their praises they magnified the qualities of men who practiced virtue. Nowadays either virtue surpasses the ability of our speech, or our panegyrics are not as

7. Cf. Psellos, *Theologica I* 91.38 (p. 357).

vigorous as in the past; therefore, the power of virtue is in danger of being seen as inferior because of the weakness of the speeches praising it. In my view, the balance [2P] between the power of speech and good deeds has been reversed both in the previous generation and in our own days: in the past, speech was more powerful than the glorious deeds themselves, and people believed that the latter were much more magnificent than they were in reality because of speech, whereas nowadays, virtue is greater than speech, and virtue is perceived as much smaller than it really is because of the shortcomings of our panegyrics. Thus I am afraid and not entirely confident in undertaking the present encomium, lest the opposite of what I expect turns out, that is, lest the speech appear inferior both to the expectations of you, the audience, concerning that man [Keroullarios], and to the truth itself concerning his miraculous achievements (this expression is more accurate). This result may detract from his reputation for virtue in the eyes of future generations, while you, who knew the man well, may get the opposite view of him than he deserves.

For me, the misfortune happens to be greater while encountering good fortune: the fact that the man to be praised is superior even to men most distinguished for virtue contributes to his magnificence, which is evident on its own, but it also prohibits my speech from being elevated anywhere near the appropriate loftiness because it faces so many achievements in which it may indulge. The eminence of his own deeds, which are far above the average, becomes an impediment: the splendor of his achievements makes it hard for others to look at him directly. However, all these factors cannot justifiably deprive that man of being remembered in the future through a speech; his splendor, while inapproachable to most people, must not cause the extinction of his memory.

Therefore, let us begin our praises. I say only this in advance: my speech is not contending with an opponent equal in strength; my only ambition is to speak in a modest fashion about his miraculous qualities, proving to all people that, although there are not many examples of virtue left in our time, this man alone has proved sufficiently virtuous to be considered equal to all virtuous men of the past and to be much admired in the present too. I think he will become a model and living image to all who try to become virtuous in the future as well.

2. It seems that all the privileges enjoyed by our great and holy father came from his ancestors, his two parents, who brought him to light, and also from his city of birth, his own natural inclinations, his way of life, character, education, magnificent soul, and all the other things that our speech is going to mention: these were all the result of a divine innovation and a higher dispensation [**3P**] made for this particular man, or a miracle. I would not call him especially blessed on account of his native city,[8] although this would suffice as praise for other people. (I do not consider the fact that he shared the same native city with so many people to be as important as his other merits, which are numerous; for no one else was blessed with them all.) Therefore, I am going to praise him sufficiently on the basis of his other endowments.

The family of his ancestors was much more virtuous than any other family. But they were unable to surpass those who came after them. This happened to them in the opposite way from what happens to streams at their springs: the water that is coming out now is much more abundant than that which came out before, as it becomes weaker and weaker the more it moves away from its source, but in our case it seems as if the stream went back to the spring, for those who came next were much more virtuous than their parents. It was necessary, as the rivers were about to be emptied into the sea, so to speak, that the streams would become much more abundant and magnificent near their dissolution.

Those who gave birth to him easily surpassed all others, but they could not defeat themselves. Although they were surpassed only by themselves, conceding the first place to no one, they were forced to give up their seats to their child. Although they stood as an example for him because they were older, they became only an image of their child's virtue because he was much more virtuous. They went on adorning him with the flowers of virtue for some time, but then, all of a sudden, took care to fashion themselves in imitation of the precision of his divine deeds.

3. But that came later. His parents were equal to each other in an admirable and divine manner. The family of one was not more illustrious than that of the other,[9] nor did they display irreconcilable characters. The one did not rush to overcome the other, or vice versa. A most peculiar thing happened: they vied with each other in the accomplishment of good deeds, but in another respect they ran together. They neglected the same things, and their objectives focused on similar goals. Their bodily forms were commensurate indeed, and the ar-

8. I.e., Constantinople.
9. We do not know the names of Keroullarios' parents. Although the family of his father was prominent, we cannot be sure whether his mother's family was prominent as well: Tinnefeld (1989) 98. Similar praise of Keroullarios' family is found in Psellos' *Letter to Keroullarios* 3.

chetypes of their souls differed hardly at all. I do not say all this just to adorn my speech, [**4P**] for I am mentioning those similarities to you, who are well-aware of both of them.[10] Is there anyone at all who did not know his father, whose virtue was a great miracle?[11] He was leading a divine life, but at the same time he was a leading figure in public affairs: he was considered worthy of being appointed an imperial functionary, being entrusted with guarding the imperial treasuries.[12] He did not blemish his public image through his moral standing or vice versa. On the contrary, each life contributed to the embellishment of the other: his virtue became greater not only through his private endeavors but through his contact with other people as well; he also ensured that his public activity was in line with his private virtue, which served as an exacting standard for it. He did not disappoint the emperor who had placed his trust in him. Far from it, in fact: he glorified the sound judgment of the emperor or contributed to his own glory as well through his good intentions. What is more admirable is the following: he resembled a stream of clean and sweet water which, when mixed with salty waters, did not become bitter but rather sweetened them instead.[13] He cast all vulgar expressions out of his tongue and soul, and maintained the grace and the uprightness of his character and speech in the midst of all the buffoonery and ensuing laxity of morals of that environment. If someone considered his mode of speaking, he would not believe that he would be able to deliver a proper speech, but as soon as he heard his speech he would blame himself for the error. He was adorned mainly by his circumspect thought, his timely silence, and his reserved manner toward those he had not met before. Those familiar with him say that he was blessed with divine visions and that, finding the gates of the temple closed, he opened them forthwith miraculously and proceeded into the main church.[14]

4. On account of these qualities he surpassed everyone, save two persons: he was equal to his wife (I cannot say anything else) and inferior to his son.

10. I.e., to Keroullarios' nephews, the implied audience of the speech.
11. Cf. Gregorios of Nazianzos, *Or.* 43.10.1–2 (p. 134).
12. See Tinnefeld (1989) 98 n. 19.
13. Psellos is probably referring to the fountain of Arethousa, whose waters mixed with the sea as it flowed from the Peloponnese to Sicily: Gregorios of Nazianzos, *Or.* 43.21.29 (p. 170).
14. The miraculous opening of real doors is a topos; in this case it may be meant metaphorically.

What I am saying may be confirmed by scientific arguments. According to science, all inequalities come out of a previous equality. Like his father, who divided his life between the practice of virtue and the settlement of political affairs, and was successful in both respects, his mother occupied herself with the affairs of the household, [5P] but she also took equal care in divine matters. She also resisted her human nature, sometimes successfully, sometimes not. She despised bodily beauty, neither cultivating nor enhancing it.[15] Sometimes she succeeded in pruning the flowers of her beauty, but her success was not complete: she was unable to hide her natural beauty completely. She lived for God and for her husband: she looked to all things beloved by them, and despised whatever was indifferent to them. Nor was it the case that God loved the hidden beauty of her soul, whereas her husband paid more attention to her visible beauty; no, he too honored her virtues, and rather for this reason showed his respect and devotion to his wife.

5. My speech, having gone back to the past, seems to have forgotten its proper subject. Now that I have dealt with that other subject adequately and at length, let us proceed to the accomplishment of our purpose. Such was the character of the holy father's parents. He was brought to light after his siblings;[16] all were persons of outstanding quality and with admirable virtues, but Keroullarios was higher than them and in virtue imitated God more accurately. The power of his parents' nature was not diminished at the time of the birth of their last child. That which they themselves experienced previously, they now accomplished: proceeding from one birth to another, they finished with the best one [i.e., Michael Keroullarios]. I have heard from some people familiar with them that some divine voices announced to them the conception of their child and its birth, predicting a divine future for him preordained by God himself. From the moment he was born, the child verified these noble predictions: he shone with beauty; I am not referring only to his soul, but to his body as well.

I know that many great philosophers do not pay attention to the beauty of the body. They choose not to praise a man who happens to be beautiful, but prefer to praise his nobler and higher virtues: the steadfastness of his mind, mature judgment, a noble soul, sagacity, resolve, and all that adorns the inner

---

15. Cf. Psellos, *Encomium for His Mother* 2.

16. Keroullarios had an older brother and sister and was born between 1005 and 1010: Tinnefeld (1989) 98 and 99, respectively.

man.[17] My view, which has the value of a doctrine [**6P**] for me, is the following. When the soul and the body compete with each other for beauty, with the soul showing off its proper virtue and the body displaying its beauty, even if the beauty of the soul is not in its own way equal to the shining beauty of the body, but much inferior to it, I say that the soul is much superior to that magnificent and beautiful body, even by its modest beauty. Now, if we have before us two men, the first shining with virtues of the soul but having an ugly outer appearance, and the second being virtuous like the first one but having blossoming physical attributes as well, I will award the prize to the second one. For even if physical beauty seems to be of no use for the virtuous soul, this is valid only for the souls that have been separated from their bodies. If the soul is still united with the body, constituting a harmonious mixture like that of the strings of a lyre,[18] the soul that has a beautiful body is better than a soul deprived of it. Therefore, in a panegyrical speech we should not despise the beauty of the person we are praising. We must also take it into account in our speech; the more beautiful is a soul wearing a beautiful body, the better it is. If our bodies were formless matter, it would be necessary to throw that shapeless ugliness far from our speech, as it would be an entity of least account and purely material. However, since we are made up of incarnated forms, we should not despise our bodies because they are made of matter; instead, we should honor them because they have a form that came from above, from the intellect, and that, having reached our bodies, became inseparable from them. Therefore, the beauty of his body must be an integral part of our praise for that man.

6. Nature, then, had made him beautiful, polishing him to a great extent, as if it had brought such a beautiful man into light only once, but then grew wary of creating such a body again. Never since his birth has nature created another man like him. But I think that it had not endowed any man in the past with such a wholly beautiful appearance, either. Let that beauty be placed before his spiritual achievements like the morning star that rises before the sun. My speech admires first the beauty that appeared at the moment of his birth; I am placing it first of all as if it were the bud of a tree that comes before its fruits. Thus, when the maturity of his soul dawns, [**7P**] I may turn the eyes of my speech to the new light, leaving aside the earlier one. He was more beautiful than anyone else, and he seemed to be unrivalled from the very beginning.

---

17. Cf. Romans 7:22 and Ephesians 3:16.
18. Cf. Plato, *Phaedo* 86a.

Proceeding further on, as soon as the prudence of his soul made its appearance, he directed the attention of his admirers to something else. The people judged his behavior through their eyes, their ears, or their attentive mind. If anyone saw or heard about only some of his deeds, or turned his mind's attention to them, he would come out the winner, but if that same man experienced all his accomplishments at once, he would be defeated at every single step, until he would comprehend what he saw. Looking at his beauty, he would be amazed instantly; but after listening to him, he would admire his speech instead of his bodily form; but if he proceeded further on, examining his mind, he would leave aside both his body and his speech and would award the prize of victory to his mind and proclaim it the winner because of the combination of all these virtues.

7. Because of his fortunate station in life, he frequented the imperial palace from a tender age, but his mental disposition inclined him toward education. He learned the first lessons adequately.[19] Afterward he moved on to the study of rhetoric,[20] not staying only with the beauty on the surface of the orations, which merely persuades; he sought truth and firm understanding instead. Even philosophy is keen to adopt such a mode of speech and does not consider it unworthy of belonging to her. He was learning to compose such speeches by using his father as a model. On the other hand, he vied with his brother, being his equal. Let me say a few things about him. Those Greek philosophers who seem to know something more than the rest attribute the differences between the children of the same parents to two opposite jars,[21] and explain any mixture of virtue and wickedness as a result of the mixture of elements taken from these two jars. However, according to us [Christians], God's creative act and providence gave equal gifts to both brothers, whose bodies and souls were similar. Their only difference was this: the older one was inferior to the younger as far as virtue was concerned, while the younger, although he emerged as the winner in the contest of virtue, could not become older than his brother. The older brother surpassed the younger one simply because of his seniority, but was inferior [**8P**] to him insofar as spiritual progress was concerned. The

---

19. Psellos is referring to Keroullarios' primary education, taught by a *grammatistes*; the key textbook was the Psalter: Markopoulos (2008) 788.

20. Rhetoric, along with grammar and philosophy (*trivium*), comprised a substantial part of secondary education; the key textbooks were those of Hermogenes and Aphthonios: Markopoulos (2008) 788–789.

21. Cf. Synesios, *Egyptian Oration* 2.6.2 (p. 155); also Homer, *Iliad* 5.697–698; and Psellos, *Philosophica Minora I* 45.54–55 (p. 163).

younger was inferior to his brother as far as seniority was concerned, but he surpassed him in prudence. They conceded the first prizes to each other, so both were winners and losers at the same time. Although their characters were somehow different, their intentions turned out to be similar. The older one was cheerful to behold: the state of his soul was reflected in his appearance, his face was graceful, and the charms that came from his mouth captivated those who spoke with him like a net from which there was no escape.[22] The younger one, to whom this speech is devoted, was more introverted; he was not captivated by his interlocutor or anyone else who wished to attract him easily. He would reflect on what he was going to say and was very reserved, not believing easily anything that other people used to say. Such were their characters. They were both eager to take from the other the gifts with which he was more endowed by nature. The older brother, being more cheerful, admired his brother's cautiousness, while the younger one, being more prudent, envied his brother's cheerfulness. They both praised the achievements of each other.

8. Although their character was different, their education was the same. The speech of both of them was equal. The intellect of the older brother was sharper, but the intellect of the younger was more accurate. The speech of the older brother was more elegant, while that of the younger accorded more with the rules of the art. Let me mention this too: the diet and clothing of the older brother were more expensive; his garments were more refined, while the other's diet was simpler, but more pleasing; his garb was suitable for a philosopher and more shiny. They divided the virtue of temperance between them. The older brother chose for himself a lawful marriage: he married the best of all women and he begat excellent children. I will refer to them later on.[23] The younger brother rejected lawful marriage, choosing to lead a life superior to the constraints of law and nature. They shared the same house, and their differences were restricted to the ones mentioned above. As far as other things were concerned, in no respect did they exist without each other. They spent from their common funds, and they deposited whatever they earned into the same account. To speak more precisely, they both spent [**9P**] from the same funds: spending some of their money generously, they became an example of magnanimity for others, while they secretly offered another sum to the poor, depositing it into their heavenly accounts.[24] Their inheritance was enough

---

22. Cf. Esther 5:2a.
23. They are the nephews addressed in the speech.
24. Cf. Matthew 6:19–20.

for them, and their property was considered adequate to cover the needs of many people.

9. Afterward the love of philosophy captivated them, and they paid great attention to the science of dialectics. They did not learn simple syllogisms only, but also became acquainted with the principles of demonstration and their first causes.[25] He [Keroullarios] was fond of prose; the older one devoted himself to the composition of metrical verses. They devoted their compositions to several men who died.[26] They made not only images of the saints, who had devoted themselves to God, but adorned these with texts in prose and verse. The older brother seemed to be more down-to-earth. I am saying this because he preferred the sciences that deal with things of this world, leaving aside the science that examines the spectacles and the beauties of the heavens.[27] But Keroullarios' mind flew also toward those beauties. Let me narrate what is not known to most people: he managed to grasp without any trouble matters that had to be explained to other people through the teachings of those wise men, who became their eyes leading them to the contemplation of things above us. He got to know both the fixed stars and the planets, he learned about the parallels of the circles, the modes and causes of the eclipses, and the disappearances of heavenly bodies.[28] If sometimes I confirmed what he had discovered without any help, he became very happy and his soul was ecstatic, since his theory had been confirmed by someone who knew those things better. Although he had not studied geometry attentively, he was able to put into practice all the theorems of that science, being more capable than any other man of constructing geometric instruments.

10. All these things took place before he was overcome by a stronger love for the more virtuous life. As soon as he realized that tending to one's morals is not a sufficient good in itself, but just a path leading to the aim [**10P**] of man, which is the contemplative life, he left those wings that fly close to the ground behind him and donned the silver wings of the divine dove.[29] He abandoned the secular life and devoted himself to the spiritual one. But as it was predestined for him to become a perfect athlete and a martyr, albeit without shedding his blood, God delivered him to the temptations of the Evil One, who had

25. Cf. Aristotle, *Posterior Analytics* 72a6–7.
26. Keroullarios probably composed prose funeral orations, while his older brother wrote funeral epigrams.
27. I.e., physics and astronomy.
28. Astronomy was an integral part of secondary education: Markopoulos (2008) 789.
29. Cf. Psalm 67:14.

asked for him to be tested, like the great athlete Job.[30] As soon as the Tempter took him into his hands, he did not submit him to partial temptations, now depriving him of his herds and then inflicting something else upon him; he did not strike him with a great wound only at the end, giving him a grave illness,[31] but rather he sent to him all temptations together,[32] inflicting the worst blow. My speech now seeks to reveal how and on what grounds the envious demon assaulted him, but I am going to be an impartial narrator. I will present his degradation as a martyrdom, but I will refrain from disgracing too much the one who dishonored him, because his soul was inclined to the spiritual life.

11. At this time the scepters of the Roman state were held by Michael [IV], the one who came after Romanos [III], I mean the Romanos who was of the family of Argyros. The morality of imperial power could be judged from two perspectives: from the standpoint of the emperor himself and from the standpoint of the members of his family, both older and younger than him. The emperor himself was lawful and not oppressive,[33] but most of his kinsmen were violent and acted like tyrants. That caused their subjects to be of two minds, as they wanted opposite things for them in different respects. They wanted them to be both alive and dead: to be alive, because the emperor was good, and at the same time to be dead in order to be liberated from the tyranny of his kinsmen. Or rather, some of those surrounding the emperor wanted him to be alive, but most of the others preferred the death of his kinsmen. Although this emperor seized power unlawfully,[34] he changed course afterward and did not strive after power and unlawful gains anymore. He followed one path first, but then took a different one, in fact the opposite one. However, those who shared his [11P] blood had a totally different character.[35]

---

30. Cf. Job 1:14.

31. Cf. Job 2:6–7.

32. That is, temptations to curse God for not standing by him, not temptations to indulge in pleasures.

33. Cf. Psellos, *Chronographia* 4.10.1–22. On the presentation of Michael IV by Psellos, see Kaldellis (1999) 56–57.

34. Allegedly by helping the empress Zoe to murder the previous emperor Romanos III Argyros.

35. Psellos is referring to the emperor's brothers, most prominent of whom was Ioannes Orphanotrophos, notorious for his cruelty. Skylitzes, *Synopsis*, p. 429.21, attributes the first banishment of Keroullarios to Ioannes himself. See also Psellos, *Orationes Panegyricae* 2.282–290 (p. 30).

Accordingly, the situation was stormy and the minds of his subjects were agitated; they could not subordinate themselves to this tyranny anymore. Let me omit all other rumors or details. A great section of the people of the City seceded [1040]: they were members of the noblest families, the most audacious and brave and their intentions were the most sharp. Before they revealed their bold plan, they abolished the tyranny in speech and installed a most lawful regime.[36] They also started discussing who the new emperor would be. Everyone refrained from proposing himself for the throne, so as to avoid the outburst of personal ambition. They put the matter to a common vote as to who would be the best choice. Now, the Ethiopians used to have a law that the most illustrious of them would be their king,[37] and this group had the same desire too, that is, to elevate to the highest dignity the man considered by God to be first among all. When the ancient Greeks needed a prophecy, they preferred to address themselves to the oracle of Delphi rather than to any other; no one called its authority into question, although that was an error in judgment on their part. In the same way, the conspirators put the matter to a vote. Everyone thought that he had chosen the best one, and they all chose the man I am praising now.

Knowing also that he would not accept the honor easily, because the man was above it, they had to pressure him to accept, as if they were ready to enter the palace, while he was still thinking about it, and they were already contending with him as he resisted. After they had crowned him and appointed him emperor in the shadowy outline of their plans, they proceeded to the implementation of their plans, like builders who start building the house after drawing up its plan. Their plan was not to kill the emperor, but to stop him from going any further and deprive him of his office, appointing the one elected by them all instead. But they took care not to confide their plan to him, because they knew that he would neither approve such a plan if he heard about it, nor praise it. He [Keroullarios] had been in his house the whole time, unaware of the plans each and all of them had drawn up concerning his person. But the implementation of those plans was much delayed; [12P] the plan was ready, but its implementation was overdue. Some of them wanted to carry out their plan with confidence, but others were hesitant, fearing the outcome. As a result a small group, the worst of all, broke away from those who had initially

---

36. The conspiracy took place in 1040: Tinnefeld (1989) 99; Cheynet (1990) 51–52.
37. Athenaios, *Deiphnosophistai* 13.20.29.

conspired. They reached an understanding among themselves and, believing that the plan could not remain hidden any longer, voluntarily exposed the plot to the emperor, though they had taken part in it. They revealed the whole plan, uncovering the plot and exposing the conspirators: they said that some of them took part in the conspiracy on the spot, while others had waited to receive the signal from afar. They warned him that he would fall into their hands if he did not forestall their attack.

The emperor was shocked to learn these things, and his soul was filled with fear. He mounted guard at the City immediately and surrounded himself with more bodyguards. He arrested all the plotters in groups and individually, kept them inside his nets, and started to interrogate them about their plot. The plotters, having been caught and being unable to escape, since they were imprisoned, revealed all in explicit terms, both effable and ineffable:[38] the first causes, their discussions, conspiracy, vote, and the fact that the man who was most suitable to be emperor because of his character, family, and other merits, had already been chosen. After their revelations were completed at this point, the emperor seemed to hold all the other plotters in contempt. He reproached each one for his plans, but as soon as he heard that last part of the plan, he became anxious in his mind and thought that the conspiracy had deep roots. He asked just a small question, whether that man [Keroullarios] had expressed his agreement with their plan. All the plotters denied it,[39] so the emperor asked why he was not made privy to the conspiracy. As soon as he learned the reason for that, namely, that it would have been impossible for that man, who had not given rise to any suspicion, to be involved in such an affair, he admired them more for their judgment but feared the integrity of that man's character. He expressed his contempt for the other plotters once more and punished them in a way appropriate to their crime, making their righteous punishment milder.

But as for him [Keroullarios], instead of praising him for his blameless behavior, the emperor inflicted a more severe punishment on him. He penalized him for the fact that all the others had acquitted him. [**13P**] He was brought to trial on charges that he did not know anything about, and he [the emperor] condemned him for a crime he did not commit. He held him responsible,

---

38. Cf. Hesiod, *Works and Days* 4.

39. Psellos is trying to exonerate Keroullarios of any suspicion of involvement in the conspiracy.

although there was no responsibility on his part at any time. What was more absurd was that he [Keroullarios] had no idea what was being said or taking place. He knew only that some people who had conspired against the emperor were arrested; however, at the same time the emperor was both his judge and his accuser. But all those who had actually drawn up those dreadful plans were not punished by him severely: some of those guilty were acquitted completely, while others were punished mildly. However, the one whose innocence all those who denounced one another had protested was punished most severely. He [Keroullarios] graciously concerned himself with the fate of those arrested, and his mind tried to find a way out for them, as was his custom. He prayed to the Lord for them to be acquitted. However, the emperor inflicted a most severe punishment on him, as if it had been he who had drawn up a dreadful plan, although he had not done him [the emperor] any wrong; instead, he should have considered the testimony in his [Keroullarios'] favor as a safeguard for his goodwill and loyalty in the future. In reality, that punishment was neither a chastisement for any wrongdoing nor a rendering of accounts for an audacious act or a bad plan, but rather it was the product of the emperor's envy of his noble spirit and because he stood high in people's esteem and was popular in all respects. He [the emperor] was afraid lest everyone choose him once again, if they decided to find a new emperor in the future; he was sure that he would not be given another opportunity to save his throne, as everyone would take the part of the other man, preventing him from judging them again in court.

12. For those reasons, the emperor judged him, looking after his own interests, and he was not a gentle judge. This was something for which one could most reproach him. Now, one might grant to the emperor the right to ensure his own safety, seeing that he feared the love of the people for the other man [Keroullarios], although that was unjust, and also seeing that he had no confidence in himself and safeguarded his throne by chasing men of merit away from office. But no one can avoid reproaching the emperor for committing another crime in addition to the bad decisions he had made concerning him [Keroullarios]; that would be sophistry. [14P] Instead of exiling him not far away from the City, so as not to be in danger himself, and providing all sorts of comforts to him and asking for his pardon, the emperor implicated his brother too, as well as all his kinsmen, shaking the ground under their feet, so to speak; he attacked them suddenly like a storm, raising up all sorts of waves against them, which submerged them completely. He transformed the house of their parents into a well-guarded prison, and shut them in as if they were

wild beasts, leaving no exit for them to escape; he just about cut off the air above them, so that they could not take wing together and attack him.

However, the prisoners did not pity themselves and did not cry for their misfortune; they only reproached the emperor for his bad decision regarding them. The fact that they were all together, each consoling the other, brought them a certain relief from the pain of their condemnation. But the emperor considered even this as a danger to himself, so he signed and dispatched the order for their separation. Then they realized that God had indeed handed them over to the Evil One, who had asked for them in order to put them to the test.[40] They would gladly sit on a dunghill,[41] provided they would be together and not parted from each other. They would prefer that to being assigned to the best dwelling-places in heaven. But the emperor made a bad decision regarding them: he did not only separate them from each other, although they had not been separated until then, being attached to each other and animated by one spirit; he placed them far away from each other, in the worst places. He exiled the older brother to a rather steep place,[42] while the younger one was sent far away and transferred to a cramped place. There he was imprisoned in a dark room. Food and even water were delivered to him in limited quantities, and the emperor appointed some awful men to be his guardians. But even this was not enough to calm his disturbed soul: he ordered him to take the monastic habit, as if offering to the spirit a man who had devoted himself to God long ago.[43] He tried to change his life, but he [Keroullarios] put up a spirited resistance to that plan, although he was most mild in other respects. He did not abhor the prospect, nor was he unwilling to choose the better life; rather, he did it out of respect for the Holy Spirit: [15P] he was ashamed to take the monastic habit as a result of his condemnation.

13. Is not all this exact testimony on behalf of God? He was considered worthy of a higher life because he had led a virtuous and pious life, and at the same time he was condemned because he was proved a worthy man. I consider those to be martyrs not only who, facing a Diocletian,[44] Maximian,[45] or

---

40. Cf. Luke 22:31.

41. Cf. Job 2:8.

42. The place of exile of the two brothers is unknown.

43. Cf. Ephesians 2:18.

44. Roman emperor (284–305), who was responsible for the Great Persecution of Christians that started in 303.

45. This is probably Galerius, junior co-emperor with Diocletian and then Augustus in his own right (305–311), rather than his senior partner Maximianus.

Licinius[46] for the sake of their faith in God, were tortured, beheaded, burned alive, cut into pieces, and eaten by wild beasts, or thrown alive into the sea, which gave them back safe, but also anyone who was punished for his good conduct, or for not being ready to agree with bad people, or even someone who is punished for a crime he did not commit, a crime committed by other people. Worthy of the crown of martyrdom are also people who, instead of resisting those who want to harm them, yield to them. But how are we to evaluate the extension of his unjust punishment? Is not this higher than any martyrdom? How are we to judge the fact that, although he had reached the peak of hardship, he was submitted to further torments? That cannot be compared to any other test of his faith.

14. The two brothers remained separated from each other. It was the first time that their natural bond was cut, and this brought them near to death. The one who is the subject of my present oration, being predestined by God for a brilliant future and able to comfort himself with his noble thoughts, managed to cure the terrible wound of this separation. He rallied his spirit and kept alive his soul that was otherwise near death. He simply held on to life under the waves and thrived even while being cut off.[47] It was as if he were swaddled by fire. He was a vineyard of God with a good stem, growing luxuriantly no matter what,[48] full of the ripe grapes of hope;[49] or, rather, he was a truly philosophic soul, devoted to God and neglecting every other preoccupation. His was a godlike mind that had advanced truly [16P] to what was beyond all intellect.[50] He did not take any care of mundane affairs, though he made an exception for his brother: he really lived for him. That seemed to be the only unphilosophical trait of that man who was otherwise devoted to philosophy. But even that was a sign of his philosophic inclination, for love of a brother is love for God, and the latter is identical to love for our brothers.

I think that complete impassibility and impartiality toward all other people is a sign of a callous, not a philosophic, soul.[51] I have not met anyone practic-

---

46. Roman emperor (308–324), responsible for the persecution of Christians in the eastern part of the empire in 320.

47. Cf. Gregorios of Nazianzos, *Or.* 26.10.7 (p. 248).

48. Cf. Hosea 10:1.

49. Cf. Genesis 40:10.

50. Cf. Psellos, *Philosophica Minora II* 34 (p. 116.18).

51. A reference to the old opposition between the Stoic ideal (complete impassivity, *apatheia*), sometimes also recommended by Christian theologians, and the Platonic-Aristotelian ideal (*metriopatheia*).

ing such a philosophy, unless it be some people who have been cut off from all fellow-feeling since the time of their birth. Yes, we must despise our parents, brothers, sons, and even our own life, if that is possible, for the sake of God, choosing God in their place,[52] but we should not cast off our family altogether. The nearer we come to God, the more we should take care of our kin. This is what the Ten Commandments clearly teach us, to show proper respect to our parents and place our neighbors immediately after God; in this way, they teach those who are subject to the law respect and friendship toward our fellow men.[53]

15. As I said, after he [Keroullarios] was attacked by this misfortune, he naturally became upset at first. However, he later turned to his own mind and then to God himself. He regained his hopes and faced up to his calamities. His brother considered all their other misfortunes comparatively small and did not lose hope, but one of his torments was unbearable, namely, being separated from his brother. He lamented for himself by day and cried during the night and could not give himself any hope; he suffered terribly, he was sad, his heart bled. He yearned for the previous union with his brother, he wanted to devise a plan so as to bring back the good times of the past, but he could not find the medicine that would give him back that union. His sadness became an affliction of the heart and his inner state deteriorated unseen. The situation was transformed into a very grave illness and his head was also affected. As if from a citadel, this tyrannical illness came out from his head and caused his sudden death. A man who was robust a short time before was now dead.

As soon as our great father [Keroullarios] learned of this misfortune, his attention to divine things was interrupted for a while, **[17P]** but he soon returned to those occupations in a more perfect manner than before. He did not pay any attention to other things, or rather, he laughed at them as a philosopher when he heard something about them. The only thing that he neither neglected nor laughed at was the death of his brother. He did not try to find some philosophic solace, comparing his own misfortunes to other graver ones of the past, because one could not discover such a thing, even if one leafed through all the tragedies. I define the enormity or insignificance of a misfortune not on the basis of what happened, but on the basis of the psychological reactions of those involved in it and of their relations to one another. I do not regard as most unhappy either a Scythian living beyond the Danube who has lost fifty

---

52. Cf. Matthew 19:29.
53. Cf. Exodus 20:12.

sons, or a Persian living beyond the Euphrates who has seen his land devastated and his dearest and nearest taken prisoner. Nature has provided the Scythian with his own philosophy, while the Persian is accustomed to such misfortunes. Rather, I consider most unhappy a common man who loves his fellow man, in case he loses what he loves most, even if that misfortune seems to be rather small to other people.

Was there anything more disastrous for our holy father than the announcement of the sudden death of his brother, beyond all expectation? He defined his own life on the basis of his brother's life; it was impossible for him not to be lost after the one who gave him his life had died. He regarded his brother as his most precious possession; it was impossible for him not to be in great sadness after he was separated from him beyond all expectation. His brother made him happy more than the sun, so how could the sun shine down brightly upon him when the one who shone more brilliantly was buried under the earth? On the other hand, how can we appreciate the fact that under those circumstances he neither said nor thought anything improper when his beloved brother died? He surpassed Job, who raised his voice, by what he said and what he did.[54] Was not such behavior worthy of a great philosopher?

Let us consider the matter in this way. The emperor forced him with violence to accept the monastic habit. Letters were written and sent to him. The emperor who gave those orders was more severe than the letters themselves. He threatened to behead him if he did not obey his orders, [18P] while the other offered his head to be cut. The emperor sharpened the iron to cut out his eyes and made it ready, while he closed his eyelids in advance, so that he might become accustomed to blindness. But it was not possible for the unconquerable to be conquered, so the emperor gave up and left, and he [Keroullarios] carried on with his noble convictions. Noble men considered his behavior noble and a sign of sincerity, whereas fault-finding men doubted his sincerity, thinking that he harbored hopes for the future. But as soon as his brother died, the fear of the emperor and the suspicions of the fault-finding men disappeared. What the tyrannical pressure of the emperor failed to accomplish was accomplished by the death of his brother. The threats from outside did not manage to persuade him to obey the emperor's orders, but that was done by his own free will. He proved to all that his entire life was a movement toward God;[55] he lived in this

---

54. Cf. Job 1:21.
55. Cf. Gregorios of Nazianzos, *Or.* 43.70.17–18 (p. 282).

world only to the brief extent that he was devoted to his brother. What was previously taken away from him now remained there, and what was left behind was taken away too. That which took place was a partial sacrifice, a burnt offering, although what I am saying may appear strange.

16. Thus he changed his life completely, adding what was less to what was more: he devoted himself to God, although he had already been devoted to him before the time of his birth.[56] Accepting the monastic habit came first, but it was just a confirmation of his prior inclination. In fact, the new clothes he wore did not change anything: the change in his dress was just an indication of his previous transformation. At that time the emperor's life came to an end [1041]; he abandoned his imperial life and then his natural one as well, or rather he was carried off from it.[57] Things then changed for the better; that is what naturally happens. The man who became emperor after him, albeit in an unhappy way,[58] released all who had been condemned for their crimes,[59] and called back to his country this man who had been exiled unjustly. **[19P]** He saw no need to fear a man who had become a monk. When he saw him, he admired his intellect and was sorry that he had now become a monk. But, as if he had inherited the hatred and tyrannical attitude of his predecessor, he did not show him any favor or generosity.

He [Keroullarios] went on living as a monk, devoted to God, to whom he had turned long ago and whom he now embraced more completely. Let me omit what that emperor decided in the meantime and how he behaved. I will mention only one episode, and then I will continue my narrative. That terrible man had committed many crimes before; he did not care about his kinsmen, he did not show any respect toward those other holy things to which we are bound by necessity or inclined by choice: he kicked out of the palace all his close kinsmen, and he subverted everything established.[60] By the end he had

---

56. Cf. Jeremiah 1:5.

57. Cf. Gregorios of Nazianzos, *Or.* 4.33.1 (p. 130). Michael IV was tonsured during his final illness.

58. I.e., Michael V Kalaphates (1041–1042).

59. Besides Keroullarios, the new emperor recalled from exile two prominent military leaders, Konstantinos Dalassenos and Georgios Maniakes, being in need of allies to replace his relatives: Treadgold (1997) 589.

60. He exiled almost all his kinsmen, except for the *nobellisimos* Konstantinos: Treadgold (1997) 589; he even castrated the younger members of his family: Psellos, *Chronographia* 5.14.2–13.

forgotten even the oaths that he had taken before God and the promises he had given to him concerning the empress, who had inherited the kingdom of the Romans from her ancestors. She had chosen him from among all the others and given him the imperial crown, but he kicked her out of the palace immediately and surrounded his power with a wall, securing it for himself alone.[61] He permitted no one to approach him, so as to be dreadful to everyone, as if he were a wild beast; the people looked at him now from afar. The aim of his last innovation became the end of his innovations altogether, since there was no other crime he could commit and nothing else could have caused his downfall more justifiably.

The entire City, not bearing the immensity of that crime and full of a divine ardor, and not only the anonymous types but the illustrious citizens as well, attacked him together truly like beasts [1042]. They were angry, and their eager desire was to tear him to pieces as soon as they saw him. Let me omit the details. Realizing that there was no other escape, for he had deprived all others of their salvation in advance, the emperor entrusted himself to the waves of the sea, as there was no chance that he could destroy it together with the land. The sea did not disappoint him but gave him back to the land,[62] which took him and surrendered him to the hands of his hangmen.[63] I do not wish to repeat the same story to you who know what had happened and have heard it many times. He was blinded [20P] and imprisoned all alone; in any case, total isolation had been his goal, although he wanted to come to it by another road. The empress, who was deposed unlawfully, was seized and brought back to her inheritance. She settled the affairs of the state by herself for a short time, and then she gave to the country a lawful and prudent emperor. God had saved him from the waves in the past and transferred him to the palace, as if it were a calm harbor. I am speaking of Konstantinos Monomachos, about whom many people will speak both in our own times and in the future. I leave to the historians the task to narrate everything concerning him. If I say something about this emperor, I hope that the man about whom I am speaking now will not con-

61. The banishment of the empress Zoe, which led to the revolt of the people of Constantinople and the dethronement of Michael V, is described by Psellos, *Chronographia* 5.21–51, in detail.

62. The emperor, frightened by the reactions of the people, left the palace by boat and took refuge in the monastery of Stoudios, in the southwest corner of Constantinople.

63. The enemies of Michael V and the *nobelissimos* Konstantinos did not hesitate to arrest the two men, who had taken refuge by the altar of the church of the monastery of Stoudios, and blind them a short time later.

sider it a useless, subordinate business. In any case, I will incorporate into my own narrative about him whatever is more graceful, appropriate to its argument, and most useful to what will be said later. Having done that, I will then continue.

17. Monomachos returned from exile in order to become emperor [1042].[64] That was the decision of the empress and the senate. But he came back from afar as a simple citizen, without pomp. As soon as he approached the City and its walls, he was installed in a luxurious camp and offered a rich meal.[65] Everything was made ready as for an emperor, although he had not yet received the crown: that was to be placed on his head at the time of his wedding with the empress.[66] In order for his reception into the palace to take place in a perfect and truly imperial way, they ordered all those who wished to proceed to him. A huge crowd then came to him, everyone arriving at a different time: some were coming in, others were coming out, and it was truly like a public feast.[67] Along with everyone else, the man I am praising now arrived too. He knew the man, having seen him many times in the past, but they had not spoken to each other. They held each other in great esteem, based only on what they had heard, [21P] and wanted to contact each other, but had no opportunity to do this. When he too [Keroullarios] came to him, he looked like an ancient hero coming to the most good-looking man; a truly good man coming to an illustrious and generous emperor. As soon as the other man saw him, he admired his monastic habit and, before speaking to him, exclaimed: "This man is fit to become patriarch of Constantinople." He prophesied the future with a tongue inspired by God. He said this and approached him, offering him his hand. As if he were his closest friend, although he had had no contact with him in the past, he kissed him. Recognizing himself as if reflected, like in a mirror, in his [Keroullarios'] shape and soul, he said that he was not different but identical to himself.[68]

64. He had been exiled to Mytilene for taking part in a conspiracy against the emperor Michael IV. Cf. Psellos, *Chronographia* 6.19.1–13.

65. In fact, Monomachos sojourned in the church of the archangel Michael in Damokraneia near Athyras, between Selymbria and Constantinople. There he was dressed with the imperial garments by Stephanos of Pergamon. See Skylitzes, *Synopsis*, p. 423.40–44; cf. Cheynet (2003) 352 n. 10.

66. The empress Zoe was married, for a third time, to Konstantinos IX Monomachos (1042–1055) on 11 June 1042. Konstantinos was crowned emperor the next day.

67. Cf. Psellos, *Orationes Panegyricae* 2.655–661 (p. 43).

68. Cf. Basileios of Kaisareia, *Letter* 165.1; also Plato, *Alkibiades I* 133b; for the theory, see Aristotle, *Nicomachean Ethics* 1168b10.

18. Offering a sacrifice of the first fruits of his reign to God, he deemed him worthy of an honor that he deserved: he shared with him the same house, eating with him at the same table. He could not do anything else, because there was no other dignity higher than this and more appropriate to his habit. As soon as by election he [Monomachos] was elevated to the throne and introduced to the palace, resembling the sun rising up to Leo [the sign], or keeping under his power the shining portion of the beginning of the circle,[69] he did not forget our man even for a moment: he remembered giving him his right hand and their agreement. He introduced him to the innermost sanctuary of the palace and appointed him to the first rank among his officers. He restored to him the inheritance of his father, giving back all the riches that he had held in the past. He gathered up again all the glory that had been scattered all over the world. The emperor ordered his kinsmen and those who had shared the trials of exile with him to come to him at appointed intervals of time. Each interval brought to the emperor just one of his kinsmen. But his visits [Keroullarios'] were not bound by any such regulations. He came to the emperor whenever he wished and not only when the emperor wanted him to come. Since the emperor was aware of the fact that he [Keroullarios] knew things both human and divine, he appointed him over both, making him a bond linking things otherwise divided from each other.[70] He thereby dealt with both of them through him.

The emperor seemed merely graceful [**22P**] and most approachable to all other people, but before him [Keroullarios] he was both that and also thoughtful and fearful, out of respect for the prudence of this man. He adapted himself to his character, which was loftier than that of the emperor. He offered the emperor advice and made suggestions to him, filling his soul with his own opinions, which the emperor regarded as divine doctrines; that gave him the highest rank in the state. What is even more admirable is that no envy touched him [Keroullarios], a thing that sprouts and grows up with all excessive things. Everyone yielded to him and granted him first place of their own free will. Seeing this, I was reminded of the story of Job, who after so many trials was given by God a greater and much more precious property. The only difference is that God gave to Job multiple herds of cattle and sheep,[71] whereas he offered

69. This obscure clause probably refers to a technical astronomical theory.

70. Tinnefeld (1989) 100 (and n. 39) argues that Keroullarios was appointed *synkellos* by Konstantinos IX.

71. Cf. Job 42:12.

to him [Keroullarios] hidden fountains of ineffable goods, which surpass the goods received by Job by far. But as for what happened next, no prudent man would dare to compare it with what happened to Job. I am wondering if greater crowns were ever awarded for greater deeds in the past.

19. That is how events unfolded, but his glorification had not yet reached its peak. It was predestined that the lamp would be placed on the lamp stand,[72] that the torch would be lighted on a high mountain,[73] and that the intelligible trumpet would sound all over the world.[74] How did God bring his plan to completion? He did not accomplish it through its opposite route—enough of that had taken place. He now found an easy, more royal road, so to speak: Alexios, that great torch of the Church, was extinguished on the level of visible reality,[75] though in reality he was lit up spiritually: he left the body he always despised and departed for God. He had meditated on his own death so deeply in advance, that the dissolution of his nature did not worry him at all. The bond linking his soul to his body was loosened quietly. Thus the heaven on earth (that is how I am calling the church of Hagia Sophia) had no sun in it, [23P] being deprived of its rays. Different people considered different candidates as more appropriate for the patriarchal throne: some were inclined to one person, others to another. Each one ordained in his own mind the man he had in his heart either because of his virtue, or because he was his kinsman, or because he was his friend.

But the emperor entertained no doubts. He did not put to the test those who were distinguished in his entourage. Rather his soul moved directly to this man [Keroullarios] like an arrow. In fact it was God's work, who had preordained him as patriarch and had sanctified him in advance, even before his birth, like Jeremiah.[76] It was he who had prearranged all these things: he had saved him from his enemies and had fenced off all roads of life that led to other directions. What is more astonishing among all of God's decisions is that he led him to martyrdom before giving him the crown of archbishop,[77] so that the crown would be awarded to that athlete both as a gift and a prize. In my view, that was the hidden meaning of his exile, the dispersal of his family, and all the other

72. Cf. Matthew 5:15.
73. Cf. Isaiah 62:1.
74. Cf. Isaiah 27:13.
75. The patriarch Alexios Stoudites died on 20 February 1043: Tinnefeld (1989) 100.
76. Cf. Jeremiah 1:5.
77. Cf. Psalm 118:26–33.

trials he suffered so gently: the result was that his accession was all the more magnificent. My speech will explain exactly how that took place.

20. The imperial decision was confirmed through some dreams sent by God. So he summoned this man to himself supposedly for some other matter, and he offered to him the patriarchal throne, believing that he was announcing good news to him. As if what he had heard was not amazing, he [Keroullarios] reacted to it with no joy at all. He even seemed to be unhappy, being annoyed by what he had heard. As if he had done nothing worthy of such a grace himself, the man who had all the grace of God in himself, and was devoted to it, said: "I should prepare myself, O emperor, so as not to be shaken by such a development. If the time you allow me for my preparation is not enough for me to receive the Holy Spirit, find someone else who is ready for that. The time is not yet ripe for me to receive such a gift."

21. As soon as the emperor heard this, he understood the meaning of his own decision more deeply. For the man was shrewd and did not [**24P**] pay attention to the denial itself but rather to the manner of it. He thought that hearing such a message with such composure, without being disturbed at all, and giving such a calm answer were signs of a steadfast soul and of piety. Therefore, he held to him more tightly than before, given that he [Keroullarios] wanted to escape, and he captured him as he was trying to escape. He captivated him while he was trying to slip through his hands, and forced him to accept his offer. Seeing no escape at all, he was persuaded against his will and agreed with what the emperor was proposing. Although he did not like it, he gave his assent.

22. I think than even if there were no other achievements for someone to praise, this would be enough to form the subject matter of a panegyric. Even if one left aside the art of rhetoric, not wishing to employ its methods for elevating that achievement, the nature of the events itself would be adequate; there would be no need for rhetorical shrewdness. Let us examine matters in this way. There are two illustrious dignities in life, that of the emperor and that of the patriarch, and no other is higher than those two.[78] That man [Keroulla-

---

78. Keroullarios was a staunch opponent of the emperor's involvement in the affairs of the Church, believing in the equality of the *imperium* and the *sacerdotium*: Tinnefeld (1989) 107 n. 76; and see also Dagron (2003) ch. 7 for a study of the patriarch's imperial ambitions. In his indictment of the patriarch, Psellos accuses Keroullarios of such ambitions too: *Orationes Forenses* 1.2419–2420 (p. 88).

rios] proved himself worthy of both, which was admirable. Although these two were most different from each other by the nature of things, most people thought that he was apt for both. Could anything be more admirable than this? But does it not surpass the art and power of speech that, while he did not desire either aforementioned dignity and was far from striving for them, he was deemed worthy of them by other people but denied the offer both times? We should not forget that many people, who were not deemed worthy of such dignities by anyone, tried to become either emperors or patriarchs by themselves; and, after being expelled and ridiculed, because they threw themselves in the middle, they were punished afterward.

But he was not one of them, far from it. He was afraid of any excesses, or rather, to speak the truth, he had surpassed both dignities through his character. [25P] It is true that the dignity of the archbishop is the most supreme and appropriate, so to speak, even for the Cherubim, but to despise all mundane affairs is higher by far than the greatest dignity of all. It is not thrones that bring one closer to God; no one is respectable because of such things. It is rather the character of the incumbent that adorns that throne; it is that which brings a man who wants to live the life of the mind closer to the one who is beyond all intellect [i.e., God].[79] Having approached him, he considered all other high dignities lower than his own rank and station. His ascent to the patriarchal throne was considered by him a descent.[80] Only his previous life was considered by him a life in God; the dignity of the patriarchy would oblige him to pay attention to the needs of practical life, to be the leader of the people and resist those who wished to break the laws. This too was divine, but it was certainly a distraction from his contemplation of God, preventing the shining of his amazing rays from reaching him.

23. He knew all this, but nevertheless he obeyed the emperor, who, however, did not so much persuade him as force him to accept. It is appropriate to say this: being happy with his prey, the emperor became more graceful and more royal than before, and he arranged for his [Keroullarios'] consecration through his scepter.[81] He entrusted the Spirit to him and surrendered that holy man to holy orders. The procession took place from the palace to the temple: some were walking ahead, others were following, both high dignitaries and clergymen.

---

79. Cf. Plotinos, *Enneads* 3.9.9.12.
80. Cf. Plato, *Republic* 539e. See also Psellos, *Letter to Keroullarios*, 6–7.
81. Cf. Philostratos, *Life of Apollonios* 1.17; also Homer, *Odyssey* 11.569.

Anyone looking at this procession would compare him [Keroullarios] to the sun and those surrounding him with the stars, so brilliant was the visible aspect of that man; but his hidden self was beyond comparison, not just merely greater,[82] because the spirit of exultation flashed upon him. He was possessed by God, but that made him neither gloomy nor broody; rather, he was filled with a spiritual joy. As soon as those who accompanied him in the procession entered the church, they placed him in front of the holy sanctuary and they stood around him like guardians, [**26P**] tending to the preliminary rituals. After those were brought to completion, it was time for him to approach the holy altar. He quickly fell to his knees, and what he said to God in a private way and what answer God gave to him, only he, who was initiated by God alone, was to know. Then he rose up, shining with a pure majestic light; his transformation was seen by all people, who attributed it to an ineffable cause. He then blessed the people and delivered an improvised speech, giving useful advice. As if laying the foundations of virtue for the first time, he began to work toward perfection.[83]

24. Having reached this point, my speech realizes that by what it has said so far about him it has hidden from sight the virtues of other people; and by what it wants to say, it will make his virtues, which we have mentioned so far, appear somehow inferior. What I want to say in advance is this.[84] Some people are devoted to the contemplative life, despising the affairs of this world, while others, not being able to reach that level, limit themselves to ordering the affairs of life, becoming more virtuous than others and serving as an example for their fellow men, whose souls they guide. Now, some have an inclination toward both lives: sometimes they turn their attention to heavenly things and sometimes they look to mundane affairs.[85] Therefore, three are the paths that lead to virtue, the third and "intermediate" one being the most perfect of all; virtuous people praise it more.[86] However, he invented a fourth

---

82. Cf. Gregorios of Nazianzos, *Or.* 7.3.8–9 (p. 186).

83. Keroullarios became patriarch on 25 March 1043, according to Skylitzes, *Synopsis*, p. 429.20; cf. Tinnefeld (1989) 100.

84. For the following, see Psellos, *De omnifaria doctrina* 72.8–13 (p. 46); *Encomium for His Mother* 3.

85. In some of his works Psellos gives his preference to that mixed way of life: Kaldellis (1999) 160–161.

86. Cf. Psellos, *De omnifaria doctrina* 72.8–13 (p. 46); *Encomium for His Mother* 3; and *Chronographia* 6A.8.1–11.

path, not discovered by anyone else. This path has been followed by the angels, who are above us, since the time of their creation by God. What was the innovation? He did not divide up his time, devoting one part of it to God and another to his fellow men: he did not forget men when he was spiritually uplifted through prayer, and he did not abandon divine contemplation when paying attention to the salvation of human souls.[87]

Natural science argues that opposite movements are divided by rest: [**27P**] what moves upward cannot then move downward unless its initial movement ceases, whether that movement originates in itself or comes from an outside source.[88] However, he managed to keep his movement the same, even when he took the opposite direction! His whole life was the exact center of a broad circle, uniting those lives that were opposite to each other and those lives that were similar. What I am saying may sound strange. This was accomplished by him and the angels alone. The angelic orders have been entrusted with the care of several nations[89] or cities, as divine scripture teaches us, and they neither abandon their contemplation of the divine for the sake of the men they protect, nor leave untended the parts of the earth with which they have been entrusted, in order to enjoy their illumination from above. Either he modeled himself upon those angelic prototypes by looking upon their nature, or he discovered that new path innate in himself. He might even have been given that gift by divine grace, which, in my view, is more probable. In any case, he led that life alone: having no other man with whom to share his endeavors, he cannot be compared to anyone else in this respect.

25. I am going to speak in the appropriate place about the other parts and powers of the virtue he managed to acquire both now and later on. But I do not know if it is appropriate to use that verb: he rather brought into action the powers of virtue that were innate to his soul, using them in the appropriate way as far as possible. Let me start from the more comprehensive ones. Who put up a more spirited resistance to the attacks of his passions, shining with his prudence? He did not regard that virtue as an intermediate habitus, but as a true extreme.[90] Who so defeated human nature, walling himself off with a much superior guard? I am referring to his abstention from all things which

87. See also Psellos' *Letter to Keroullarios* 1.
88. Cf. Aristotle, *Physics* 264a19–33; Proklos, *On Plato's Timaios*, vol. 1, 289.
89. Cf. Deuteronomy 32:8.
90. Cf. Aristotle, *Nicomachean Ethics* 1170b6–7.

give rise to a passion opposite to virtue. I think that I can pass over the fact that he harassed his body by wearing a threadbare cloak and neglecting his bodily clothing. He did not undress in order to bathe, despising all treatment of the flesh, enjoying only roughness and all other greater hardships, which [28P] gave him pleasure and even thorough enjoyment, because many others had emulated such a life. I do not want to present him as emulating others, but as someone who opened new, more important paths. But the fact that he educated his imagination not to be adapted to low spectacles but to accept only the higher forms is beyond any human example. Something that cannot be imitated by any other is higher than all archetypes. I am going to explain what this was, so that everyone will understand it and know how he led his philosophical life.

26. As we are composite creatures, the rational part of our soul is mixed with an opposite aspect, which, though irrational, can be tamed through reason. I am referring to the part of the soul that seeks visible beauty. This is useful to man, a composite being, for the purpose of procreation. As we said, it is united with our reason. But if it acquires strength in itself, it may defeat the rational part, going beyond its proper limits, and sweep reason along with itself. But if our reason, which is the best part of our soul, puts a curb on it and silences it, and then manages to turn it to its own direction, making it forget its nature and embrace what is good instead, as if taming with reins a wild beast that will keep quiet even after the reins are removed, then the irrational and desirous part, tamed by our reason, not only throws off all external visions but takes on the shape of the internal, higher ones.[91] In this way, he made his irrational desires obey his reason, and he even managed to cleanse his imagination of bad desires.

I will reveal one of his secrets, which has remained unknown until now. He confessed it to me, because I was his closest friend. When he was awake, the power of his natural imagination was afraid of him, but many times when he was asleep it was excited. Being only a rational soul, he put up a fierce resistance to his irrational part. [29P] He either reproached it with insults or repelled it with his powerful reason. When some nefarious Powers, material and underwordly ones, were allied with it, he repulsed them as well with the weapons of his mind. Thus, at the time of his sleep his mind was alert. The passions and the demons were so afraid of him that they did not dare ap-

91. Cf. Plato, *Phaedrus* 254d–e.

proach him during the daytime; being powers of darkness and shadow, they needed the help of the night in order to attack him. I know that all those who fight against pleasure tend to sweat a lot, being very anxious; they are gloomy; their eyes are dry; they look sullen and do not like to come into contact with other people. But he, even though leading such a life, was full of grace. His speech was sweet and pleasant. He was affable, and his spirit was full of joy. His freedom from emotion, a result of his inner struggle, enriched his soul. He did not complain of suffering during his struggles, but his spirit was content and happy with all that he accomplished.

27. Let my speech return to its initial point. Who else was awarded such crowns for his struggle against the passions? Who else was so full of grace after his struggles? Who else had such a high spirit? I am referring both to the divine one, which fills the eye of the soul with light, and the secular one, which has to do with practical and public life. Nothing escaped his attention, either of the higher things—assuming it is necessary to spell this out—or of the mundane things pertaining to practical wisdom and general learning. His heart was expansive; in fact, the same gift had been given to Solomon from above.[92] He seemed to possess an accurate knowledge of all things divine, but had also examined our lower nature. He went from the oak tree to the hyssop, and there his contemplation came to rest. But he did not despise the roots, juices, and all the other things to which Solomon paid attention. Like all experienced orators, he took care to find the appropriate time for each act, and he divided his educational activity according to the times: he permitted himself freedom of speech as occasion served and adapted his speech to his interlocutor's character. That power was not just an art, it was a true science and a most precise philosophy.

It is a matter [30P] of mere technique and even sophistry to take the occasion into account and adapt yourself to the circumstances in order to cheat the audience; but if you wish to benefit them, this is a philosophic, spiritual approach. Of course, philosophy itself is always the same; she does not adapt herself to various circumstances or subjects. However, this does not permit us to despise ways of teaching and admonition that take circumstances into account. This is neither a forfeiture of the rights of philosophy nor a turn for the worse, but is a most accurate form of philosophy, which a leader of the people must possess. Now, sometimes he went against the current, and many people

92. 1 Kings 2:35a; also Gregorios of Nazianzos, *Or.* 43.73.13–15 (p. 290).

believed that he abused his outspokenness. In fact, that was just an excessive application of the teachings of his higher knowledge. A teacher must examine the circumstances most carefully: if things are deteriorating, leaving him no possibility to benefit his students, he must use a more pointed form of speech and stand up to the dangers.

28. He was not willing to repay the emperor for making him patriarch, as we said above, with his total subordination, as if he had been done a favor.[93] He was not grateful to him for the grace of the Holy Spirit. Thinking that this gift had come from God himself, he considered the emperor just a member of his flock, though the leading one. So he started benefiting his people, beginning with the emperor! If someone wants to impart velocity to a body, he starts from the head, if he is a good scientist: he cleanses it from all bad humors and wipes off the ducts of its senses, through which the spirit of the soul comes into contact with the organs of the senses.[94] In the same way did he think it necessary to put the soul of the emperor into order, the head of the state, so that health may be restored to the whole body of the people. Let no one suppose because of this that he was not a philosopher but an ungrateful man: he repaid the emperor for the favors that he had received from him. Were his admonitions to become virtuous, his advice to avoid bad thoughts, his encouragement to do what was beneficial and pleasant for his people, **[31P]** not a much more important and perfect reward, most appropriate both for the emperor and the patriarch? If the patriarch had obeyed all of the emperor's wishes, most of which were harmful, then the fault would not lie with the emperor but with the patriarch, provided the latter had such bad intentions. Even if the patriarch was only indulging the emperor, I do not think anyone would acquit him. If someone pushes someone else over the edge, instead of restraining him, then the one who pushes is much guiltier than the one who falls. In any case, he was favorably disposed toward the emperor as one of his own people, and was not in bad odor with him; this may be proved by the fact that he confronted all dangers with him, sharing all his misfortunes. To some extent, the fact that the emperor was rewarded with those crowns at the end was due to him [Keroullarios]. But let me not mention those yet. Let my speech return to its own road.

---

93. On the troubled relationship between Keroullarios and Konstantinos IX Monomachos, see Tinnefeld (1989) 101–102.

94. Cf. Psellos, *Philosophica Minora I* 55.1159–1176 (p. 275).

29. Who knew better than him when it was time to speak freely and when to give ground? He made use of both in due measure. Who was more grateful toward his benefactors? He repaid them, either by giving them a good advice or taking care of them in an appropriate manner. Who was more just than him? Other people, considering the teachings about the virtues as mere fragments without any connection to each other, have a desire to attain just one virtue isolated from the others. For example, they may be just in some respect, but at the same time their cruelty is greater than their justice. However, the virtues are interrelated, and one may be more beautiful because of another that is near it. If a virtue is separated from its neighbor that safeguards its beauty, it will not remain the same but will change into its opposite, if we may use such terms; in the same way, if a small shield does not stick with a greater one, it will be conquered by the shield opposite to it, which will then take its place. For this reason, he [Keroullarios] made justice more humble through his philanthropy. His judgments were most accurate because he was neither bribed nor mislead by those he favored. He compensated the inferior part by giving it his own support.

God has implanted paradigms of political justice into our very souls, which are images of higher concepts, in anticipation of the perfect and ultimate judgment that will take place there. But he [Keroullarios], being the arbitrator between soul and mind, [**32P**] awarded to the mind the first prize and to the soul the second prize. By mind I mean either the intelligible illumination, or the peak of the intellect, or the substantial and separate mind, or the greatest part of the powers of the soul.[95] The soul is inferior to all these things I have just enumerated. Even if it is higher than the least of those parts, because a whole is higher than any parts, it is still inferior to the mind, which is higher. He made use of both soul and mind in an impartial way: his mind went before his soul, and through mind he approached God.[96] The body is an instrument of the soul, but no part of the mind may be employed as an instrument. A soul united with a body suffers, so to speak, a division similar to that of the body, but the mind cannot be divided in any way. As soon as God approaches the human soul, which is a low nature, he is not united with it directly but through the intermediary of the mind. Later, he [Keroullarios] stood again as arbitrator between the body and the soul; he subordinated desire to reason, and through

95. Cf. Proklos, *On Plato's Timaios*, vol. 1, 246; Simplikios, *Commentary on Aristotle's "On the Soul"*, p. 286; Psellos, *De omnifaria doctrina* 32.3–5 (p. 30).

96. Cf. Psellos, *De omnifaria doctrina* 33.2–4 (p. 31).

spirit he strengthened his reason, which was a bit weak. But he brought both his spirit and desire under the supervision of his reason.

Having accomplished those judgments within himself first, he then proceeded to arbitrate the disputes of others. He offered himself as an example to the litigants, or through his reason made a distinction for them between what was good and what was bad,[97] giving first place to the former and subjugating the latter to it. He proved that our nature is not made up of equal but of unequal parts, because otherwise there would be no strife inside us, since our mixture would have been governed by equality, or vice versa. His mind was always flying toward God, and his soul was following him. His body did not offer resistance; to the contrary, it strengthened his soul through the practical virtues, which led up and moved upwards too. Having employed justice inside his own exemplary soul, he exhibited it through his political virtue as if in an image. Therefore, in public affairs, especially in those that fell under his jurisdiction, he dispensed justice according to the divine laws, or, to put it more modestly, he followed the ancient laws and their subdivisions.

[33P] The heavenly world is divided into higher and lower orders: the higher ones are near God and are illuminated by him directly, while the inferior orders, which are not in a position to receive that illumination directly, are illuminated in a way adapted to their needs through the intermediacy of the orders above them. In turn, they transmit that illumination to the orders that come after them, and so on. In this way the supramundane group of nine orders leads up to the final liminal station of the angels. The same takes place in ecclesiastic orders: some clergymen are trying to contemplate things divine or are flying toward them, others make themselves a comfortable residence for God, while others still manage to enact or accept something of the higher orders.[98] Among them, he was established as the leader like God: he was divided among them in a way appropriate to each, and, like a judge, he arbitrated supernatural affairs in an extraordinary way.

30. These things are known to very few people; his activities escaped the attention of most people. On the other hand, he could settle their quarrels quickly on the basis of the holy canons, and managed to persuade the litigants to stop their quarrels and accept his decision, because it was accurate and just. He followed the traditions of the Fathers so closely and respected the orders of

97. Cf. Gregorios of Nazianzos, *Or.* 43.1.8 (p. 116).

98. A theory borrowed from Pseudo-Dionysios, *The Celestial Hierarchy* 4.2 (p. 21.9–14), 6.2 (p. 26.11–13), and *The Ecclesiastical Hierarchy* 1.2 (p. 64.23–65).

the Apostles so much that he considered them to be the voice of God, outroaring both our hearing and our soul. Some men, who stand out among others, believe that virtue is something simple and uniform, making no distinction among its several subdivisions and not knowing that the virtuous man proceeds from a lower level to a higher one. Even if they make progress themselves, they are not aware of it. But he [Keroullarios], before proceeding to the higher level and while he was still at the front door of the lowest virtue, made an enumeration of the various ascents of virtuous men and defined each one of them with its proper measure. As he himself reached the end of this or that particular virtue, he grasped its complete fullness and the beginning of the one that came next. Setting out from the practical virtues, he cleansed himself and subjugated his body intellectually to his soul: in this way he contemplated supernatural realities and [**34P**] became a theurgist of the higher mysteries.[99] He considered the virtue of a theurgist to be most appropriate for an archbishop, for the one who approached God could not proceed through the practical virtues (this would be irrational), but at the same time he should not abandon the realm of the body just because he was near God. Contemplation is an illumination that proceeds from our proper nature, but theurgy is a virtue in the image of God himself because it deifies the initiate or helps him to imitate God, as far as his own nature permits him to do so.[100]

Deification is not the same for all and does not bring all to the same level of divinity. Rather, as soon as the soul of each person develops all its powers, reaching that level of perfection appropriate to itself, it will be given the sort of deification that is suited to it.[101] It cannot go beyond the ranks of an angel, and even an angelic order cannot proceed beyond an order higher than itself; nor can that higher order go beyond the one that is above it. That would cause a total disruption, and the world would not be called a *kosmos* any more. Some people speak about a natural virtue that comes after the practical one, which consists in the contemplation of the inner meaning of all beings, not in a scientific but in a spiritual way. Thus, one comes to an understanding of what corporeal and incorporeal are and of how they come together, and of their principles.[102] A man who possesses those virtues does not do so in order to

---

99. Cf. Psellos, *De omnifaria doctrina* 71.1–11 (pp. 45–46).

100. Cf. Psellos, *Philosophica Minora II* 38 (p. 132.9); Plato, *Theaetetus* 176b.

101. Cf. Pseudo-Dionysios, *The Celestial Hierarchy* 1.3 (p. 9).

102. Cf. Psellos, *De omnifaria doctrina* 92.1–12 (p. 53); *Philosophica Minora I* 50.82–83 (p. 189).

enjoy that vision (that comes later on),[103] but through them, as if these were clues, his soul soars toward the contemplation of higher realities.

He [Keroullarios] did not neglect this virtuous practice either, having me as his companion and collaborator.[104] He divided everything that I know into its proper parts. If someone revealed to him the secrets of nature,[105] he became very happy with it as no one else, and then he proceeded to the clarification of some obscure points on the basis of what he had already discovered. If some-one else had told me that about him, I would not believe it, because those things are normally attributed to higher natures, but as I myself was an eye-witness of each of that man's achievements, I am saying something that I both believe myself and discourage anyone from calling into question.

It is possible that the subtle distinctions of my speech, interpreting his achievements in varied ways, have made them appear more admirable, but [35P] the truth is that the facts speak for themselves. The contribution of my speech is minimal, akin to giving various beautiful names to a most clean fountain or employing terms denoting terror for describing a wild beast. Of course I can make a magnificent subject appear trivial with my speech and adapt what is beyond nature to the demands of my present oration,[106] but I would be ashamed if I did not grant them their proper magnificence but trans-formed them to suit the limitations of my speech. In any case, there are many and various styles of speech, some of them lofty, others low. The good orator must adapt the style and the content of his speech to the various circum-stances. I will try to make use of both of them in due measure. If my style be-comes loftier, this will be because of the nature of my subject, not the magnifi-cence of my speech but the man himself who accomplished those things; the magnificence of my speech is simply a result of these achievements.

31. That was the situation, or rather that was how he dealt with these matters, and actual deeds followed as a result of his contemplation and—how might I put it?—his elevation to God. Where [. . .] these things, but that man despised not only money and all sorts of possessions, but even his own body. He was most generous and high-minded in other respects, and he displayed these quali-ties to other people, who might profit more from him [. . .] of the virtues. His

103. Cf. Psellos, *Philosophica Minora I* 31.122–123 (p. 121).
104. Cf. Psellos, *Poemata* 1.125 (p. 6).
105. Cf. Psellos, *Philosophica Minora I* 31.92 (p. 109).
106. Cf. Synesios, *Letter* 5 (p. 16).

way of life, retinue, and all that accompanies such things were appropriate to an ascetic who lives on a mountain. No red carpets were spread for his bed—far from it. He wore a ragged garment on his shoulders, and his undergarment was a rag too; he never changed them, but rather alternated them. What was even more admirable and amazing for me was that although those garments were equal to or even worse than the garments of most people, they still blossomed with an ineffable beauty. He who wore them, although he had brought into his possession the most precious materials, preserved these garments intact.[107]

No experienced cooks prepared seasoned dishes for him, and his food was simple. I mention things of which [**36P**] I was an eyewitness, although when I went to him he welcomed me in a more pretentious manner, because he wanted to entertain me both by sharing his table with me and by the way he welcomed me. In any case, the food they served to us was the same. Only during great feasts did he take the opportunity to entertain high dignitaries or to honor some clergymen in the customary way. Then he tried to offer a more luxurious table and proved himself more lavish and extravagant than any other person. I have already stressed this above, referring to his soul, which was adapted to various circumstances. I want to repeat what I have already said about it in all frankness once again: whatever he wished to do was done in an inimitable way, or rather, in doing what he ought to have done, he was unequalled by anyone else.

32. Let me start from matters of a higher order. When he needed to fly up to God, he was raised up like an angel; when he needed to pray to him, his senses did not function anymore, everything was quiet: only his mind went on functioning, burning with a divine love. But when there was need for him to come down to earth in order to come back into contact with men, albeit all the while still contemplating God, then his nature was divided into mind and senses. Everything was done in an appropriate way, and everything was truly extraordinary. Sometimes he lived as an ascetic, because virtue was his constant companion and because he loved the supreme good, and sometimes he lived luxuriously, on account of custom. So he constantly changed his behavior. If one saw him involved in secular affairs, he would not consider him able to live another life, but if he saw him leading an ascetic life, he would consider him able to live only that life; if he had the opportunity to see him in both states, he would go away admiring him. Such was his adaptability to all circumstances.

107. The meaning is obscure due to damage in the manuscript.

All people recognized his supremacy in every field, but he was also superior to anyone who had specialized and gained supremacy in one particular field. I do not know if any other men of old neglected their body to such an extent, having overcome all the necessities of nature, but that was certainly the case with him, who had overcome his nature in a supernatural manner. What was more amazing was that he was not reminded to take food by his own body, but he himself reminded his body to take food, so as to be vigorous, but not to live pleasantly. He did not despise his body as an enemy,[108] [37P] but he took care of it because it was his collaborator, and he kept peace with it as long as it was at peace with him, not violating his treaty with it. In spite of being treated courteously but not extravagantly by him, the body too kept its peace with him; being benefited by him, it was grateful, supporting the spirit and keeping its power intact. If someone were to raise the option of justified suicide,[109] I will respond to him, expounding our own doctrine, namely, that no one is permitted to loosen those bonds himself before God commands it. The contemplation of death and the effort to withdraw from our own body is not accomplished by destroying its natural union with the soul, dividing from each other those two entities which have been united by God for their mutual benefit; rather, it is accomplished by not living like an animal, but living the life of the soul, resisting the natural temptations of our body, destroying our passions, or at least resisting their attacks.

33. I have something more to say about that union, and this is not a digression from the subject I promised to deal with. Nature and soul have a different attitude toward the mixing of opposites. Our nature, having woven the body in our mother's womb, bound it to our soul, while our soul, being mixed or entangled with our body[110] (I do not know how to describe that), is bound to it with a second bond, the inclination of our desire. Therefore, there are two natures and two bonds: the bond of our body to the soul, and the bond of our soul to the body. These bonds can be untied in a similar manner to the way they were tied originally: nature, at God's command, unbinds the body from the soul at the time of the so-called death,[111] while the soul undoes her ties with

---

108. Cf. Plotinos, *Ennead* 2.1.3.1.

109. A reference to the title of Plotinos, *Ennead* 1.9; also Psellos, *Philosophica Minora* I 38 (p. 128.19). The relevant teaching comes ultimately from Plato, *Phaedo* 62b–c.

110. Cf. Psellos, *De omnifaria doctrina* 34.9 (p. 31), 35.4 (p. 31).

111. "So-called" because the soul lives on.

the body through philosophy, contemplating not her natural and forgivable death but a supernatural and higher one. He [Keroullarios] was always dying in that way, not just once, directing the energies of his soul toward the contemplation of creation.

34. [**38P**] The Apostle Paul, who became everything for everyone, won over almost everyone.[112] On the other hand, that man [Keroullarios], though sometimes working against himself, attained the same end. He gained people's favor, not by indulging sinners but through his intransigent attitude toward their failures. Although in other respects he adjusted to the circumstances, he was adamant about this: he recognized no difference between a poor man and an oppressor, but, like Phinees, he kept the same stance toward both.[113] His ardor and passion were always undiminished. He did not yield even to the emperor, who sometimes fell into error, although he loved him: he fought against him for his own sake, appeasing his anger and mollifying his passions. If the emperor broke an agreement, the patriarch reproached him immediately: at first he invoked the law (which was a more suitable approach), then he reproached him, and finally he castigated him vehemently and openly. One cannot adequately praise his tendency to be inexorable and severe toward the emperor in correcting him. But if the emperor treated him with insolence, he endured it gently, and when the emperor repented of that, he forgave him his fault. But if he was dismissed the first time he castigated the emperor, he was not discouraged and did not confine himself to simply performing his duty: he went on resisting him, and his soul was upset because he had not accomplished his task completely. He suffered from a very painful wound that could not be cured, unless he had the opportunity to speak freely and accomplish his purpose. But although the emperor was very angry at the beginning, after he was appeased and came to his senses he was not unfavorably disposed toward the patriarch for preventing him from doing what he wanted; as he had now been turned to a better path, he was grateful to him for restraining him and making him better.

35. People are willing to acknowledge all the other virtues of that great father. No one will call them into question. But some people, whom he opposed, accuse him of being severe [**39P**] and persistent in his anger. Therefore, I am going to say what I know regarding this very matter, namely, his severity, which

---

112. Cf. 1 Corinthians 9:22.
113. Cf. Numbers 25:7–9.

they bring as an accusation against him, by explaining what sort of dispensation he employed when dealing with the people. Since his heart was set upon a single chief purpose and burned with an ardent love for the good, he wanted no one to be deprived of virtue; he wanted each person to be godlike and to take advantage of the Passion of Christ for his own salvation. Wishing to reform all those who were in a bad state, he behaved like a teacher: he whipped them with his speeches and intimidating face; he terrified them and brought them to reason with his stern look. All this was prescribed by the teaching of the Holy Gospel. He did not rush to throw off his stern mask so that no one would be able to realize that his behavior was just pretense, because he was not really indignant; he was only adjusting to circumstance. So those who did not know his character and method of dealing with his flock thought that all this was for real and not a simulation of anger; thus they became better over time, being educated by such a stern teacher. Some people, not knowing this, believed him to be quick to anger and hard to be appeased. I will reveal a secret so as not to be thought of as trying to spin the truth with my speech and hide the truth. I took the liberty of asking this great father once about his behavior, because I wanted to imitate him, even to the point of being led astray. I asked him why he gave such a different impression of his soul in that respect alone, while in all other cases he overflowed with goodness. The patriarch looked at me calmly, nodded his head, and said: "If I did not act in this way, I would not win over the souls of so many people. Otherwise, if my soul were not totally free of that passion, I would be afraid of that behavior too."

36. He was unconquerable, very hard to catch no matter what wrestling holds were used against him; he was altogether superior to them. What we can understand about the man, we admire, but if we cannot understand something, we are at a loss. We do not pay attention to the best of all seasons,[114] nor do we wonder if God thunders in the spring or if the weather is sometimes paradoxically clear in the winter, [**40P**] relieving our gloominess. Moses, being a human being, ignored the divine dispensations and prayed to God to cure his sister who became a leper, but God accused Moses for the hastiness of his prayer, employing an example taken from human nature.[115] My view is that the natural characteristics of our soul include neither changing our behavior easily nor remembering the wrongs of our enemies forever. However, some

114. Presumably summer.
115. Cf. Numbers 12:10–15.

people call the former goodness and the latter firmness. In any case, if someone uses these within the bounds of reason and good judgment, giving the impression that he is dissimilar to himself, that man is worthy of great praise and admiration. He himself [Keroullarios] testified to the fact that these qualities were alien to his character and were not a personal flaw, and that he employed them in order to educate his people by using an ineffable dispensation: many times he rushed to defend immediately those who came into conflict with him, if something happened to them. If he had really been angry with them, he should have agreed with the emperor or even incited his anger toward them. Far from it: as if being unaware of the dangers they had to cope with, he offered them his own support.

37. That is his defense toward those who did not understand his good qualities. All men who are illustrious and great in virtue are prominent for one or another particular virtue, and that one quality stands out when its possessor is compared to other great men. His distinctive trait was mildness;[116] then come magnificence and munificence. This cannot be understood unless I describe one of his many deeds that stemmed from that particular virtue. Besides, the story is pleasantly entertaining. Every year a great feast took place in the holy church of the Apostles.[117] The archbishop of Constantinople used to take part in it. He came accompanied by his usual retinue and divine splendor. After holding his habitual intercourse with God, he started inspecting the church from above and around, admiring its images and the hand that had painted them. Truly, the contemplation of the icons of that church is a delight for anyone who loves beauty. **[41P]** Not only have the various colors been combined and separated in an accurate representation, but, if one wants to examine matters more deeply, he will discover various philosophical concepts hidden inside those images.

After he [Keroullarios] was satisfied with all the amazing things he had seen, he peeped out from the gallery of the church downwards, appearing suddenly to all those who were inside the sanctuary or standing outside it. All trembled to look upon him. Some rose from their seats, while all those standing crossed their hands and brought their feet slightly together. To all those who were looking at him as he appeared suddenly from above he seemed more godlike

116. See also Psellos' *Letter to Keroullarios* 1.

117. Probably on 30 June, when the feast of the Holy Apostles is celebrated according to the Orthodox calendar.

than before. Among them was someone standing by who looked the patriarch straight in the eye, not being ashamed at all; he behaved like a vehement rebel! At first the patriarch thought this was due to an oversight and did not reproach him at all. But when he realized how impudent the man was, he ordered that he be brought before him. This was not done without violence. Some of the holy attendants arrested him as if he were accused of something, and they constrained him to move, insulting and mocking him. The man was frozen with fear and almost dropped dead before judgment had been given. He did not know how he would stand before the archbishop who would be his judge. He expected to see rivers of fire sweeping him along toward the tribunal,[118] a deep darkness, and the angels standing by and giving evidence of his crime.[119] As soon as he approached the dais of the archbishop, this man stood in front of it terrified, expecting the worst.

But look now upon the divine soul of the patriarch, which cannot be adequately praised. He spoke more mildly than usual and did not reproach him for what he had dared to do, not in the least. He called him to himself with a gentle voice and—what a miracle!—was reconciled to the one who had insulted him. He even gave him his own hand together with the grace of the spirit, and made him a clergyman. Will anyone consider *that* behavior severe? I think that all will rather call it pure mildness and natural goodness. How can anyone regard the indignation that he showed toward sinners as a real vice of his soul and not a timely façade, considering that he offered greater gifts to those who insulted him, [42P] instead of being angry with them? A man who used a great sin as an opportunity to show the sheer magnitude of his soul and his mildness could not behave otherwise in the case of a lesser offence, unless his deceptive severity had a deeper meaning that could not be understood by the many. Was it possible for a man, who did not permit even the slightest passion to enter his soul, to dwell upon past injuries? If remembering past wrongs is a lasting anger, it is impossible for such a passion to be born in the soul of someone who has no anger at all.

38. If one wants to know the truth, who among all people was perceived to be more benevolent than he? Who was so eager to fight for the sake of the people? Who was so willing to face danger along with those who were in dan-

---

118. Daniel 7:10.
119. Cf. Matthew 13:50 and 25:41.

ger? He shared mentally in the torments of the tormented, and his soul was wounded together with those whose body had suffered. He would gladly have surrendered himself for the sake of the freedom and salvation of his flock, putting into practice what Paul had taught.[120] Having mentioned his philanthropy and his zeal for the practice and cultivation of that virtue, I want to dwell upon that subject for a while, in order to give you a pleasant narrative. The emperor was once in serious trouble. One of his kinsmen[121] attacked him with a very strong army from the west. I am addressing you who have known the anger of that beast and his unrestrained charge and assault. Things were going from bad to worse for the emperor: the worst of all was that the whole army had sided with the rebel. That man, taking heart because of the multitude of his own army and because the emperor had no army at all with which to confront him, was in a hurry to start the attack. So he threw everything into commotion. The City was almost surrendered to him. Our only hope to remain free was offered by our walls.

The emperor looked like a man shut in from all sides. The siege was vigorous. We decided to resist the enemy with the small part of our army that had remained with us; some [43P] generals persuaded the emperor to do that.[122] But as soon we clashed with them, we retreated into the City and shut ourselves in there, nearly causing the total retreat of all those who were inside our walls.[123] If a divine power had not restrained those who were victors that day from advancing forwards, our great City would have been captured together with its men, and all things would have been seized by them.[124] Such a disaster had fallen upon the emperor. No one could console him except for the tongue and hand of the patriarch, so to speak. He [the patriarch] gave him courage when he fainted, restored him when he had abandoned hope, promised him salvation, made predictions concerning the future, supported him when he was faltering, gave him back the strength of his soul when he was near death. As the patriarch had predicted, the arrows of the enemies turned

120. Cf. 1 Corinthians 9:19.

121. Psellos is referring to Leon Tornikios, nephew of the emperor. His revolt against Konstantinos IX in 1047, the siege of Constantinople, and the subsequent defeat of the rebels are described in detail by Psellos, *Chronographia* 6.99–114.

122. Skylitzes, *Synopsis*, p. 440, attributes that plan to the *mesazon* Konstantinos Leichoudes; see also Cheynet (2003) 366 n. 93; and cf. Psellos, *Chronographia* 6.112–114.

123. This event is described by Skylitzes, *Synopsis*, p. 440.

124. See Cheynet (2003) 367 n. 95.

against themselves, and the long chain of the revolt started to crack here and there. The army was dissolved, and the rebel was surrounded. He became a suppliant and was brought to the emperor in chains. The emperor's fear disappeared, and he was filled with a burning anger. Thinking on their bold acts, he wanted, and had effectively decided, to cut them all into pieces.

But opposing all the others, the patriarch, fighting also against the momentum of the moment itself, asked the emperor, who was the victim of their conspiracy, to have mercy on the conspirators and save them. They were about to be thrown into the sea, to be burned, or to be buried alive, but he saved them from such monstrous punishment and safeguarded their liberty against all expectation. After a pardon was granted to them and the emperor became reconciled with them, so to speak, the emperor started to be angry again. The patriarch appeased his anger to such an extent that the emperor grew afraid of what he had done to some of the rebels previously and thought that he might not be able to repent for what he had done even to those who had *not* been adequately punished. I am referring to the two chief rebels.[125] The emperor wanted to burn them after cutting off their heads, like the heads of the Lernaean Hydra,[126] but the patriarch did not permit him to do what he wanted. To tell the truth, the patriarch was unaware of the emperor's wish; otherwise, the emperor would not have proceeded to such a punishment. He forestalled the impaling of the chief rebel at the last moment, when he was already placed on the scaffold, and he did that not in a quiet and discreet way but [**44P**] with a loud ruckus.[127] He managed to bring him down from the scaffold to which he had been led up and mollify the anger of the emperor, which had become great once more. If this is not the largest sign of his philanthropy, I ask to be shown a greater example; then I will keep quiet. Otherwise, I attribute that virtue in its entirety to him alone.

39. But I almost forgot his greatest virtue. To what am I referring? His zeal for the faith, which was hot and even burning: it was consuming his soul with

125. Leon Tornikios and Ioannes Batatzes, Tornikios' main supporter; see Skylitzes, *Synopsis*, p. 442.76–77; cf. Cheynet (2003) 367 n. 97. Both of them were blinded.

126. The Lernaean Hydra was killed by Herakles; cf. *Corpus Paroemiographorum Graecorum* vol. 1, p. 169.1–18 (Zenobios 2.83). In all probability, the emperor, after blinding the two men, wanted to execute them, considering their blinding an inadequate punishment.

127. According to Tinnefeld (1989) 101, this is the only concrete evidence of Keroullarios' opposition to the emperor Konstantinos IX. See also Psellos, *Orationes Panegyricae* 1.146–150 (p. 8).

ineffable flames and was also setting fire to the souls of the enemies of the faith, burning them completely with a strange fire coming from heaven, like the one that burned down the priests of shame.[128] What I want to say may be evident and well known to all of you, but I am writing it down for the sake of future generations, so that they admire his ardor for religion.

Old Rome quarreled with the new one, and not over trifles, either.[129] The matter was not to be overlooked, as it had to do with the most important of our pious doctrines, the theology of the Holy Trinity. Those supporting the other position *seem* to be speaking reasonably, and the difference seems not to be that great. But their position is entirely impious. I do not know whether there is a greater difference than this one between the two sides. Instead of confessing, as they ought to, that both the Son and the Holy Spirit proceed from the Father, each one in his own particular manner, and bring back to their principle those two persons who shine together, being equal to each other, and giving them their proper names, they argue correctly that the Father is the principle of the other two persons, but, subjugating the Son and the Spirit to the Father, they claim that the Son comes from the Father while the Spirit proceeds from the Son in some way.[130] That hidden heresy was first invented by Areios;[131] then it was expounded more accurately by Eunomios,[132] if we are permitted to use the term "accurately" instead of saying "in a more impious way." Eunomios made that teaching the foundation of his impious doctrine.

Other people did not consider that thing to be something terrible, and its development probably escaped their attention, but our defender of the faith and ardent fighter for the Word of God could not tolerate that. So he fought for the sake of the mother city, Rome, trying to save the true doctrines, fighting accurately [45P] and ardently against her for her own sake. He tried as hard as he could, advising her, sending her letters, urging her, using scriptural

128. The priests of Baal burned by Elijah (1 Kings 18:38).

129. This introduces an account of the "schism" of the two Churches in 1054, which was not an event that many Byzantine sources noted. Under Psellos' name is preserved a long poem against the Latins: *Poemata* 57 (pp. 407–415). However, the attribution of such a bad poem to Psellos seems doubtful.

130. The doctrine of *filioque* that continues to divide the eastern and western Churches.

131. The famous heretic of the fourth century AD, a priest at Alexandria.

132. A follower of Areios, leader of the Neo-Arians (Anomians), and an opponent of Basileios of Kaisareia (the Great) and Gregorios of Nyssa.

passages, employing various arguments, trying with all means to persuade that nation to agree with us, so as not to see the mother quarreling with her own children.[133] But in spite of all his efforts he did not manage to persuade them. Those castigated became even more impudent. So he burst out, confronting the insolence of the heresy with the accuracy of the orthodox faith. How did he do that? It is actually an entertaining story.

Some of their leading clergymen[134] dared to quarrel with us [in 1054] about our ecclesiastical jurisdictions and to compete with us in doctrinal matters, trying to prove that they were cleverer than we in such things . For the sake of their faith they were ready to fight against us, constructing various arguments, misinterpreting the Holy Gospel, and even falsifying the holy texts to support their theory. Their heresy was tritheism or even worse. How can God be an entity that comes out of its own privation? How can God be an entity before which a greater entity is placed, which divides it from its first principle? How can they say that they believe in one God when they separate his own products from the first principle instead of bringing them back to it, and transform the initial equality through division into inequality? They confronted us with these impious doctrines, but they could not find anyone to defeat. After they clashed with the leader of our army, this great father, they were defeated at the time of their first attack, so they retreated all together.[135] Ashamed of their unexpected defeat and retreat, they did not dare to confront us openly any more. Being cut off from our fellowship, they shot some arrows of words against us, but these fell upon a reflective surface and turned back against them. As soon as the holy father became aware of those words, or rather that trap, he cut their arguments into bits, and he excommunicated from the Church those who had committed a manifold impiety and placed them under that most frightful curse.

40. [46P] I can admire this too. And if I compare it with another incident and his general attitude toward the divine, I am even more amazed that he had managed to discover something even greater than that. Look at this, in order to

---

133. On the correspondence between Pope Leo IX and Keroullarios before the schism of 1054, see Tinnefeld (1989) 105 n. 64.

134. Cardinal Humbertus of Silva Candida, Friedericus of Lothringen, and the archbishop Petrus of Amalfi were sent to Constantinople in 1054.

135. A reference to the excommunication of Keroullarios, Leon of Ochrid, and the *sakellarios* Konstantinos, which was placed by the three Roman envoys upon the altar of Hagia Sophia on 16 July 1054. See Shepard (2008) 601–602.

understand what I am saying. The pious faith belongs to all people, who were gathered from dispersion into the same faith, invited by the words of the Gospel. No one is more pious than another. Some people who have a better and more accurate understanding of our doctrines may be more prominent than others, but as far as simple confession of faith is concerned we are all equal to one another, enjoying the same honors. I am not referring to the fact that he [Keroullarios] knew the doctrines better than other people, since all are in agreement on that point. I do not consider him higher than all others for that reason, but for another, even greater one, which I cannot express as perfectly as I wish since our tongue is not in a position to express all our thoughts. I am going to explain as best as I can what happened to him regarding religion, of which I myself was often an eyewitness.

He was close to God, but not only due to his accurate knowledge of the doctrines. Let me try to define what is ineffable in a few words: he was dependent on God in an unspeakable and supernatural manner. I do not know when this took place, that is whether before or after he learned the doctrines most accurately. Through his ineffable thoughts he was always dependent on God. He showed this through the symbols as well, especially when speech proceeded out of his mouth attended by the wings of an archbishop. When he fixed his eyes on that, his heart was absorbed by what was happening during the liturgy, and he was elevated up from the earth almost one meter. Realizing that the words of his mouth were not separate from himself, but at the same time that it led all those who were separated from him to a better union with himself, he said something that was both humane and sympathetic. What was it? I entrust it to your sympathetic ears: "The traitor [Judas] was bad indeed and the most ungrateful of all people. At the same time, more than anyone else he became the cause of our salvation. I hate him for his treason, which is only natural, but at the same time somehow I have pity on him, because he became the cause of our salvation."

I have not said this without reason. I do not tell the story in order to honor him even more, but in order to show to you his innate love for things divine. I do not admire a man who writes pious treatises, expounding the doctrines accurately, weaving arguments against the infidels, and being most **[47P]** knowledgeable, but who does not display a reverent attitude toward these things, instead using his tongue in a haughty manner for explaining things divine, while his heart is far away from their divinity. But he [Keroullarios], using a few words for things that surpass the power of speech and mind, was able to comprehend the intelligible realities through the supreme power of his mind. Now, I want to speak in more detail about a habit of his soul that I have already mentioned, namely, that he lived above the earth but at the same time took part in our worldly lives; the one did not diminish the other, but both were equal. Let him remain above us in reality, while we will bring him down here only in speech.

41. He considered all men his kinsmen and took care of them all in an appropriate way. But he took special care of his own kinsmen, being bound to his family through the natural bond of love. The throne did not make him more magnificent and inaccessible to them, nor did the dignity of archbishop lead him to hold them in contempt. He continued to behave toward them in the same manner that he behaved to all people before taking on that high dignity. At the beginning he behaved toward his other acquaintances with reservation, avoiding them as if they were not the same people he knew before. But he discovered a new way of relating to the sons of his brother.[136] They were both good-looking, but their souls were more beautiful than their bodies, and they were both close friends of mine, I who am writing the present speech. They were the hearts, so to speak, of his soul: they gave life to him and they received life from him as well. They also received from him the name which is attributed to the literal "innards" of the body.[137] They lost their father when they were still in the prime of their youth and hardly remembered him. Therefore, they looked to their uncle, trying to imitate his character. It did not take long for them to achieve that, as their souls were apt for copying his manners. He [Keroullarios] wanted to form their souls by impressing his own character upon them, but they were equally eager to receive that impression. Let me do his kinsmen some honor for the sake of him. [**48P**] At the same time, I will have the opportunity to introduce into my speech a lesson in philosophy.

The impression they both received from their uncle was one and the same, namely, they became better than most people, being eminent among them, but they imitated his character in a different way. The good was impressed upon both of them, but each one adapted it to his own character. The older one was a truly divine man: his tongue did not speak anything wrong, and his

---

136. Their names were Konstantinos and Nikephoros: Tinnefeld (1989) 98–99 and n. 27. Psellos sent some letters to the older one, Konstantinos, who was his friend. See also Psellos, *Oratoria Minora* 31 (pp. 117–126).

137. *Splagchna* means internal organs but also what is most dear to one.

ears did not receive any bad rumors from depraved men. He was always the same, not adapting himself to the times. He liked righteousness and did not know of anything wrong. His fellow men were not suspicious of him, and he was not suspicious of other people. His soul was simple. He did not pay any attention to the affairs of other people, and he hated meddlesomeness.

That was the character of the one. The other one was a man of graceful character and elegant in his dealings with others. He had an ability to look into the hearts of other men, finding out their true character on the basis of their outside appearance. He was not accessible to all people, but only to those with whom he wished to come into contact. He was not quick to become someone's friend, as he did not give his friendship to all people easily but only to those he had examined carefully and tested. Afterward, he laid down in them the most stable foundations of a friendship. He was shrewder than anyone else and had a sharp intellect. He was able to divide his thoughts. He was devoted to his brother, who was greater than him. He praised his brother's manners more than his own. The great father respected their characters both when they were still children and later too, when they became adolescents. Since they had good but different characters, as I have said, he became their mutual bond so that their differences might not disrupt their similarity. He adapted himself to both of them in a clever way and transformed their differences into a unity. He also brought them to drink at the fountains of my discourse, and they drank from its water abundantly. They learned the arts of speech, and they climbed up the mountain of philosophy.

42. But my speech is not about them, it is about him. Its purpose is to gratify him, examining in detail the goodness of his soul, or rather it wants to show that he possessed all the virtues, although virtue has many subdivisions: one may be more appropriate for a soul that has been altogether freed from the fetters of its body; another one may be more suitable for a soul that has proceeded beyond our nature through philosophy; **[49P]** and another more fit for a soul that lives still with the body and adorns it. He did not take possession of just one of those virtues, refusing to take the other. Nor, after reaching that one virtue after a short flight, did he suffer the so-called "shedding of the wings."[138] Instead, he took possession of all of them, both together and individually, in a profound way and each in the most appropriate way. He surpassed all virtuous men, and each one even with respect to the quality at which he was best. In

---

138. Cf. Plato, *Phaedrus* 246c.

summary, he surpassed everyone in every respect. He became the greatness and glory of the dignity of the position of the archbishop, which is the most elevated of all dignities by nature and its lofty character. He did not adorn it with speech, nor did he expound many philosophical teachings about it. Rather, he had the appropriate character for that dignity. The virtue of his soul and its magnificence were fit for that greatest of all dignities and rivaled its elevation. No one can adequately describe the respect and reverence shown to him by all the people, their intimidation mixed with love before him, and their fear mixed with joy when they approached him.

43. Well, I do not know what to say, as I want to write two sections, one referring to his ascetic life and another one dealing with his perfect conduct as archbishop. Although there is no difference between them with respect to their goodness, it is easier to combine identity itself with difference itself than to be both an ascetic and an archbishop. The monastic life is hidden away from most people and ineffable. The purpose of the monk is to keep his soul concentrated inside, abandoning most social relations, and to be directed toward God always; quietness is the foundation on which one can be raised up. An archbishop must have these virtues but must be able no less to address all people. The governance of many people is not the same as speaking to God alone. He should employ all methods of education for the people whom he must lead to virtue; he must speak frankly before the powerful and resist tyrants. He must elevate the humble and put down those who are impudent and insolent.

The matter at hand here is how the monastic life can be combined with that of an archbishop, or rather, how *he* combined both in his own person, blending the special characteristics of each one [50P] without falsifying any of them. Those Greek authors who seem to be more important than the others argued that our soul has two parts, one higher and another inferior. I am referring to the rational and the irrational parts.[139] However, they did not manage to explain how these two are combined into one. But he explained it not with arguments but with his own deeds. How? He did not accomplish each one of them in its turn. Let me say it plainly and in few words: his devotion to higher matters did not prevent him from governing the multitudes, and, conversely, his dealing with public affairs did not impede his rising up toward God. These two are not really opposites of each other; the first has to do with contemplative virtue, the other with practical virtue. Contemplation must be

---

139. Cf. Psellos, *De omnifaria doctrina* 61.9–13 (p. 42).

restrained through action, and action must be adorned by contemplation. Likewise, the subordinate aspects of each one of those virtues must be linked together closely. This man did not at all forget the perfect life of the monk as he improved the souls of his flock, cleansed their lives, and generally led them to the good life with all the means at his disposal. All the while, as he was doing this, his mind was flying winged toward God. And when he was devoted to contemplating the divine, he did not neglect the salvation of his people; to the contrary, through his contemplation he secured several means for facilitating their cleansing.

However, he despised everything that had to do with his body, because he had acquired a vision of the intelligible beauty.[140] The Greeks called this an Idea, and placed it after the Good itself. In my view, it is identical with the Good itself; I call it Intelligible Nature. He had no conception of Forms combined with matter. He also loved and admired the proper composition and graceful style of speech, because he considered it a clear reflection of the Good itself.[141] His wish was to compose such beautiful accounts. Let me now add to the speech something about myself. He loved my compositions more than anyone else. If a man had memorized a passage from one of my improvised speeches and recited it by heart, he was very happy to listen to him and became much more graceful; he would virtually embrace that man. [**51P**] He especially appreciated those passages of mine whose subject was most esoteric[142] either because it was hidden from the sight of most men or because it was something highly specialized. Before he heard my account, he expressed amazement that I had something to say about that, as if he did not know anything about demonstrations in technical fields. But as soon as he heard my account, he expressed his admiration once more and said that he would be amazed if I did not talk in that way.

Sometimes he came near to the fountain of my speeches, because I gratified him with my frequent visits to that great father; I gave him something from my own cargo, and I took another cargo from him, as if in a commercial exchange. I cannot describe the joy with which he was filled at the time.

140. Possibly an echo of Plato, *Phaedrus* 250d–254c; cf. Psellos, *Philosophica Minora* I 7.106–107 (p. 25).

141. Cf. Plotinos, *Ennead* 1.8.13.9–11.

142. Psellos had dedicated to Keroullarios a treatise on alchemy: Tinnefeld (1989) 124 and n. 177; but see Musso (1977) 9–10, who argues that the treatise was addressed to the emperor Michael VII Doukas.

Sometimes he secretly tested me. He had heard that I could improvise on questions referring to divine things and that, having memorized the ancient commentaries on them, I added to them something I had grasped by myself. So he asked me about the meaning of some scriptural passages, the exegesis of which he had learned from the ancient interpreters accurately in advance. After hearing what they had said and what I had added to them through my own research, he embraced me like a father, kissing my head many times. He gladly exchanged all his knowledge for my own wisdom and honored me excessively.[143]

44. But he was sad that I was wallowing in the inferior affairs of this world, spending time at the court. I was willing to weigh myself in his scales, but I could not do so, because the palace had a claim on me too. That was the cause of a certain quarrel that broke out between me and the patriarch later on.[144] I am going to defend my position with a speech another time. I cannot now deal with that matter, because I am composing an encomium, not an inquiry. I can say only the following. If I am permitted to say so, he spoke less philosophically than I did in responding to him. I am addressing his own soul, who knows that: he is a jury that cannot be cheated. What I gave him in return for his disposition toward me was not only equal but greater than his own offering, to the same degree that this man was greater and more important than me. And may I never encounter any man from whom I may draw some profit, if I did not derive anything from his river of goods, [52P] while he too drew something from my own source. May I never draw any profit anymore if this is not true. However, the magnitude of his love for me and of my own love for him was the cause for things taking another turn; people who envied me managed to estrange him from me. Let my digression stop here. What I have said may serve as a defense to him. Let truth dispel the shadows of doubt, if any traces of it remain shrouded. I have not yet brought forward the circumstances that may vindicate me. I have not yet employed the art of persuasion that can be used in a geometric way. I have not yet mentioned the wave that swept along many people and me as well, almost drowning me. My mind has not given an oath; therefore, my tongue is free to speak.[145]

---

143. In his *Letter to Keroullarios* 3, Psellos complains that Keroullarios does not give his erudition any attention!

144. One should remember that Psellos composed the indictment against Keroullarios.

145. Cf. Euripides, *Hippolytos* 612.

45. My speech has arbitrated these matters to a slight extent. I did not bring forth my apology, I just mentioned some events that happened at the time so that my oration may not be left colorless. It will go back upwards, because it has already moved too far downwards. I have many things to say about his accomplishments when he acted according to reason for his own good reputation or in making a special dispensation, but I decided not to mention them all, to keep my speech within bounds; still, I took care to mention acts that have a limit within themselves.[146] Let me omit, then, how many of his qualities were supernatural and surpassing Mind; or his raptures during his prayers, and how he managed to follow both roads of virtue, being in the middle of them. This is a virtue of the true fathers, this is his extraordinary and solemn attribute. Let it be unspoken how he spoke to God, leaving his body behind. No speech can adequately praise his hidden activities at night, either when he was ascending to heaven or was being taken to paradise where he heard ineffable words.[147] Let me speak only about those things that are attainable by us and easy to believe for my audience. That part of my speech has finished then, and it now makes a new start.

46. [53P] The time for the emperor to pay the ultimate debt had come [1055].[148] He was undone and breathing his last. His nature had not been exhausted, but the limits of his life had been reached. The emperor begged to be left alive, but death was inexorable. He was full of plans at the time of his death,[149] but all these were quickly cut short by death. The man was dead, but it was as if power had been taken from him some time before. Everything hung in the balance, and the scales tipped in the other direction.[150] In the end, Theodora was favored [1055–1056],[151] and even his own kinsmen almost abandoned the dead emperor, for that was gratifying to the empress. They had

---

146. The meaning is obscure.

147. Cf. 2 Corinthians 12:4.

148. Konstantinos IX died on 11 January 1055: Tinnefeld (1989) 118 n. 140; also Psellos, *Chronographia* 6.202.

149. Konstantinos IX wanted to proclaim Nikephoros the *proteuon* emperor, but he died before bringing his plan into completion: Attaleiates, *History* 51–52.

150. Some collaborators of the emperor, wishing to fulfill their master's plan, tried to proclaim as emperor the *proteuon* Nikephoros before the emperor died, but their plan was forestalled by Theodora's supporters: Skylitzes, *Synopsis*, p. 478.85–95.

151. Theodora, the last surviving member of the Macedonian dynasty, daughter of the emperor Konstantinos VIII, reigned from 1055 to 1056.

been opponents, and even at the time of his death she was not reconciled to him.[152] But our father, although he had many reasons to bear malice against the departed, went to the deceased, though no one had called him. He did not despise him as a man lying dead on his bed, but approached him with the proper respect, as if he were sitting on the throne, holding an assembly for the election of magistrates. He crossed his hands and kissed him, shedding many tears from his eyes as if he were defending himself on matters about which the emperor should have spoken in his own defence. Then he assembled his clergymen, and they sang the prescribed psalms and prayers. Afterward, he covered him and buried him magnificently.[153]

But it was predestined that the situation would change again. The patriarch, being afraid lest something bad happen, started to lay down the law for the empress. At first she followed his injunctions, considering them as a law given by God, but then she changed too, bringing forth her own laws that were different from the laws of our father and even ran counter to the canons. That was not of her own will, but some ambitious persons,[154] boasting that they were straighter than a measuring rule, influenced her and persuaded her to adopt their views. Our father said that the state needed the soul and mind of a *man*,[155] but they overlooked his desire because it was not profitable to them. He was speaking about what was needed for the state, but they were striving after what was profitable to them. Therefore, there was a general dissent [**54P**], and there was no agreement about a common goal. The friends of the empress did what they wished, or wished what they did. The patriarch did not collaborate with them, not agreeing with what was taking place. He kept his own rules, being devoted to the intelligible life that had been given to him from above and that he had chosen himself. He neglected all other things.

47. After a short time the empress also reached the end of her life [1056].[156] Let me omit what took place at the time, because I have respect both for her

152. At *Chronographia* 6A.15.5–7, Psellos states that Theodora respected Monomachos.

153. Konstantinos IX Monomachos was buried as a commoner, according to Skylitzes, *Synopsis*, p. 478.92–93; see Cheynet (2003) 394.

154. Among them was Leon Paraspondylos, the most important of Theodora's courtiers: Tinnefeld (1989) 119 and n. 143. Psellos had sent many letters and a poem to Paraspondylos: *Poemata* 28 (p. 295).

155. This is stated also by Psellos himself: *Chronographia* 6A.6.1–5 and 6A.17.6–8.

156. Theodora died on 31 August 1056: Tinnefeld (1989) 120 and n. 151.

and for the man who was chosen by her as her own successor.[157] I was present for all of this, and I am ashamed to tell the truth about the events of that time. Let me say just this. She was entrusted with the election of whoever was good, and with her eyebrows alone she nodded her approval of what had been decided by others.[158] She preferred as an emperor a man chosen by her own collaborators above the others. Silence moved her tongue, and the interval that she would have used for speaking was taken as a sign of her approval. All those initiated into these secret plans knew what had taken place, but other people did not know the reason. In this way Michael became emperor. The empress survived for a short time and then died.[159] The great father came to perform her funeral and to give her successor laws by which to rule.

But let me mention what I almost forgot to say: while the empress was still alive, she spoke her final, imperial speech, and then fell into silence. The man chosen to be her successor needed the great hand of the holy father in order to be crowned, and he asked him to come with all his heart, imploring him in a manner more appropriate to a humble man than an emperor. But the patriarch—O for his soul, that surpassed all goodness of character!—did not rush to do what was asked, not being afraid of the man who prevailed in the fight for the throne. He did not neglect or think lightly of their unkindness toward himself, but paid more attention to the empress who was breathing her last than to the weighty business of the succession. He asked if the appointment of her successor was made by her, or if she had deliberated about it, or at least if it was approved by her. As soon as he arrived and found her still alive, he asked her just a small question that she was in position to answer, [55P] whether she had chosen her successor or not. Seeing her in the agony of death, he said: "O empress, do not be in a hurry to answer my question; just give a nod of agreement indicating your satisfaction with that choice." She gave such a nod, and the patriarch was assured. Then he proceeded to the emperor and performed the service established by ancient laws for the coronation of the emperor, placing the crown on his head. Then he embraced him, improvised some advice appropriate for the circumstances, and retired, leaving his words as guardians of the new emperor.

48. The situation had changed, but at the same time had remained the same. The reign of the one [Theodora] had come to an end, and the reign of the

157. I.e., Michael VI Stratiotikos, 1056–1057.
158. I.e., by the influential Leon Paraspondylos.
159. Cf. Psellos, *Chronographia* 6A.20–21.

other [Michael VI] had begun. But that was the only change. The status quo of the state remained the same under both emperors: the officers entrusted with imperial correspondence remained the same; the superintendent of the whole,[160] the court heralds, those initiated into state secrets, and the guardians of the backstage dealing were the same as before. There was no change at all. The key point was that our father took no part in the affairs of the state. Everything was breaking down because there was no one to sustain them. I am not going to say anything bad about the emperor. Some others may care less about his good character, and they may use plenty of words, accusing him. What I will say is that he can be compared to the most virtuous men on account of the simplicity of his manners and his unskilled soul. His character exhibited all good traits, and, if one were to compare him to other emperors, far from them humbling him he would bring shame upon them.

But he did not know how to hold the reins of the state.[161] I must confess the truth. He did not know how to restrain or steer the horses that pulled the chariot of the state;[162] he was rather impelled by them than impelling them himself; he could not lead them, but was led by them, or rather he was led astray because he did not know this art of charioteering. Therefore, he entrusted the governance of the state to others, while he was living like a private citizen.[163] I am resorting to more human qualities in order to judge the whole situation [56P] accurately in a manner befitting a prudent man. In any case, things were predestined to take this turn by God, and I am astonished to realize that no situation may take another turn than what is predestined. In spite of that, no one may be acquitted by us if he commits a sin in that situation.[164] Therefore, I may criticize how the whole situation turned out, even though it may not be morally reprehensible in some respects. But one may reproach it in a speech for all the horrible things that took place afterward and destroyed everything. So let no bad thing be said about it; thus my soul will calm down, because I am not accustomed to accusing people.

The appointment of the emperor is not to be blamed at all. No accusation against him may be leveled. And let all those who gave him the imperial power

160. I.e., Leon Paraspondylos.

161. Cf. Psellos, *Chronographia* 6A.7.3.

162. Cf. Psellos, *Chronographia* 7.56.6–7.

163. This is confirmed by Attaleiates, *History* 52–53, and Skylitzes, *Synopsis*, p. 480.37–40.

164. Psellos seems to be making the point that the emperor was not a bad man, for all that he was incompetent.

and took care of the affairs of the state be considered good men and capable administrators, and let their intentions be considered most honest. Divine providence will pursue its own purpose, and things will come to their present condition. My goal is not to examine the cause of those events. I refer to them not for their own sake but only in order to bring my speech to its appropriate subject. As if bringing the holy father into the light myself, I discussed the beginnings of his existence; then I went on to promote him and discussed various events that took place at other times; finally, I placed his light upon the lamp stand[165] and made some digressions there, too. After discussing important events in which he was involved, I am now coming to the end of his life. It is now necessary for me to narrate some other events, in which, or because of which, he accomplished great things, and after which the true servant of the great God offered his own life as a sacrifice to the Lord. I will have to go back a bit in time.

49. For a long time the soldiers had not considered the situation of the state to be tolerable. All of them together and each one of them separately [**57P**] complained because the emperor was always chosen from among the other side, I mean the civil servants. Even when a decision was to be made concerning the head of the army or the commander of a military unit, leadership was entrusted to men inexperienced in war. Those who lived inside the cities received greater offices than those who endured the hardships of war. When the need arose for some to conduct hard battles and resist adverse fortunes, those who lived in Constantinople could sit back and relax as if in a great castle, while those who lived far away from the City in the countryside suffered terribly. For these reasons they were ready to protest against this situation in a most violent manner, and they lacked only a spark to set off their explosion. And then it happened. No one asked them their advice concerning the appointment of the new emperor; they were held in contempt;[166] and the leadership of the army was entrusted to other hands. All this was the cause of that great thunderstorm, which would have almost burned and destroyed the entire state, if God from above had not taken notice.

The revolt did not resemble any past mutinies of the army. This time the entire army revolted, not just a part of it. Those who held the first and second

---

165. Cf. Matthew 5:15.

166. According to Skylitzes, *Synopsis*, p. 483.18–20, the emperor refused to appoint Isaakios Komnenos and Katakalon Kekaumenos to the office of *proedros*. Psellos gives a somewhat different story, saying that the emperor insulted both men (*Chronographia* 7.3.10–25). The version of Psellos is confirmed by Attaleiates, *History* 52–53.

ranks, the leaders of the companies and their deputies, those who fought hand-to-hand with weapons, the javelin-men, rock-throwers, experts in sieges, even the lowly slingers, both nobles and the humble, had all together formed one formidable army against us. It was the most important and powerful part of the eastern army. They did not consider themselves as mutineers but as lawful pretenders resisting usurpers. They chose the best one among themselves as their leader, and they obeyed him as if he were an emperor, submitting themselves to him [Isaakios I Komnenos].[167] That is what they were busy with.

Now, the emperor [Michael VI] and his associates were filled with fear, but no plan could be drawn up even though the great patriarch was at hand, the chief element in all actions, the leader of the Church, the man who had the greatest dignity, being both a father and a leader, the most virtuous of all people, possessing both that virtue that leads to God and the one that is appropriate for the conduct of public affairs. All who have even a limited knowledge of these events know well that [58P] the patriarch took a middle position between the two adversaries; he was adamant and so powerful that the party to which he offered his support would prevail. Who could be more useful as a mediator, if they decided to seek refuge with God? But they did not make a good decision. Therefore, the link was broken. If the patriarch had not made the right decision at that time, throwing himself into the middle of the dangers and managing affairs in a discreet way; if he had not arbitrated the dispute justly, restraining vehemence here and improving the situation there, the ship of our state would have sunk and we would all have drowned together, as the waves were huge, rising up to the sky. My speech will briefly explain how all this transpired.

50. The emperor drew up some battalions left in the western provinces and sent them against the rebels. A war broke out between the two armies, and the two sides clashed with each other. They fell on each other in packed formations, and a cloud of dust rose up.[168] Many soldiers were killed, rivers of blood flowed, all things were mixed together; there was no end to the disaster. Some were killed now, others were to die later; they pushed and pushed back in their struggle to kill; for some this calamity was against their own people in defence

167. On 8 June 1057, the officers of the eastern provinces, Katakalon Kekaumenos being prominent among them, acclaimed Isaakios I Komnenos emperor (1057–1059); see Tinnefeld (1989) 120.

168. Cf. Homer, *Iliad* 3.13.

of themselves:[169] sons fought against fathers; people attacked their own countrymen; everyone was stained with the blood of kinsmen. There was a mighty noise, but the danger was greater than the noise, and everyone was threatened with a very quick and sudden death. In the end the rebels won, and they put our men to flight, defeating them completely.[170] Some of them barely survived to bring news of the disaster. What happened next? They announced the disaster to the emperor, who fell down as soon as he heard it, abandoning all efforts to resist. However, he still did not ask for the only medicine that could cure that wound. The people of Constantinople were agitated and joined the rebels outside.[171]

The great ship of our state was in great danger, threatened not only by the rough sea, but also by the fact that even those who were responsible for keeping it on the right track had fallen into the sea. Those people, who had brought everything into disarray, [59P] did what the emperor had not done in advance: they asked the holy father to stop the earthquake. It really was an earthquake: the rebels shook us from outside, and the people inside were agitated.[172] All had the same aim, but they quarrelled with each other and both committed and suffered the worst crimes. They went over to the victor and had surrounded the loser like wild beasts; they wanted to take him and tear him up. They could not catch him, so they besieged him in a dreadful manner, lighting a fire against him from afar. They armed themselves, took up swords, did terrible things, and threatened him with their speech.

In the end, they invaded the Great Church [Hagia Sophia]. Men who had never before carried weapons were ready to fight and armed for war. They came to the church[173] both to find shelter and to resist the emperor. They took refuge there in order to be saved, but at the same time they were ready to fight against him, killing all their enemies. But look now upon the governor there, and admire him. He was not frightened by the sight of this mob, he was not afraid of that invasion of the citizens, or rather of the barbarians. He was not

169. This clause is obscure.
170. In the middle of August 1057: Tinnefeld (1989) 120. On these events see Psellos, *Chronographia* 7.3.1–43; Attaleiates, *History* 53–54; and Skylitzes, *Synopsis*, pp. 493–496, whose account is the most detailed of all.
171. Cf. Gregorios of Nazianzos, *Or.* 43.57.10 (p. 246).
172. See the similar description of these events by Psellos, *Chronographia* 7.40–43.
173. In the early morning of 31 August 1057: Tinnefeld (1989) 121.

terrified by that onrush of evil, but started calming the tempest down, trying
to save the great ship of the state as far as possible. He was speaking to the in-
vaders from above,[174] placating their anger, restraining their impetus, and trying to persuade them to obey the emperor,[175] arguing that it was not good to
fight when there was still a chance of making peace. That was the initial plan
of the good governor, worthy of a patriarch and great of soul. What more
could he say or do in the midst of such a grave situation, and surrounded by
the churning waves of the sea?

But those below were shouting loudly. There was general confusion and
sounds could not be heard distinctly. In any case, their voice was calling out to
cut the emperor into pieces and to give the throne to the one who had won the
battle. They said that if the patriarch was opposed to that plan, they would
take the responsibility for the crime themselves, leaving the holy father free of
any guilt. At the time, as he was trying to hold the helm of the ship of our state,
other waves were raised up, and the church was a true bedlam. All kinds of
people came in: magistrates, senators, clergymen, all sorts of them, and those
of inferior ranks, ending up, they say, with the trumpeters and the heralds of
the army. Both young and old men, [60P] decent and impudent, educated and
uneducated, were all gathered there. There was no difference among them now,
there was a general agreement. All were equal to each other, having invaded
the church together for the same purpose. Our father, realizing that the situation was beyond control, took hold of the ship helm more firmly and began
to steer it in a expert way. He could not save the throne of the emperor, seeing
that the providence of God clearly favored the other man. So he took care to
save the life of the former emperor and to ensure that power was handed over
to the new ruler bloodlessly. He was clearly annoyed by the plan of action he
was being forced to adopt.

So he dropped a hint to the old emperor—how else can one put it?—
describing in vivid colors the magnitude of the disaster, saying that it was up
to him to decide: he could either take refuge with the patriarch himself and
save his life, or he could wait to see how things would turn out. The emperor

174. Cf. Skylitzes, *Synopsis*, pp. 498–499.
175. This is not true. Keroullarios was deeply involved in the conspiracy against the
emperor Michael VI; his whole attitude testifies to his barely hidden support for the
rebels: Attaleiates, *History* 56–58. Psellos tries to exonerate him, presenting him as bow-
ing to the pressure of the mob in order to save the life of Michael VI.

listened to this message. I do not to know whom to admire first, the patriarch who found the proper solution, or the emperor who made the proper decision concerning himself. That decision alone made up for all his former mistakes; it was equal to or even greater than all his other moral qualities. What, then, did he do? He put up no resistance to the times. He did not choose to shed blood in order to save himself and keep his power, although he could have done so, exchanging his own power for the lives of many. He placed at God's disposal the power that he had received from him in the past, persuaded by the holy father whom he trusted as a guarantor of his safety. He calmly laid aside the imperial garments that adorned his body and, with an untroubled mind, took up the redeeming monastic habit instead.[176] Then he proceeded to the great shelter provided by the great father, dressed as a monk, without dissimulation. As soon as the latter learned that, he began to act as a guarantor. He went out of the church and met the emperor who was then arriving; he gave him his right hand and then pulled back. The patriarch then embraced the emperor, who was trembling with a divine fear, and cleansed him with his tears.[177] With due respect and honor he led him into the patriarchal residence.

51. If anyone knows of behavior better or more suitable than this, I would admire his inventiveness.[178] But I, who was an eyewitness of all these things, thinking them over now once more, am unable [61P] to discover what was the most admirable of all the actions of the patriarch, or of his omissions. Surely the fact that at the time of the dispute of the two great opponents he managed to save the first, who was in great danger, and make the second one emperor is a sign of greatness and lofty sentiments. In this way he calmed down the turmoil and saved the earth from the earthquake. The fact that he did not permit the usurper to enter the City[179] before he provided guarantees for the previous emperor's safety, and that he brought the latter to himself quietly and protected him behind the wall of the church, was something everyone should have done; however, only he was able to accomplish it. If he had inclined to one side of the scales, the other one would have been completely destroyed.

176. On these events, see Tinnefeld (1989) 121 and n. 162.

177. Attaleiates, *History* 58–59, records the ironic reply of the ex-emperor to the patriarch.

178. In his *Indictment against Keroullarios*, Psellos accuses him of duplicity and fraud for his involvement in these very events: *Orationes Forenses* 1.1338–1588 (pp. 50–59).

179. Isaakios I Komnenos (1057–1059) was crowned emperor by Keroullarios in Hagia Sophia on 1 or 2 September 1057.

If he had supported him who was only formally emperor, resisting the one who already had power in his hands, he would still not have blocked him [Isaakios] from becoming emperor, as he was beloved by the entire people, and nothing would have been saved, because the usurper would have swept all things along with him like a rapid river, especially the one who had exchanged his own safety for the throne. However, things happened as they should have happened, and no prudent man will reproach what took place. The two adversaries resembled two channels: the one poured in, the other flowed out. The rebellion was transformed into a lawful power and the earthquake came to an end. The tempest died down and everything was calm again. Then the new emperor took hold of the affairs of the state, and the great father thanked God for transforming night into day and the storm into calm weather.

52. So far the patriarch was resisting some malicious men in order to defend certain others. But from now on the whole sea was raised up against him, not only some waves here and there. Since he had lived an extremely holy life in the appropriate way, all that was left was the crown of martyrdom. The man who ran in the stadium of virtues and was awarded the relevant crown on the podium there was to be awarded the crown of martyrdom as well. God gave him that, too. When the end of his life approached in a hidden way, he was deemed worthy of the best prize. My intention is to narrate what happened to him and explain who was guilty of it, but I am not in a position to do so with moderation. Why? [62P] Both the one who committed the crime and the one who suffered it were admirable men for their virtues, each in his own way. The emperor can easily be compared to the most important emperors of the past, and is found superior to some, while to others he is equal, and he is only a little inferior to some others. His only stain was the way in which he took possession of the empire. He had many gifts, but the most prominent of them all was his steadfastness. This was evident from his appearance too: he resembled a high and unbreakable pillar in the palace;[180] in a novel way he held up the entire state on his head.[181] But his good was mixed, as has been said. Let me use the phrase of the Prophet: bronze is mixed with a potsherd.[182] No one is invulnerable except for God or maybe the angels as well. Man does not always have

---

180. Cf. Pindar, *Olympian* 2.82.
181. On the plans of Isaakios I Komnenos to restore the military might of the empire, see Shepard (2008) 603.
182. Cf. Daniel 2:35.

the same views. He is a changeable animal and can easily take the opposite direction from the one he followed before.[183] But this is not the only cause of the
crime committed by the emperor against our father. There is something else
too. Perhaps I am the only one to have understood it, and I am going to share
that knowledge with you now.

53. I will explain it by using the example of the strings of the lyre. Those
of them with the same tension are discordant; to be concordant they must
have a different tension according to set scales. The latter are harmonious or
concordant on the basis of the higher or lower scales. What I want to stress is
this: men of a similar character cannot agree with each other, unless one has a
stronger and the other a softer character. Let us imagine two men who are
both brave, who vie with each other for the first prize; is it possible for them to
ever agree with each other? They can be reconciled only if one of them yields
to the other, recognizing that he is stronger. But that could not take place in
our case: the emperor was not to be persuaded easily to take the second place
in the state. On the other hand, the patriarch [63P] had a lofty view of his dignity. The emperor wanted to subordinate him as he had subordinated all others, but the other one [Keroullarios] was intractable.[184] The former dared to
order him to shut his mouth, but the latter spoke more freely than before, not
adapting himself to the circumstances.

The patriarch was sincere and wanted to benefit all people, but the emperor was suspicious of his relentless determination and was afraid for his
throne, seeing that the people quickly took the part of the patriarch and were
influenced by him. I am not able to say whether he had contrived measures
against the patriarch in his mind in advance and in a hidden way. Although I
came into contact with the emperor, who entrusted to me his secret plans, I
did not notice such a thing. He exploded suddenly; no one had suspected such
a thing before. And he dared to do those terrible things. You are aware of the
siege, the blockade, the unjust abduction of the patriarch,[185] the shame, the

183. Cf. Plato, *Letter* 13.360d–e.

184. Keroullarios regarded the emperor Isaakios as his own creature: Tinnefeld (1989)
121. See the summary account of these events in Psellos' *Chronographia* 7.65.1–7.

185. The patriarch was abducted by soldiers from the monastery of the Nine Angelic
Orders in early November 1058: Tinnefeld (1989) 122 and n. 166. Attaleiates, *History*
61–67, describes the events in detail, drawing in all probability from this funeral oration
of Psellos, and not refraining from criticizing those who helped the emperor in his en-
deavor (i.e., Psellos himself).

accusation brought against him. You know that the patriarch surrendered himself to his tormentors like my own Jesus.[186] He did not try to resist the multitude of the palace soldiers sent to arrest him by inciting the mob of the City into rebellion, a much greater throng. He did not push the soldiers away or reproach those who were to arrest him, but endured his humiliation as if it were a feast; he was proud of his martyrdom. He was willing to suffer first of all for the sake of the people, so that no one may suffer for his own sake.

54. I saw the man at that time and shed many tears at the sight. How could I not? The spectacle would make even stones cry. They dragged the patriarch in a shameful manner, and everyone who wished to could also pull him; they mocked and humiliated him, a man who had risen to heaven through his virtues, who made into gods those whom he initiated, who was godlike, whose character was like no other, whom no one could imitate, who anointed both emperors and priests, not by pouring the oil from a drinking horn,[187] but pouring it from his own much nobler source. I cried from the center of my soul when I saw him, but admired his brave character and composure. He remained unharmed by those who wanted to cut him to pieces. He was not troubled at all. He gathered up his thoughts and realized that it was necessary for him, who was a partaker of the divine nature and of things divine, [64P] to drink the same cup as the Word,[188] of whose baptism he had partaken. I am referring to the temptations he suffered unwillingly. He was not angry with those who had abducted him; he was not insulted at all; he was almost thrown into the sea,[189] but was not afraid of the waves. He hoped that a whale would suddenly come and swallow him, but not do him any harm; he hoped that the beast would leave him on a beach unharmed, as on the other occasion.[190]

55. He himself was completely unruffled,[191] but the news stirred up so much indignation among the people of the City against the emperor, who believed that he had subdued the unassailable, that the fire of fury would have destroyed everything, and that the City, that eye of the universe,[192] would have been extin-

186. Cf. Gregorios of Nazianzos, Or. 39.1.1 (p. 150).
187. Cf. 1 Samuel 16:13.
188. Cf. Mark 10:38–39.
189. He was taken first to Prokonnesos and then Imbros: Tinnefeld (1989) 122 and n. 169.
190. Cf. Jonah 2:11.
191. The same word (analotos in Greek) is employed by Attaleiates, History 65.
192. A common designation of Constantinople: Gregorios of Nazianzos, Or. 43.10.9 (p. 72).

guished had the patriarch not extinguished the fire through his prayers to God. Because of this, the emperor became afraid of arresting that man without having brought any accusations against him; so he tried to invent accusations, but matters turned upside down for him against his plans. As he had condemned him to exile without trial, he decided to condemn him formally after passing the verdict.[193] So he proceeded to a judgment, after reaching a decision, transgressing the laws, inverting the order of justice, and trampling down the courts. He treated what was the highest thing in the state in the worst manner, for the sole purpose of making the verdict fit the punishment.

I must underline once more what I said at the beginning of my account about these matters: no one could reproach that emperor, a brave man whose royal virtue was inimitable, but I cannot praise that action, although at the same time I forgive him for his decision. He decided to act so because he was afraid for his own safety. He considered a baseless suspicion as a real fact, persecuted the man he suspected, and a terrible audacity provided an outlet for his boldness. He invented an accusation afterward, something that he should have taken care of in advance. But his anger had not let him act so, so he invented an accusation afterward, or rather he falsified the good intentions of the patriarch to suit his own beliefs. The fictitious evidence that was brought against the one who suffered was itself a testimony to his innocence, and the one who had committed the crime defended himself by citing his own deed! Our father did not [65P] know anything of the things of the past or the present that were brought as evidence against him. However, the emperor convened a council of all the wise men and the best scholars, and he collaborated with them in order to prepare an indictment against him [Keroullarios].

No one can reproach anyone among them, if he employed the correct divisions in the proper way. First of all, every action can be interpreted in a good or a bad way, which is why the orators can speak persuasively: one and the same action may be interpreted differently.[194] Second, most of those convened had the highest opinion of our father's novel actions, which were adapted to the various, most difficult circumstances. But the desire of the emperor to interpret his actions in one particular way forced them all to accept his view.

---

193. Psellos' own *Indictment against Keroullarios* is probably an expanded literary version of this accusation.

194. A hint by Psellos that he had written the indictment against the patriarch himself! On the presentation of the powers of rhetorical deceit by Psellos himself, see Kaldellis (1999) 132–141.

If anyone accepts my judgment concerning the actions of our father and the reactions of the emperor afterward, I would dispel the cloud that hung over the patriarch, and also all suspicions that were entertained by the majority. A man whose actions are inspired by God, whose actions follow divine laws, cannot be accused of anything. At the same time I do not judge the emperor severely, but forgive him. He was a victim of his own mistaken views and could not see the truth; in fact, he acted more against himself, not against our father. All those who backed him up were swept along by his power and the circumstances. If someone was saved from the thunderstorm, he was safe not because he managed to escape from the conflagration but because the fire did not deem it worthy to pursue him.

In any case, when circumstances later changed, they revealed that the speeches of accusation did not reflect the disposition of their authors, who supposedly had an unconquerable spirit: they too changed their minds. Those who seemed previously to have become servants of the other side [the emperor] were subsequently freed. Of course, our father was not offended at all by their writings accusing him; moreover, the fact that the accusers repented of their accusations later proved our father's innocence more clearly. It was necessary that he [Keroullarios], who had long since been armed in advance with all the other virtues, would fight as a martyr to the end; it was necessary for the emperor [**66P**] to be flawed because of this particular sin; and it was necessary for all who had spoken wrongly, led astray by the circumstances, to be seen afterward as having acted unreasonably. That is how things happened. All others remained in place, but the patriarch, who was elevated to heaven and spoke to God himself, was broken up among the elements of our world.

56. He was given by the sea to the earth, and the two exchanged him between themselves in a miserable way. The one made the father suffer more than the other. The sea disturbed the father with her waves and tempests; it propelled the ship not to ports and beaches but only to the promontories and to the rocks under the sea. On the other hand, the earth was transformed into a prison for him. Wherever he disembarked, he was shut into dark rooms. A man who was entertained by God in heaven in comfort and in freedom was now enclosed in a small place here on earth. The Tempter, who had boasted to God that he would force him to commit at least one grave sin or at least speak a bad word,[195] if God but surrendered the patriarch to him in order to make

195. Cf. Job 1:9–12; Luke 22:31.

trial of him and permitted him to employ all the means at his disposal, did not neglect any torment that he could employ against him, including earth, sea, winds, bad climate, malicious and beastly characters, insults, the absence of anyone to comfort him. Anyone else would have died a violent death under those circumstances. This man who once ate with God was now tormented with hunger. He lacked a second garment to wear, but he did not care so much about that.[196]

What is indescribable is his isolation from all men, the fact that he did not speak to anyone, that he did not have any books, that he could not take part in the liturgy, without even the possibility of breathing freely. To which sufferings of the martyrs can those things be compared? But what was in store for him was much worse. A frightful jury was prepared, severe judges were appointed to vent anger. All men and all tongues were mobilized against him, and every device was contrived. Some were already in motion, while others were being prepared; [67P] some were to be mobilized in the future. All were gathered there like the Giants in myth,[197] not to cut the earth into pieces or destroy the pillars of the sky, so that the universe could be destroyed and the world lose its beauty, but in order to destroy just one man in this world. Such was his power, equal to that of all other men, in spite of the fact that he did not offer any resistance to them. He contrived no plan against his adversaries; in fact, he did not quite grasp the meaning of that whole commotion. What frightened them was not his resistance, but their inability to destroy his serenity. What annoyed our father was neither the tongues of all those people, nor the various ploys invented against him, nor the turmoil of the men on land. He was, however, sorry to be imprisoned on the island of Imbros, not because it was not a proper prison for him but because there was too much noise due to the waves and the sailors, for this prevented him from praying.

57. But his tortures had peaked; no torment was enough for him. Every form of torture was invented by the Evil One. Only three friends came to Job, that great athlete,[198] but he [Keroullarios] was visited by everyone: they came to him in waves, each one of them separately and all together. But it was predestined that at the end of his tribulations he would be rewarded with the greatest prize, the Great and Superior Ascent, not with the double punishment

---

196. Cf. Matthew 10:10; Luke 3:11.
197. Cf. Hesiod, *Theogony* 664–686.
198. Cf. Job 1–2. Attaleiates, *History* 63–64, also compares the patriarch to Job.

of the sinners, about which he did not care at all. God sent him a message, explaining the reasons for his suffering and promising him the indestructible crowns. God told him that since nothing on earth was equal to his great achievements and victories, the kingdom of heaven would be given to him as a reward for his deeds on earth,[199] and there he would live together with the saints; this was the only reward worthy of his achievements. The manner in which that prophecy was made was supernatural and most graceful.

The court was to meet outside the walls, in a region by Thrace.[200] They were afraid to hold a session inside the City, lest there be a disturbance. As the judges were drawn from all [**68P**] over the earth, it was ordered that he [Keroullarios] be transferred from the sea to the mainland. He wanted the ship to anchor in the port of Madytos, because he had a hidden purpose relating to his salvation, which my speech will reveal; however, his abductors led the ship straight on according to their instructions. The patriarch was sad; the arrows of sadness pierced his heart. But then God gave a sign that things would take a turn for the better: he ordered the winds, currents, and waves to lead the ship in another direction. Through their skill, the sailors struggled to keep it in the prescribed direction, but the ship, as if it had changed its mind, went straight to Madytos, offering resistance to the oarsmen. In the end, the ship defeated the sailors and anchored in Madytos, according to the wish of our father.

58. Why did his great soul so ardently wish to go there? There was a bishop there not long ago, who was seemingly a man but in truth an angel or a god in reality. His soul was truly divine, his bodily life only a sideline. He was devoted to God, being a sacrificer of the great sacrifice, a true overseer of the mystery. His character was simple, like Jacob's,[201] he did not spend his time in the marketplace, and he did not possess the cleverness of the men who did. He knew things divine in a divine, supernatural way. His name was Euthymios.[202] He was glorious for his behavior; his speech was flavored with spiritual salt.[203] He offered his soul as a sacrifice to God, and he was divided between the heaven and the earth: his soul became a supernatural, ineffable entity, while his lower aspect, I mean his body, became miraculous. That is something both note-

---

199. Cf. Matthew 3:2.

200. Actually, on the Asiatic coast: Tinnefeld (1989) 122 n. 170.

201. Cf. Genesis 25:27.

202. Euthymios, bishop of Madytos, lived in the tenth century: Tinnefeld (1989) 123 n. 171.

203. Cf. Colossians 4:6.

worthy and admirable. Springs gushed out of him all over: not potable water, like that which springs out of the hollow parts of the earth, but a clean and clear myrrh, which one could not compare to anything else. It was transparent, its smell was pleasant, and its other qualities, different from those of other perfumes, were inimitable and supernatural.

Our divine and great father was very close to this great bishop Euthymios [**69P**] in an ineffable way. There is a hidden, spiritual kinship, besides the bodily one. Similar characters indicate spiritual kinship. Quite often a man brought up in Europe may have a character similar to a man born in Africa, although great lands and seas separate them. Our father had read the texts referring to his life, and recognized his own soul described in them, and he was elevated from earth up to heaven, or rather he came into contact with that blessed man there and became very fond of his company, although he wanted to keep this intercourse a secret. So he wanted to see his body too, the shadow of his soul and the source of the myrrh, and to kiss his tomb, out of which gushed that river which gave such joy to the Church.[204] As soon as God brought him to that place, he was filled with a spiritual joy and pleasure. He cast all sorrow out of mind and entered the holy shrine as if inspired by God. He approached that bodily spring, bowed his head and embraced it, addressing him as if he were alive in a way hidden to most people.

It was night, so he commanded his company to sleep somewhere in the area as was usual, while he kept his eyes open, which resembled two stars illuminating the body of the saint and being illuminated by it.[205] But at the time of the appearance of saint Euthymios, God made him sleep for a while, so that he might see the saint with the pure eyes of his mind. The saint made his appearance. His face was graceful, light came out of his eyes cheerfully, and his eyebrows revealed a graceful character. He was smiling, and he wore the garments of a bishop. He embraced the patriarch joyfully and filled his heart with an ineffable joy. He then gave him the happy news: "O servant of God and archbishop, stop worrying about your trial and defence. You have already defeated the Tempter. The crown is ready for you on high.[206] Your dwelling place among us in paradise awaits you." Thus he spoke and left the patriarch when he woke up. It was early in the morning. He stood up, and his face and soul were transformed. The man who [**70P**] was entrusted with watching him was

204. Cf. Psalm 45:5.
205. Cf. Plato, *Timaeus* 45b.
206. Cf. 2 Timothy 4:8.

amazed, as he saw him godlike and asked about the cause of his sudden trans-formation. The patriarch said only this: "God has already called me to himself and is taking me out of your hands." He then asked him to lead him to the place assigned to him. He revealed his dream to only one person, to whom he entrusted his innermost thoughts. The guard had the ship ready to sail, and they reached the place where the trial was to be held, or rather the place of his transfer to a divine place.

59. One of two things could then have happened. It was possible for him at the time of his trial to lose his case and to be forced to abandon his throne, being defeated by so many enemies in an effort to defend himself against all the judges and advocates and accusers who would try to support the fictitious indictment, and to resist the emperor himself. That could not have happened, of course, but it is necessary for me to mention it so that my speech may con-sider all possibilities. It was also possible, on the other hand, that the entire phalanx of his enemies would be broken by him and retreat, unable to bear the shame of it. That was not his wish: he did not want to put so many people in danger for his own sake. For those reasons God above found the best solu-tion: the divine jury proved more powerful than the human one, and the one taken to be judged was taken to heaven in order to be crowned.

Let us examine the matter from another perspective so as to realize that death was not just the end of his life, but rather a transfer to another place brought about by the providence of God. Let us imagine him hypothetically either remaining quiet at the time of his trial or defending himself against each one of the accusations. There is no middle ground. If he remained quiet, he would thereby destroy himself: from his own point of view, that would be-tray the dignity of archbishop, while the others would consider it a manifest defeat. If he tried to defend himself, however, and was defeated, that would be a double humiliation for him, both in having to defend himself and at the same time being found wanting by his accusers. But if he managed to prevail and defeat his numerous adversaries all by himself, strong and powerful as they happened to be, he may not have been personally humiliated, but he would have been regarded by most people as an ambitious man [71P] simply out to preserve his patriarchal dignity and throne.

God took care to undermine the enmity that most people had for him, so that not the slightest suspicion could be held against him and no possibility would be left for anyone to say that his victory was only partial and that his ambition was greater than it. These are the sorts of accusations brought up by bad people, full of envy for men who are superior to themselves. Therefore, God undermined that enmity along with the patriarch's own ill-feeling against his opponents, or rather, he performed a miracle that cannot be adequately admired: he stopped the emperor's drift toward that bad direction and prepared for the patriarch a ladder that led up to himself, so that he could ascend with ease to heaven, his soul being light as a bird, being free of the burden of his body. God did not wish for him to be rewarded on earth for his struggles. He did not want him to take back the throne that he had *yielded* (that is the proper expression), which he already despised, as he offered no resistance to those circumstances. That was not the proper reward for all his struggles and tribulations, or rather of his martyrdom; for those, the just arbitrator rewarded him with heavenly Jerusalem.

60. I am circling back to the same highlighted notion in my speech, not because I want to give the impression that I am more ambitious than the majority. For how could one seek after honor by writing a speech for that man? Such a speech would be defective in all respects and would be unable to reach the highness of that man. Rather, I am doing this in order to show that his death was predestined, as were all the details of his life that were miraculous: his parents, his virtues, and his devotion to the good. On the other hand, the details of his death were also preordained by God, and that will be proved by the facts themselves. The man who had seen divine things with his own spiritual eyes was transformed by God and became even greater, more steadfast and stronger, resisting all attacks.

At last his journey by sea reached its mainland destination. The distance between the two lands by sea was small, and a Zephyr wind drove him gently across the waters,[207] giving joy [**72P**] to the patriarch and not causing him any fear. He drew courage from this. And then what? Finally, he reached the land for which he did not have any desire. That is the most beloved sight of all who risk their lives at sea, but there at sea the patriarch had been in no danger; to the contrary, everything had been happy for him and most according to desire. He disembarked in tranquility, his movements were steady, and he entered the dwelling place that was ennobled due to him. I do not know whether he had another divine and ineffable vision or else had predicted what was going to happen. He realized that his powers had begun to abandon him, and predicted

---

207. Cf. Aischylos, *Agamemnon* 692. According to Tinnefeld (1989) 122 n. 170, Keroullarios was brought to the area of Abydos, where he died.

his own death to all who were present there with him.[208] What happened next? But how am I to describe this? Shall I offer a lament along with tears, showing that the Great Giver of Light was extinguished and the great trumpet of the Word of God was about to be silenced? Or shall I narrate his death calmly? But it was no death at all; it was rather an ascent, or rather a deification.

Even though I wish to imitate his passion by using a supernatural mode of speech, I cannot restrain my flowing tears. I am reminded that this great Light of Truth (what else can I call him?) was ready to migrate to another world; the brave fighter was migrating from the dwelling places here on earth to those on high. Thus, I will act as a just arbiter.[209] I will yield to my passion, but will also adapt myself to his steadfastness. As soon as he saw the angels surrounding him, ready to act as his retinue, he reconciled himself with his oppressors. How pious was his soul! What a man was he! How powerful his memory even in that dreadful hour: it was spiritual rather than based on the senses. He reconciled himself with his tormentors, as if he gave his right hand to his malefactors and forgave them all for all he had suffered, including the emperor himself, the judges, those who insolently turned their tongue against him, the advocates, those who misinterpreted the laws, and the capable orators, who could defend two opposite positions. He forgave all who had a complaint against him, if there were such men. He freed all those who had been cursed by him [73P] of their spiritual bonds. He permitted those in exile to come back to the spiritual Jerusalem;[210] he brought the prisoners back from captivity and liberated them from all dangers.

Afterward he prayed for his people, raising his holy hands up to God. The great sacrificer and archpriest offered the whole world as a last sacrifice to the great archpriest and sacrificer. Then he sacrificed his own soul calmly, as if he were offering a gift to God, or rather giving him back his own deposit untouched and unharmed, in fact greater than it was before. The feelings he incited had two aspects: he joined the higher world and left behind our own,

---

208. According to Tinnefeld (1989) 123, Keroullarios died on 21 January 1059. However, Attaleiates, *History* 65–66, says that Euthymios of Madytos, appearing to Keroullarios, had predicted that he would die before the Nativity of Christ on the day of the commemoration of the feast of those who had pleased God. Therefore Keroullarios died before Christmas 1058, on the Sunday before that feast, when the Orthodox Church commemorates those who had pleased God in the time of the Old Testament.

209. Cf. Gregorios of Nazianzos, *Or.* 2.1.16–17 (p. 86).

210. Cf. 1 Ezra 5:7–54.

which was a cause for grief and joy simultaneously, for rejoicing and for sullenness. It was reasonable for the angels and the souls of the saints to be joyful and to share in his happiness, as they would be initiated into the great mysteries like him, and would receive the rays of the holy light. But a deep darkness[211] covered the whole earth, as if the sun had gone down. We were darkened too, because we could not see our star and the savior of our souls anymore.

O you who left behind the noises of this life as you rose up, reached the end of your struggles, and relaxed. You exchanged the shadows of divine things for their reality itself, which cannot be destroyed. You followed rivers up to their source and migrated from the earth toward heavenly beauties. You left the rotary motion behind and have already been initiated into blessed visions. O you who conquered all the virtues, now you received your just rewards for each part of that virtue; or rather, you reached the peak of the Idea of Beauty, which is the culmination of all others, being most simple and first of all.[212] You saw the essence of truth, which cannot be described by our speech but is reality itself. You united your whole existence to God. You left behind the created world, devoting yourself to the study of supernatural entities. You were beyond nature and becoming, even while still alive. Now you became even higher than them, being illuminated and enlightened by the light of the Holy Trinity directly,[213] and you enjoy the first source of beauty, seeing the nature of the good which is beyond everything.[214] O you who despised all things of this world while you were still in this [74P] world, and you did not pay any attention to glory, magnificence, the sublimity of thrones, bodily beauty, applause and acclamations, or any of the things that are to be found here in such excess.[215]

Even when you were involved in the worst situation, you vied with the best of all men of the past: you became a martyr like them; you emulated their piety and their outspokenness, and for this you shared in their passions. You too were dethroned from the patriarchal throne like the trumpet of the Theologian,[216] or rather you yielded to the pressure of many people as if by way of dispensation. You imitated the grace of Chrysostom,[217] the great soul of

---

211. Cf. Exodus 10:21.
212. Cf. Plato, *Symposium* 210e.
213. Cf. Gregorios of Nazianzos, *Or.* 11.6.20–21 (p. 342).
214. Cf. Plotinos, *Ennead* 1.6.6.15.
215. Cf. Gregorios of Nazianzos, *Or.* 42.19.15 (p. 90).
216. Gregorios of Nazianzos, archbishop of Constantinople (380–381).
217. John Chrysostom, archbishop of Constantinople (398–404).

Athanasios,[218] and all the other bishops either before or after them who decided that it was better to abandon their thrones, which they had not, however, occupied illegally. All the other souls that rest in heaven envy you, because they were not deemed worthy to become martyrs, or because they do not have any rewards, not having suffered the same torments here on earth. O but how shall I address you? What more can I add to all those gifts you have now received from God, to that perfect reward of the future, or even to the supernatural and divine rewards you received in life? Very few have received such rewards here on earth.

Your body was not destroyed after it was separated from your soul, it was not broken up into the four elements out of which it had been created. That supernatural composite that you were did not go back to being air, fire, earth, or water. Perhaps it had not been created out of these materials to begin with, and that is the reason why it has not been transformed back into them. That is an audacious thing to say. Let the vain theories of the pagans go to hell.[219] They depict the Creator as borrowing some parts from the elements at the time of their combination to each other, and taking them back at the time of their dissolution. I am using their own words. But you proved that there is no such strange borrowing, no such strange refund. You go on living after death both as a soul and as a body; your body has changed neither its color nor its form. I am referring to the form appropriate to an archbishop, for your right hand is making the sign of the cross; some of your fingers are stretched out while others are bent, giving the sign of peace to all people.[220]

[75P] You broke the hearts of the people at the time of your death and are now more popular and revered than when you were alive. The emperors look upon you with admiration and patriarchs embrace and bless you. The emperor who had honored you with exile—a discreet way of putting it—came to your grave and offered his apology for his deeds as best he could. He embraced your body as if you were alive, shedding many tears; he asked for your forgiveness and was forgiven indeed. What can I say about the other emperor?[221] While you were alive, you were his spiritual father. He patterned him-

218. Archbishop of Alexandria (328–373) and defender of the Nicene Creed.

219. Cf. Gregorios of Nazianzos, *Or.* 7.16.11–12 (p. 220).

220. Attaleiates, *History* 65–67, gives the same detail, drawing in all probability on the text of Psellos.

221. I.e., Konstantinos X Doukas (1059–1067).

self upon you. You gave him your virtues and were his guide toward the best. And you go on guiding him even more now that you are dead. You predicted that he would become emperor, and you explained it to him through ineffable signs. You prepared the imperial crown for your niece,[222] and married her to that future emperor. That divine couple resembles two shining stars that have come together. At the time of their marriage that light was fainter, but now it shines in the palace. You offer them guarantees of their salvation and that their family will go on governing the empire. They did not respect you as a great man only when they were private citizens, but even now that they wear crowns they approach you as a supernatural man and saint. They stand on either side of your tomb, approaching your body with fear and respect, and they do not dare to look at you directly.

The earth cannot cover you as it does all other men. The hands of the people clutch at you, and they refuse to count one who is still alive among the dead. They regard you as a living being and address you full of joy and admiration together. How may I describe the reverence that your successor holds for you,[223] that great sacrificer who is also the sacrificial victim, that great trumpet that rings across the earth? Although his virtues surpass those of all other people, he recognizes that you are superior to him and honors you with annual feasts; he had established that practice and is the first who keeps that law.

61. No one should ever have been compared with you, who are inimitable. Or rather, we should never compare you with mortal men. God gave you a virtue that is inimitable, and so in the same way we should have offered you an unrivalled encomium. But [**76P**] let us come to this part of the speech too, so that my text might not be defective. The fruits of spring are ready on the trees.[224] The church [Hagia Sophia] has been awarded one special season of the whole year, the spring, just as heaven has received its supernatural prototype. But it has a defect if we compare it with its archetype, that is, true spring, even though it is still beautiful and supernatural. The grapes of the archetype are real, the branches too, the furrow is full of true ears of wheat, the plants have real flowers, the apples are real too. The grape offers its juice to anyone

---

222. The empress Eudokia Makrembolitissa was probably a daughter of Keroullarios' sister: Tinnefeld (1989) 98 n. 24 and 99 n. 29.

223. I.e., Konstantinos Leichoudes.

224. It is possible that something is missing before this phrase. The transition to the description of the paintings of the church is rather abrupt.

who wishes to drink it, and the ears of wheat are ready to be stored in the warehouse. All spectacles are true indeed, not mere images. Here too there are many grapes, and most are ripe; the flowers on the plants have a variety of colors, but if anyone wishes to touch them it is proved that they are mere images; he has been tricked by them.[225] If what we see is hidden inside, that may be an achievement of ineffable nature. But the transparency of the curtains is such that they give the impression that spring has really come. The nature of the stones is equal to the art of painting and to the abundance and blossoming of spring. He created all these adornments to such an excess that he was adorned by them too, because they proved that he was very clever indeed.

But what now am I to do with this secret? Shall I keep it secret or announce the divine vision of that man to your pious souls? If I compare it to the most perfect philosophy, I realize that it applies to all its parts. But O my admirable and beloved man,[226] why do you not reveal that vision, which you saw with the eyes of your mind in an ineffable way? Why do you not address us all with courage, why do you insist on keeping that divine vision a mystery? Are you afraid that some may not believe it but consider it a delusion of the night? But that vision was beyond your powers, if you permit me to speak so. Although your knowledge is immense and your mind is very sharp, it is not suitable for grasping such a sublime vision. If you permit me to act in this case, too, in the way I acted before, and allow me to use [77P] my own tongue to reveal your divine vision, I will tell it, trying to liken my voice to Daniel's for your sake.[227]

You were contemplating the form and magnitude of that church with the open eyes of your mind, not in their material aspects but rather in their higher and better versions; that might have been not just an act of contemplation, but rather a symbol of a higher vision.[228] You were not in the middle of the church but in the upper part of it, in the galleries. You were contemplating (let me again use the words of the Prophet), until two thrones were set down. Their form was admirable, their beauty inimitable. On the first was seated the great father, while the other one exalted a young man. Let me here use the words of

225. Psellos is describing the floral wall decorations of Hagia Sophia.

226. He addresses here one of the late patriarch's nephews, who had this dream and was present at the time of his uncle's commemoration, which, according to Tinnefeld (1989), took place on 21 January 1060. I would argue that this event took place a month earlier: see n. 208 above.

227. Cf. Daniel 7:7.

228. Cf. Gregorios of Nazianzos, *Or.* 28.19.26 (p. 140).

the Apostle: his garments were shining.[229] You considered him to be like a divine and supernatural angel. You were terrified as soon as you saw that and were almost frozen with fear. But your uncle embraced you calmly and restored your courage. Then he asked you about those whom he liked very much or those whom he took care of while alive. You answered his questions. Then you remembered that the holy father used to reproach those of his friends who had died for not caring to send him some knowledge of the divine mysteries that were hidden by the heavenly veil; they did not send even a hint to his imagination while he was sleeping, so that he might know what the ascent of the souls and the end of their travel were and what the meaning is of the pure dwelling places of paradise. Remembering all this, you took hold of the holy father and said to him, not being at all disturbed by the miraculous spectacle: "I have not lost my senses. I know that in sleep I have left my senses behind. I know what happened to you as well: I know that you are dead and I do not regard you as alive. Tell me where your soul is, where your dwelling place is. Do you enjoy any divine visions? What is the brilliance you possess now?"[230]

You spoke like this, and wanted to know more even than that which you asked. The holy father wanted to say something about the ineffable mysteries, but he did not dare to reveal anything without the permission of the angel who was superior to him. He asked the young man if he agreed to let him reveal something of the mysteries, **[78P]** permitting him to speak. You also implored him, moaning and filling your eyes with tears. But the young man was inexorable and did not permit him to reveal anything. He said that this was not permitted at all, because all these things were hidden in the treasuries of heaven. You shed more tears, and your brother, who appeared suddenly, helped you too. The angel could not reject your entreaties anymore, so he allowed your uncle to reveal something of what was hidden, so as not to leave you completely ignorant. He, however, did not speak. He just brought out of his bosom a book in the form of a roll[231] and unrolled it in its entirety. Nothing was written on it, but it was colored with an undefiled pigment. The angel

---

229. Cf. Luke 24:4.

230. A similar dream of Psellos himself is described in the *Encomium for His Mother* 20. Psellos had seen his father in a dream and had asked him where his soul had been transported after death; see Angelidi (2006) 161. Psellos explains a similar vision in *Theologica I* 30.69–145 (pp. 124–126).

231. Cf. Ezekiel 3:1–3.

said to him: "If you do not want to say anything ineffable, write down something in that book." The father wondered how he could write. And the angel replied to him: "Write it in the blood of martyrdom." The father stretched out his right hand and used his second finger as a pen. The angel curled up that finger and stretched out the third and middle one as a pen. The father wondered where to start. The angel said: "Use the words of Paul. Make them the starting point of your speech and then go on." And the words of Paul were the following: "Blessed be the Father of our Lord Jesus Christ, who is blessed unto the ages; I am not lying."[232] You thought that he would write something more, but he furled the roll once more and added just one more word at the end: "good." Then he offered it to you and said: "You recognize my handwriting. Read it to the others and give to them a clear proof that you received it from my own hand." After saying this, he flew up with the wings of a Cherubim.

It was already early morning, and you woke up. You were filled with fear and anxiety, but at the same time you were happier and more excited than ever before. You told me what happened to you, and I more profoundly explained to you the meaning of your vision. The vision is not only true, but it is filled with hidden meanings. No envious man can persuade me not to believe it. [79P] I am initiated into those hidden doctrines, having read books concerning matters divine, and I have known something of those ineffable and hidden things. Let me boast of it a bit. The church in which you were initiated is the symbol of true initiation and of the mysterious and hidden vision. The galleries in the higher parts of the church are a sign of the supernatural vision. The thrones indicate the prophecies of the Word of God concerning the resting place of the righteous. The young man with the godlike face was a true angel, a herald of the Word.

My speech wants to say something about philosophy at this point. All perfect gifts come from above according to the divine Apostle.[233] The dispenser and presider over all these goods is God, but from different sources of the good different recipients receive them in different ways. Some supernatural powers are placed after God, and these offer the most perfect gifts to those worthy of them.[234] Bodies are created by nature, but nature has the last rank in this creation; the proper divisions take place above. Souls are united with their bodies,

---

232. Cf. 2 Corinthians 1:3; Ephesians 1:3.
233. Cf. James 1:17. See also Psellos, *Philosophica Minora II* 38 (p. 144.8–10).
234. Cf. Pseudo-Dionysios, *The Celestial Hierarchy* 3.3 (p. 19.18).

but they do not exist before the bodies: they are woven together with the bodies at the time of their creation.[235] Let us not try to explain this any further; the simple words of the Gospel surpass the wisdom of those who live on earth. At the time when we receive our souls, some angelic powers are appointed as our guardians: they guide us toward the good, explaining to us the divine commandments. Some greater and more perfect powers succeed them as soon as we make more progress, ascending toward beauty itself. In the end, when our soul is to be divided from our body, some other powers are entrusted by God with that task at the predestined time. After the soul is separated from the body, other powers take our soul. Holy Scripture calls them "uplifters" and "guardians."[236] I am always referring to the souls of virtuous men, leaving aside for now the souls of the others. They bring them up to a certain point, depending on whether the souls are more or less clean. They bring them as close to God as possible. Other angels take them from there and give them their proper resting places. I am not referring to any material places like the ones on earth. [80P] These are higher intellectual places. There they may have a preliminary vision of the reward we will receive at the time of the final resurrection of the dead. Perfection will be attained at the end of time; however, virtuous men have a possibility before that of glimpsing behind the divine veil. The angel who is their guardian leads them to those visions and controls all movements of their intellect. His decisions are fulfilled by the souls.

That is why our holy father was accompanied by that young man who was his superior; he had a similar seat to his, and our father acted under his control. The angel did not permit him to reveal the mystery, but was adamant in refusing that in spite of all the implorations. The reason is not any impudence on his part. Here too the explanation has something philosophical about it: the world that lies above visible nature and its orders is not visible to our eyes and our mind cannot grasp it. How can anyone imagine something he is unable to grasp with his mind? Imagination is inferior to intelligible knowledge. But even those souls do not have the option of going wherever they wish. They are under the power of their guardian angel and cannot go out of their resting place, unless the angel permits them to do so, because God has a secret plan. There is law prohibiting them from revealing those mysteries to any man. But if God permits them to do so, they do reveal something, albeit

---

235. This is the Orthodox view: see, e.g., Psellos, *Poemata* 55.87–90 (p. 393).
236. Cf. Psellos, *Philosophica Minora I* 38.19 (p. 139).

within measure; however, a soul entrusted with keeping those mysteries cannot move beyond a certain point. That is why the holy father did not answer the question of his nephew immediately, and why the angel did not give him permission immediately.[237] But as soon as permission was given from above, the angel gave his approval and the holy father did what he was ordered to do, and nothing more. The words of Paul, which were used as a preface, were a guarantee of the truth. And the letter was brief, since what is beyond is ineffable. Of the two fingers, the one was pulled back, and the middle one was stretched and entrusted with writing the letter; this was a symbol of the cross, which is in the middle, and gave an indication of the right decisions of God.[238] What is in the middle has neither excesses nor defects. The blood of martyrdom is easily [81P] understandable, but it has a hidden meaning too: only the souls of the martyrs, who are superior, are entrusted with the revelation of the mysteries. Our father appeared in the form he had at the time of his death so that the vision might not be considered a fraud. Thus everything was appropriate to the divine doctrines, everything was supernatural.

62. That is the end of my speech; may what suffices reach its completion. O great patriarchal soul, to whom the present speech has been devoted, please have mercy on me. Forgive my audacity in writing this speech and my ardent desire that I alone dared to write this encomium for you. Help me from above and guide me toward God by cleansing me during this life.[239] At the time of my death, place me in your own place of rest. That will be the greatest happiness. If another place is allotted to me, may that not be different from your own, but similar to it. That is a gift of God, who loves mankind, to the souls that are brought near him; it is awarded to them in the name of Christ our God; glory be unto him into the ages of ages, Amen.

237. Presumably there is "lag-time" in the communication between the angel and God.

238. Cf. the form of the cross made by the dead fingers of Keroullarios' body: section 60 (74P) above.

239. Cf. Gregorios of Nazianzos, *Or.* 24.19.27–28 (p. 84).

3 Funeral Oration for the Most Holy Patriarch Kyr Konstantinos Leichoudes

Anthony Kaldellis

Introduction

The Life of Leichoudes. We know little about the life of Konstantinos Leichoudes beyond broad outlines, and this funeral oration, which highlights abstract virtues over historical data, is our main source for it. He was born around 1000, in Constantinople. In 1043, he was chosen by Konstantinos IX Monomachos (1042–1055) to be his *mesazon*, a kind of prime minister who ran the civilian branches of the government on the emperor's behalf. While Leichoudes certainly offered his support and patronage to the circle of scholars around Psellos, including Mauropous and Xiphilinos, we do not know any specific policies or acts that we can attribute to him as *mesazon*. Around 1050 (the dates are unclear), he had to step down in a context of tension and hostility, and seems to have been replaced by a political enemy (Ioannes the *logothetes*, about whom we know little). Mauropous, Xiphilinos, and eventually also Psellos lost their favor at the court and left or retreated. Leichoudes turned to private activities in retirement. He returned to politics in 1057, when he was chosen by Michael VI to accompany Psellos on an embassy to the victorious rebel Isaakios I Komnenos. When Isaakios deposed the patriarch Keroullarios in 1058, he appointed Leichoudes to replace him, allegedly at Psellos' own suggestion. Leichoudes served as patriarch from 2 February 1059 to 10 August 1063. Little is known about his patriarchate; he does not seem to have made any controversial decisions, although he was hostile to the Monophysite communities of the empire.[1]

The Funeral Oration for Leichoudes.   For all that Psellos affects a funerary delivery (in section 19), the oration was actually written after August 1075, because Xiphilinos is described as deceased (in 4); therefore, it was written more than twelve years after Leichoudes' death. Compared to the two other patriarchal orations, it contains more abstract and somewhat generic descriptions and praises of its subject's character, intellectual merits, and political and ecclesiastical career, so that we learn very few facts about him. The oration follows the standard panegyrical order, but it is rather perfunctory when it comes to Leichoudes' birthplace (Constantinople) and parents. It stresses his education, because it was wrapped up with the education of Psellos himself and his friends Mauropous and Xiphilinos. Like the two other orations, it then consists of two broad "movements," one political and the second ecclesiastical, with a hiatus between the two. Leichoudes is presented as consistently perfect, an idealized embodiment of Psellos' own ideals. For more on Psellos and Leichoudes, see the general introduction.

Like the others, this oration survives in MS Parisinus gr. 1182. It was first published by Sathas (1874) 388–421. The present translation was made from the new critical edition prepared by Ioannis Polemis for the series Bibliotheca Teubneriana (*Orationes Funebres I,* ed. Polemis, pp. 82–114). An Italian translation, based on the Sathas edition, with valuable introductions and notes, was published by Criscuolo (1983). Otherwise, the work has been little studied. The bold numbers in the translation correspond to section numbers in the Polemis edition; the bold numbers in square brackets, such as "[82P]," correspond to the page numbers.

---

1. *ODB* 500.

Funeral Oration for the Most Holy Patriarch Kyr Konstantinos Leichoudes

1. [82P] I have undertaken to praise a man, and adorn him with a funeral oration, whom I deem greater than any eulogy and whom I came close to comparing to Higher Beings on account of his good repute in all the parts of virtue. He was greatly favored with happiness, both that which comes down to us from above as it overflows from divine mixing bowls,[2] and that which we ourselves contribute toward the provision and perfection of every kind of good. I will also add things that come to us from the other side,[3] for they too contribute a portion of our overall happiness, at least whenever intellect presides over them, by using them as instruments to promote virtue in the circumstances of life. For his soul was not content with just two or three good qualities, as is the case with others (where, moreover, they are contrived), but every part of virtue flowed into him, and he availed himself exceedingly of every one in such a way that he did not succumb before their multitude but was rather invigorated, even though their influx was immense. And if the man being praised had lived in the distant past, someone might suspect that the speech has been fabricated arbitrarily and that the "facts" it presents should be measured only against the speaker's rhetorical power. For in matters that we cannot easily perceive ourselves, we do not easily place our trust. If such a person seems to have lived somewhere, he is ranked among the prodigies of nature; the event is not attributed to moral choice but rather even to a supernatural miracle. But as this speech is contemporary with the man being praised, and as virtually everyone is aware of his good repute with respect to his good qualities, we will not be apprehensive that we may be exaggerating and thereby make our words

---

2. Cf. Synesios, *Letter* 140 (p. 245).
3. Presumably from the body.

seem untrustworthy, but rather we will fear that we may fall short of the proper measure of praise due to him. We are not like teachers addressing an audience ignorant of the facts, but instead we stand here to be corrected by them, who censure us when we fall short and who will be paid by us in full.

I have heard many people question whether our times are even remotely comparable to those past [83P] when it comes to the production of virtue, but I would not immediately agree because virtue can be practiced in secret. I am convinced myself, and enjoy the expert testimony of everyone else too in my support, that this man alone, by the multitude and the greatness of his good qualities, could compete against all the men of the past together when it comes to the perfection of virtue. So precisely where my speech seems to succeed, there in reality it will falter, and right where one thinks it hits the spot, there indeed it will be in great difficulty. For my speech will lack the strength to attain those qualities of which this man partook through the breadth of his nature, and it will even turn out contrary to its own intention.[4] Its intention is to reach the full measure of the things he accomplished, but it is defeated by the man's vigor and his ambition to seek the good, and his praiseworthy qualities are not even limited to that. Setting aside all the other ways in which one might tackle his praise, whether one traces his genealogy up to lofty or down to lowly, earthly origins, whether one considers him in his own right, or understands him in the light of divine providence, still he will remain unmatched by any speech.

2. At this point in my speech I am reminded of the most famous orators, who were highly skilled in crafting their speeches. Whenever they wanted to compose an encomium for a particular person, they thrust forward those qualities for which he had a good reputation, while those in which he was not successful they either overlooked or, making mention of them, did not place them among those things for which he was exceedingly praised.[5] I admire these men for the technical skill and subtlety revealed in their approach, but I believe that they do not suffice for the full development of the art of praise. Perhaps they never encountered such a man, in order for them to flourish in every topic of praise on behalf of a man who had flourished in every part of virtue.[6] But *my*

---

4. Cf. Plato, *Republic* 343a.

5. For the ways in which orators tweak the truth and mislead in pursuit of panegyrical objectives, see Psellos, *Chronographia* 6.22–28, 6.161.

6. Thus the excellence of Psellos' subject will enable him to surpass the famous ancient orators.

speech blossoms and thrives in all respects,[7] including the founders of his family, from whom he derived his origin, his fatherland, the noble qualities of his body, and those of his soul, in which he seemed altogether extraordinary, in which, indeed, no one at all attained an equal standing. I am as far from [**84P**] saying the same things that most orators do as they are [from the truth] when they seize upon a tiny pretext[8] and exalt what they have found with their power of speech, not tailoring their encomium to the measure of the person but rather according to their own rhetorical power. I, however, given that the factors that contribute to his good fame are many and not at all easy to enumerate, and are so splendid as to be comparable to the Great Giver of Light,[9] will not go through each one in detail but, touching upon one as much as is reasonable, will then move on to the next. What, for instance, could I say about his fatherland, that City which presides over all other cities, to which one could ascribe only God as its founder and protector? I speak of New Rome, more august than its elder counterpart, in which he was born and which he recognized as his first mother, an appropriate one indeed.

3. If, next, we were to enumerate his ancestors, both those to whom he was born and the rest of his family, we would find them all worthy of reverence, and each surpassed by his descendants, with the last in line [Leichoudes' father] more celebrated than the others by this fact alone.[10] For he [i.e., his father] reached the peak of every virtue and attained the full measure of every blessing: he seemed undefeated by anyone in either respect, for there was nothing left in which he could advance any further, but he was bested by his son at both. Now, in the case of his father and his other ancestors, happiness came when they were mature adults—by happiness I do not mean what the many think, namely, the one found only in tall thrones, mounds of money, and an excessive abundance of property, but also that which is expressed in spiritual advantages, by which the inner man is adorned.[11] So that was his [Leichoudes' father] condition with respect to those things, and in time all things matured for him; as for the other one [Leichoudes], he began to contemplate the good while even his fingernails were tender.[12]

7. Cf. Himerios, *Oration* 68.11.

8. Cf. Euripides, *Iphigeneia at Aulis* 1180.

9. I.e., the sun, as opposed to the lesser one, the moon.

10. I.e., the fact that he came after them. Nothing is known about Leichoudes' father outside of this oration; see also below for his father.

11. Cf. Clement of Alexandria, *Paidagogos* 3.1.

12. I.e., at a very young age; cf. *Greek Anthology* 5.129.

A certain person who saw him after the swaddling clothes had been removed marked him as one who would exhibit wondrous qualities in life. Such was my impression of him too, even before he reached his perfect peak, and all the proof I needed I saw in his eyes. But it is not yet time to discuss these matters. Nevertheless, a mere shadow-outline of him would be superior [85P] to the fully developed form in others. For, just as if his soul were not deeply mired in the depths of the body but set over it from above, both his speech was articulate and also the parts of his soul did not blur together but were already distinct, and their distinctness was clear and unambiguous. The child presented a shadow-outline of what was to come, placed as a gift of nature before those who would mold him. When he began to receive preliminary instruction in the most fundamental lessons and practiced as a pupil the rules of orthography, there he showed the greatness of his nature. For he caused some anxiety to his teachers, not because they might have to lower their standards and offer less than a perfect education, as though he were not fit to receive it, but over how they could impart to him the most sublime lessons, since his soul had a great capacity. In his case alone was the soul greater than the body, understanding most of the lesson in advance and giving his initiators the opportunity to progress further. Thus he mastered the mysteries and surpassed the initiatory rites in precision. While others of the same age were barely capable of learning the alphabet, his faculty of comprehension was more precise than the most advanced lessons.

The myth relates that Phaethon took the chariot of his father the Sun and drove the horses off the straight path, burning up a great portion of the ethereal realm. This man, by contrast, mounted the chariots of discourse, given to him in part by his father and in part by his teachers, and neither diverged from the fixed path—far from it—nor abandoned it when struck and bruised, unless he occasionally surpassed it also by the extraordinary skill with which he handled the chariot. According to the myth, the Giants hurled their missiles against heaven,[13] but the true account has them give way before heaven. What is the meaning of this? That when the first fuzz of his facial hair began to sprout, the others, who had long beards and heads turned silver by the abundance of gray hairs, were all defeated by this child. When they joined the greatest contest and [86P] the time came for the race and the struggle fought with words, they entered the ring with broad chests and wide shoulders,[14] like the

---

13. Cf. Hesiod, *Theogony* 664–686.
14. Cf. Homer, *Iliad* 3.194; Sophokles, *Ajax* 1250–1251; *Greek Anthology* 16.303.5.

comrades of Typhon and Prometheus, while the child, who did not reach up to their knees, bravely wrestled with them, and then advanced forward from the starting line and, putting a difference of sixteen feet between himself and all the rest, prevailed, not only because he pulled ahead but also by not being led astray by anything. His nature thus declared, I believe, the directness and steadiness of his resolve in higher matters.

But he did not then seem to have left the contest; rather, as though he had announced an even greater challenge, he immediately stripped down to face it. Admiring both the beauty and the art of speech, he devoted himself to rhetoric in both respects, running, as it were, with a swift pace. To such a degree did he revive it, I could say, slightly exaggerating, with more beautiful formulas than did he who first assembled all of its parts into a wholeness.[15] So great a predisposition had nature given him for skill of this kind. For his mode of speech was a prodigy of technical skill and a treasure and ornament of rhetoric. When it had sharpened the persuasive power of his words, he became equally skilled in both impromptu speeches as well as those that are prepared and planned out in advance. He was immediately admired by the orators, and that which the art did not give to them he could devise expertly. He practiced many rhetorical subjects and especially those in which the challenge presented itself in manifold ways; here he revealed clearly the central node of the argument *and* introduced the rest of it by way of a supplement.

4. But how could one fittingly admire him in this respect? Who at all could make his skill with words into the subject matter of an art that produces encomia in his honor? The histories tell us that Perikles was a natural speaker, and many praise him excessively, saying that, although he was not trained in advance to be a powerful speaker, nevertheless his public addresses were all "thunder and lightning."[16] But this man was so superior to Perikles that, even though he had [87P] received preliminary instruction in the art, it did not regulate his speech to any great degree. Instead, he expounded better rules to those who were learning from him,[17] and when he made public addresses he did not flash with lightning like the other man, hurling fire upon those present; rather, he surrounded them with light and removed the shadows from their souls; he did not thunder, "shaking their souls and throwing them into confusion."[18]

15. This is presumably Gorgias or some other founder of the rhetorical tradition.
16. Cf. Aristophanes, *Acharnians* 531–532; Plutarch, *Perikles* 7.1.
17. Not students, but anyone who observed his speeches, including teachers of rhetoric.
18. Cf. Aristophanes, *Peace* 320; also Aischylos, *Prometheus Bound* 994.

Instead, he addressed them in a harmonious manner and adjusted himself perfectly to the attitudes of his audience. No one could say that he had vanquished the auxiliary troops, but not Hektor.[19]

Hektor fought face-to-face with the son of Peleus [Achilles], but across from our man were two brave men [Xiphilinos and Mauropous], spear-bearing warriors[20] devoted to the very same studies, who, with their noble arguments, deprived the others of confidence in any matter. But even together they were defeated by his speech and judgment, though they so surpassed and excelled all the others. Yet I would not be able to say by what margin they were defeated by him. For the difference between him and them was less than the difference between them and everyone else. Still, his post was a senatorial one, while they ran alongside him on the ecclesiastical side.[21] I was still young[22] when I met both of them, and they had by then matured. At the time I had just barely begun my basic education, while they had entered into the contest of rhetoric. Both these men, named Ioannes, were venerable and peers with respect to culture, but were different to the extent that the one [Mauropous] valued rhetoric more than the other, and philosophy less. As for the other man [Xiphilinos], my speech has already revealed his approach.[23] In any case, they were equal in every respect when it came to the perfection of virtue. One of them [Xiphilinos] had already matured in age and education, and he brought his temporal existence to an end in perfect virtue [in 1075], while the other [Mauropous] still has life left in him. Not only is he conspicuous among other wise men, but he is also one of the most prestigious bishops: the metropolis of Euchaïta obtained in him a virtual founder and protector. To him I owe an encomium suitable for his life, but I have postponed it until now, fearing lest I seem to be late on my payment or to have paid back less than I owe. In fact, he rose up from the same family as the one being praised now,[24] just as though they bloomed together from the same roots, giving rise to the question of whether he became more revered on account of the other, or whether the other acquired the glory

19. Cf. Homer, *Iliad* 2.815, 3.456.

20. These terms are also common in Homer.

21. This is likely an anachronism, as Xiphilinos was probably not ordained before he became patriarch.

22. Literally, "had not yet reached puberty." This must refer to events in the 1030s.

23. Presumably philosophy rather than rhetoric, unless this is a reference to Psellos' *Funeral Oration for Xiphilinos*.

24. The kinship between Mauropous and Leichoudes is known only from this passage.

of noble birth from this relationship, [**88P**] or whether an equal account must be given of their dignity. That which I would emphasize is that each returned to the other what he received and the exchange was repeated in turn.

5. But my speech, which has detoured far from the road that leads to the man we are praising, immediately now returns to its original point.[25] Competing with such men, he [Leichoudes] showed himself superior in education, in his ability to compose an argument and study it, to mix styles together, to vary his speech with a number of figures, to assemble concepts together in rhetorical periods and then to unfold them in a single rhetorical exhalation; to pick the right words and bring them together harmoniously; at one time to sound out thunderously, while at another to make his voice pleasant and smooth, and to render his discourse harmonious and rhythmical. And when he had won an illustrious victory in this contest as well, he turned—his third phase—to study the law, thereby going from one art to another art: from one that strikes on both sides of a case to one that cleaves to only one of the two sides, and from one that cuts language up into its elements to one that has need of that very ability to cut. Those who enter from there into the inner sanctum of legal studies, or who were then preparing to enter contests at law, seemed to be like those people who throw themselves at the study of physics without knowing anything about the science of nature, by which I mean (just to be clear) the *Physics*.[26] Or they are like those who decide to learn about mirrors and optics without the principles of geometry or the basic elements of the science about them.

But *he* grasped the ladder by which learning ascends:[27] which the first level was, which the one after that, and from which one he had to transfer his footing to the next. Thus arming himself carefully through the study of rhetoric, he turned to the art of law. He thoroughly mastered the lessons that he finished regardless of the field into which he advanced. For runners gradually run out of breath as they race along, and a wheat stalk at first grows up from the ground at an equal and steady pace, but then it is held back by the many nodes that it forms, as it its own breathing takes blows and has panic attacks. But the racetrack gave way to him as he advanced, and the farther he went the more he took wing, since his nature was not blocking him from claiming

25. The term *deomenon* here is possibly corrupt.
26. I.e., the work by Aristotle.
27. Cf. Iamblichos, *De communi mathematica scientia* 10 for the ladder image; also Psellos, *Oratoria Minora* 18.45–47 (p. 67).

[89P] more but rather was eagerly claiming even more. Just like those who start building their proofs from axioms and who then advance on to further proofs by using already proven theorems as axioms,[28] so too, he used the theorems that he had finished working out as axioms to the next ones that he tackled.

He did not pounce upon the laws like a lion, gorging himself on them, feasting on them, tearing them apart with his teeth and shredding them with his claws.[29] Rather, he led his education upward according to the art [of rhetoric]. What in the art are topics and problems are in law the so-called model actionable cases; just as it is necessary to refer every and any rhetorical thesis to one among the enumerated political questions, so too, every political problem is referred to one type of actionable case; also, just as associations and divergences will now compose their differences and later divide from each other, so too do they join together with each other and then again separate. Most people are hampered by their own lack of skill and thoughtlessness, but his prior facility with methodical exposition made him an expert in every field. Thus he joined together these political arts [rhetoric and law] and made each more dignified through the other; and, due to both of them, he himself appeared to everyone as more honored and most perfect. There are many who are accomplished in these arts, and there will always be more who are experts in one of the two, but they deliver less and are held back more, as their mind secrets away concepts in its deepest recesses and their tongue is not up to a flowing delivery. But which of *his* qualities should one admire first? His mind that grasped everything with precision or his speech that delivered it in such an orderly way? His intelligence that analyzed everything gathered inside or his tongue that brought forth to the outside what had been analyzed? The magnitude of his soul or the elegant stream of his voice, which made room for everything properly distinguished and was never cramped? O, his speech perfectly reflected his inner thinking, saying everything without omitting anything. Thus was he made known in public by his nature, his skill in the art, his prudence, and all his other qualities.

Immediately most rose up from their judicial posts to honor him [90P] and made way for him, just as the sophists had done earlier when he had been studying their discipline. Whatever he decided *was* the law for the men judging cases, and his interpretation was for them a lesson and an object of study; he

---

28. Cf. Aristotle, *Posterior Analytics* 90b24–25.
29. Cf. Homer, *Iliad* 11.176; Euripides, *Cyclops* 248, *Elektra* 146; *Greek Anthology* 9.244.

alone was the standard for orthography, for the art of rhetoric, and the norm for legislation. He completed the orators by bringing them something of the law and introduced most parts of rhetoric to the judges. He brought definition to the unlimited scope of the one art, and he made the other, bounded art irrefutable through the use of antitheses. Thus he wove together through each other those arts that seemed to be distinct from each other, and he brought together fields that were generally taken to be discrete and supposed to have no part of each other. So I must now briefly discuss and examine in his case that which I observe in the case of many others and which causes me to be perplexed about the issue. What is it that I am now saying and that my speech is hinting at? Well, every soul has a seed within it that makes it suitable for one pursuit and unsuitable for another. Thus, many people are naturally inclined toward practical affairs right from their very birth, as if from an advantageous starting point, whereas others are inclined toward verbal skill. The latter have a ready tongue, the former work well with their hands. We can say the same about the various arts: some people readily mastered one, while barely even glancing at the other; they often learn the one that they deem best[30] but quickly spurn the other as inferior. When I come across the philosopher Aristotle writing in a panegyrical mode, I do not know what to say in his defense. He had so much wisdom, he specified with precision the scientific method, furnished us with most of our accounts of proofs and dialectic, and inquired into nature and things that take place by nature—but he was lacking in all literary grace.

So while others are often significantly deficient, our man was as diligent a student of philosophy and the other disciplines as his natural capacities allowed him to be, so that he could in some way respond to students in those fields; then, he sallied into rhetoric and the law wholeheartedly and with a noble impulse. Reason testifies and philosophy proclaims everywhere that the soul contains the basic principles for all fields of knowledge[31]—for the image has to be similar to the prototype [i.e., God]. But there [in the prototype] these principles are all fully exposited and active, or, rather, in the prototype they exist [91P] in an even higher mode, whereas in our realm of images some things are opened and revealed while others are shut closed, and so we are adept at some of them while others we take on in a weaker way. But *his* nature was suitable for everything, though it paid special attention to the graces

30. Presumably rhetoric.
31. Cf. Psellos, *Philosophica Minora I* 18.43–44 (p. 60).

of language, as if Providence had long before endowed him with administrative reasoning, which he was later to so cultivate. It deliberately furnished him with the very things that ought to adorn a political life,[32] and later, when he turned to the more exact practice of philosophy, it stored up in him a more exact knowledge of philosophical reasoning. What a beautiful statue he was for life,[33] dedicated to public affairs by all the different parts of the Good.

6. But my speech has paid much attention to his manner of speaking and may seem to have overlooked his other attributes: the blending of his personality traits, his orderliness, lifestyle, conduct, and prudence. But who was comparable to him with respect to each of those virtues? Who, with a tongue so well trained to speak well, knew how to keep it quiet at the right moment and prefer a timely silence, thereby triumphing through modesty over the ambition of nature? Who allowed others to speak freely on topics on which he himself was quite capable of taking up the argument in turn[34] through his natural greatness and mental sharpness?[35] If he ever so much as thought to speak about things he knew, he would immediately blush all over, as if feeling shame on behalf of others. Who ever was assisted on all sides when speaking by grace, intelligence, voice, speech, and also a natural harmony—because an orator must have a bit of that too, so that he was constituted and prepared on all sides to achieve persuasion? Whoever was comparable to him even to a small degree when it came to the perfect mixture of his character, since this good quality does not come to be in us but is innate from the beginning, as are shapes and colors in rose gardens? In this way was the man prepared long in advance to govern the affairs that Providence would entrust to him: the ship was bound to show up so that the expert could come aboard and perform the science of command.

Indeed, the reign and the life of the emperor of that time [Michael IV] had reached their limit [1041], [92P] and the one after him [Michael V] began to reign even though he did not know the art of ruling; nevertheless, he had just mounted the chariot[36] and began to fear the things that he did in fact later suffer. He turned to no other man except to this one, only he did not go so far

32. Cf. Plato, *Republic* 506b, 540b. This may refer to rhetoric, which was believed to adorn political orders.

33. Cf. Psellos, *Chronographia* 6.125, on Konstantinos IX Monomachos.

34. Cf. Plato, *Republic* 336b.

35. Cf. Gregorios of Nazianzos, *Or.* 43.14.4 (p. 146); *Or.* 7.7.7–8 (p. 194).

36. For the image of the chariot of the state, see also Psellos, *Chronographia* 4.14, 6.193, 7.57.

as to have him mount the vehicle. Instead, through the influence of others he drove the chariot of state badly, lost his grip on the rails,[37] and came close to breaking the very wheels. This would certainly not have happened if our man had taken hold of the reins with him. But perhaps it was destined for these things to happen in this way and for the entire family of that man to be destroyed, a family that had intruded itself into the state. In this way, decisions made above came to fulfillment. In fact, Providence had decided to bring about the most excellent order in the political scene, to distinguish with clarity things that were confused, and to infuse the world with a genuine royal splendor. Therefore, something bizarre happened that has never been recorded before. Over all the notables, men who were ready to take the throne and were all but in charge of political affairs, preference was given instead to a man in exile [Konstantinos IX Monomachos]:[38] by a common vote, he was brought back to his fatherland and at the same time raised to the throne [1042]. His name was the same as the one who founded our Heavenly City [Constantine I], and his family name was fitting too, as being the one who would face danger in advance and alone for the state, a worthy fighter beyond everyone else, fighting in single combat for the common fame of our people:[39] it was from this that he had taken on that name as if it were a victory prize. Even before he reigned he was adorned by the magnificence of his good judgment and, after receiving the throne, he exalted it even more with power. He vanquished all the emperors in all respects, surpassing everyone in the nobility of his mind, while the loftiness of his royal mind-set made it impossible for anyone to even come close or rival him—and this so that the division [between his own will and his royal status] would be equal and balanced.[40]

For he [Monomachos] did not suppose that, just because he had risen above everyone in the loftiness of his power, he had accordingly changed his nature and somehow became superior to all things combined that he was now chosen to rule. The business of the monarchy seemed to him to have many parts: he saw that one part was adapted to battles and foreign wars, another

37. Cf. Sophokles, *Elektra* 746.

38. Konstantinos Monomachos had been exiled under Michael IV (1034–1041) to Mytilene, on Lesbos. He was brought back by Zoe and Theodora in 1042 to marry the former and ascend the throne.

39. Monomachos in Greek means "single-fighter," or gladiator. It was a family name, not earned by Konstantinos, though that is the conceit of this section of the oration.

40. This clause is obscure.

was inclined toward peace and the careful management of the administration, and a third to something else. So he placed generals in charge of one, judges in charge of the other, orators in some positions, [93P] and capable advisors in others. But so that the state not be broken into pieces, and so that the unitary supervision of all these things not be divided up by necessity into these separate pieces, he decided to tie this multitude together with one knot, in such a way that their highest points all converged there.[41] And searching for the one who might suffice as a cord from which to suspend them all, he discovered the true Golden Chain, I mean, the admirable man whom this speech concerns. This chain he affixed to the heavens, not like Homer's Zeus,[42] with arrogance and great boasting, but rather as the most exact and prudent among all the emperors might suspend it, to join together the many divisions; thus, the man who appears at the top of the chain holds it up by himself, while the chain in turn binds together and affixes everything to itself by the succession of its links. Thus, then, did the emperor decide, and thus did he hit the mark with all that he decided, so much so in fact that of the many prior reigns that we know about from the histories, including the varied modes and methods that they used for governance, not one measured up to this one: neither in the excellence of their planning nor by the ends which their magistracies were known to have pursued.

7. But at this point in my speech, now that I have come to what ensued, I am like those people who have suddenly jumped up to sail out of a harbor and into a vast ocean.[43] Up to here my speech has ridden smoothly through level fields, even if at times it has appeared skittish or has exhibited some spirited whinnying and daring boldness. But from here on the course is uphill, and the ascent poses varied and multiform challenges. Thus I may seem to be panting even before I tread upon the foothills of the mountain; I am almost out of breath and despair of reaching the commanding heights that I decided to set out toward and to climb. All these qualities of the man, which my speech has declared up to this point, were but provisions for what was to come and preparations for the future, just as if one were about to drive a chariot and so prepares the vehicle in advance, polishes the axle to be as smooth as possible,

---

41. Cf. Plato, *Phaedo* 60c.

42. Cf. Homer, *Iliad* 8.19–20, 23.115.

43. Cf. Gregorios of Nazianzos, *Or.* 43.65.3–5 (p. 268); for the expression, see also Plutarch, *Cicero* 6.4; *Alexander* 31.5.

rounds off the wheels, and bends their rims made of the highest quality oak,[44] all so [**94P**] as to drive it into battle with confidence. The preceding was for the sake of everything to which my speech now wants to turn. For all that his preparations were superior and his points of origin were keen and sharp, the outcome was by no means lesser.

When he [Leichoudes] was placed in charge of public affairs and took hold of the reins [in 1043], he did not experience what many do. He was not shocked by the multifaceted nature of command, nor did he fail to understand the causes behind actions. Not only did he understand them well, but he knew in advance what the outcome of each decision would be. He also mixed nature in with public affairs and, when each of the aspects of political power seemed to correspond to an element of the soul, he entrusted one part to the other part. As if he had grown eyes all over his body, he observed affairs from every possible angle, or rather he fixed the single eye of his soul, as if it gave off light,[45] to watch over all sectors of the political sphere, and thus he both closely examined everything and pieced it together. O, what an accomplished and manifold nature he had! He campaigned along with the generals, stood in the front lines of the company of troops, fought ahead of the whole phalanx, held up a shield in support, struck the enemy from the flank and broke up their ranks—not doing these things in person, of course, but by giving suggestions to the men put in command of the armies. He belonged to the party of peace,[46] calmed tempestuous seas, and mollified swelling waves. He unified in himself what had been ruptured, kept separate things that are best kept apart, contributed ideas for upholding the common interest, brought order to present affairs, gave excellent counsel about the future, clarified ambiguous laws, produced written decrees for appointments to office, promoted the best men to the magistracies, managed the public taxes that had been imposed, and set limits for each item of public business. He assumed many forms in dealing with his subjects: to some it was as if he was giving himself wholeheartedly, while with others he was aloof; to some he was intimidating, for others he lifted the gloom; to some he seemed severe and grave with authority, while

---

44. Cf. Homer, *Iliad* 4.486.

45. Cf. Matthew 6:22. This also refers to the mythical creature Argos, who was covered in eyes.

46. As opposed to Keroullarios; for him as a man of war, see Psellos' *Letter to Keroullarios*.

others rejoiced in him and approached him casually. He appeared differently to people with different mentalities, so people who had different dispositions encountered him under different aspects.

I myself saw many who were complaining about one among the many items of public business and cursing the task [95P] on which they had embarked. But the landscape of his soul was devoid of such things and incapable of admitting them, and, if he seemed to have grievances, they arose for him when he did not have *more* public matters to which to attend. Not once did he shrink from making decisions on the various aspects of governance, and, if he briefly became irritated at the way things were going, he would immediately take it all up again. It was as if someone wanted to philosophize in the study of all fields: such a person could easily accomplish that so long as he did not grow weary at the very outset; he would have to persevere for a while when it came to first principles and the basics. So, if one absorbs the most fundamental lessons, one soon becomes an expert in optics and mirrors, an engineer in the company of Archimedes, and, when it comes to balances, understands everything that Hipparchos and Heron discovered and for which they became famous.[47] Thus, after having understood everything with the greatest possible precision, he [Leichoudes] dispensed justice to all as if he had turned his eyes to the imperial decrees and was receiving from there the rules that guided his decisions.[48] To those who asked, he would not immediately give an answer about their legal interests, but would first seem to enter into the oracle chamber, and then recite the oracles as if from before the tripod.

Because of all this, the emperor's own authority gained in dignity. When it came to matters that the emperor did not know, it was through him [Leichoudes] that he gave the impression of having mastered them. He was infused with majesty in a twofold way: first, his imperial authority came from above, but also, second, the fact that he exercised it in the best possible way was due to that man. Often he [Leichoudes] would array around him a truly imperial formation and seat him up high; then, down below, he would range around those who had come, in separate groups, to supplicate the emperor or who were there to ask about their disagreements. In some cases he himself[49]

47. Hipparchos was a second-century BC astronomer and mathematician, who worked mostly on Rhodes. Heron of Alexandria, of the first century AD, was a mathematician and inventor; a number of technical treatises were preserved by the Byzantines under his name.

48. Cf. Sophokles, *Trachiniai* 158.

49. Probably Leichoudes, but switches in subject are unpredictable here.

gave the response by turning his ears to the emperor, as if he were receiving the signal from him, while in other cases he indicated to him [the emperor] how to decide in each case. So the latter was the emperor in both ways, in his appearance and in actual fact.

8. He [the emperor] was gifted by nature in many ways. His mind was as sharp as that of any other emperor, his talk was pleasant, and his manner more graceful than that of anyone else, so that there was **[96P]** something even imperial about him. But when it came to affairs of ultimate importance, he would follow our man's advice. The order that prevailed in the public sphere was the sign of how perfectly everything was being managed and governed, as was the resolution of differences, the contributions that were levied for the treasury, the fact that subjects were governed lawfully; that barbarians were quiescent or put down by force; and the circle of Rome's authority expanded and took in many of the barbarian lands, all of which he [Leichoudes] accomplished and [. . .] through that man's interventions and hard work. But in exercising power in such a way that no one would have expected, and showing that power agreed with him, did he perhaps in the process become alienated from himself or in any way change his convictions about living a restrained life? Not in the least—unless we say that the change was for the better. I state this not because I heard it from someone else; rather, I followed it all from the beginning myself and rely on the testimony of many who were in his audience. He was constituted by his very nature for the better life, to which he was bound in the end to ascend, but, assigned first by a Higher Power to other occupations, he neither neglected them nor hesitated to carry out what had been decreed. His mind was sharp even though his character was venerable beyond his years and steadfast, and the magnitude of his glory did not distract him from his duties. The complex interweaving of state business did not cause any diminution in the appropriateness of his actions. Even as he was being tested in the most pressing business, his disposition was that of a man at ease; if he ever strayed outside of this, he would immediately recover his composure.

His clothing was neither excessive nor casually shabby. It always aimed at proportion, what a wise man would approve. His food was neither sumptuous and devoid of good taste nor, like a man in want, was his table frugal. He walked in an orderly way and spoke brilliantly off-the-cuff, just as his natural capacity of speech directed him. He dignified his voice with melodic rhythm; his rapid flow was steadfast, and yet his steadfastness had momentum. Often many would be surging all around him like waves, men who had only just now begun to attend him, but he made no enemies at all. He smoothly divided his attention among them all. **[97P]** In fact, his prudence, which was by nature dynamic, was strengthened even more by his involvement in public affairs, so that through his greatness he could prevail over men scrutinized in action, and, by participating in so many fields, he surpassed those who had lofty opinions. Actually, it was in part by his natural adeptness that he prevailed over the most notorious of the latter group, and in part it was by having traversed all fields that he performed better than those who had come before. No one from the wrestling grounds managed to hold him down, nor any of those skilled in lofty conceptions; instead, each person was defeated by each of his manifold skills. But the most distinctive aspect of his nature, that which I now present before all, is that if he ever grew angry at someone and reproved him, he immediately regretted it, changed his prior decision, and embraced him with no delay, the very same person whom he seemed only a moment ago to push away and dismiss.

As for the notion that he coarsened his standard of living and, in fact, his entire life by imitating Phokion and Cato,[50] or by emulating the justice of Aristeides in his many positions and acts of authority,[51] thereby ending up in a position similar to that of the most destitute, well, I myself would neither say that nor be entirely happy with it [if others say it]—for where would that leave his liberality? Such a thing perhaps was appropriate for the lives of those men who received power in a hereditary succession (where indeed could have they dismounted the chariot of Roman power[52] in pursuit of high-minded honor?). Our man, by contrast, who was placed by others in the vehicle of state power, how could he have decided to live with no money? The amazing thing was that he received money from no person and took care that both his soul and his palm remain free of unjust gain. He had no regard for himself and transferred his ancestral property to others, living only from what he was legally entitled to receive. The sea is not diminished by evaporation, because it receives the currents of rivers,[53] but the wealth stored up in his honorable soul was incalculable, though he received nothing from the outside except only what was reasonable.

9. So much, then, for those matters and for how his life seemed to have been fashioned from a new mold. No malice ever upset him nor **[98P]** did envy even

---

50. Cf. Plutarch, *Phokion* 3.6–7, for a comparison of the two statesmen.

51. Cf. Plutarch, *Aristeides* 6.1 (Aristeides' justice was proverbial).

52. Cf. Synesios, *Dion* 16.3 (p. 181).

53. Cf. Aristotle, *Meteorology* 346b24–31; Pseudo-Kaisareios, *Questions and Answers* 75.

dare to bend the bow against him,[54] but it was instead as if everything and everyone feared him; nothing at all stood in his way or undercut his straight path. No matter where he went, deep gorges were immediately filled in and steep lookout-points above the clouds were instantly made smooth.[55] But just so that he alone not remain untargeted, whether from those shooting from above or from below, a shot of the following kind was made against him [ca. 1050], which was really a blessing. It served two purposes: first, by being shot at in a minor way he was thereby placed outside the thick of the shooting and firing range;[56] second, so that, looking to his future career, he would have sufficient defenses when it came to enduring injustice. The goal of Providence was to raise him up to the patriarchal throne and make him a shining light for the entire world. Just as we are sometimes transferred to a different life where we end up, a different one from where we had planned to go, so too he, being led by the Holy Spirit to something else, made his beginnings elsewhere so that he could be trained in lesser matters before taking on greater ones. It is in the same way that philosophy requires one who is going to live philosophically to become aware of this lower life before the more perfect ascent of his soul;[57] he is to put his bodily conduct in order in the proper way, so that in this way it acquires mastery of itself, and only after that is he to go up to God.

While this is the purpose of the whole enterprise, it does not take hold of its goal right from the start but begins from the inferior things, and only so does it attain those that are more than perfect. That is why he too was first tested in the inferior positions of authority, so that he might take hold of the superior ones by advancing along the proper path. It was at that point that he invisibly shot at him—whoever it was who fired that shot—but he managed to hit not the heart or the liver: he merely grazed the skin. Now, I admire the emperor in all matters, but this one deed of his I cannot praise, namely, that this man, whose quality he had ascertained by testing him in so many matters, he accused soon after he had taken cognizance of him. He removed him from his position of authority, not of course by seizing him from the foot and hurling him over the divine threshold, as epic poetry would put it,[58] for he respected the man's virtue and hated that he had to do this. He did not just throw him

54. Cf. Gregorios of Nyssa, *Life of Moses* 2.260.3–4 (p. 284).
55. Cf. Isaiah 40:4.
56. Cf. *Corpus Paroemiographorum Graecorum* vol. 1, p. 242.12–13 (Diogenianos 4.71).
57. Cf. Plato, *Republic* 539e.
58. Cf. Homer, *Iliad* 1.591, 15.23.

off but gradually nudged him off the chariot, so that his change of status might still earn him respect. The whole matter was [**99P**] managed so, and a divine solicitude was exercised on his behalf to make it the case that he would no longer carry out this ruler's decisions in the future—and about them I need say nothing more—and also so that, when the emperor passed from this world and was buried, he [Leichoudes] would not be roughly treated at the hands of many, or, at any rate, by their mouths.[59] Thus he stayed out of the killing of men,[60] kept himself away from the blood, and could laugh at—how shall I put this?—those whose souls were destroyed and who died badly. Or rather, to tell the truth, there were cases when he took pity on them, but it was not possible to extend them a helping hand, as they were impelled to war and were glad to fall in it. It was enough for the man, in place of any other purification, that being slighted by the emperor here below made him better known to the One above.

10. And then what happened? A flood of evils transpired in the time when he stayed out of governance, though not yet the gravest of all the hardships, and the emperor's life withered, and a deteriorating disease led him toward death [11 January 1055].[61] In addition to that, the emperor regretted all that he had decided regarding our man and often cursed those who forced him to do it. But there was nothing that he could do about it, given that his strength was draining away, except that as he was dying and being led away from here he would exhale his breath and cast his glance solely upon him. Thus the one man [i.e., the emperor] completed the time allotted to him and departed, while the other man [Leichoudes] immediately showed himself to be unperturbed by the waves. He remained safely in the harbor, and, though everyone was calling him to a second term of governance, he paid no attention to this in his mind, and in the end he prevailed and proved stronger than those who were pressuring him. So from that time onward he held a lesser position, just as Themistokles did with respect to Eurybiades,[62] when nevertheless it was he [Themistokles] who commanded the admirals and ruled the rulers on account

59. I.e., he would not share in the guilt of Monomachos' later policies and make enemies.

60. Cf. Homer, *Iliad* 11.164.

61. The terminal disease and Monomachos' difficult final years are described in Psellos, *Chronographia* 6.200–203.

62. Cf. Herodotos, *Histories* 8 (passim); Plutarch, *Themistokles* 7.3 (Eurybiades was the Spartan nominally in command of the allied fleet in 480).

of his prudence. And when this regime [Theodora's] too came to an end [31 August 1056], and a different emperor was brought in to govern the whole [Michael VI], our man again did not take hold of the tiller. Instead, he instructed those who were posted there how to be the best pilots. So long as they were receptive to his instructions they sailed through and around in the most expert way, [100P] but when they did not accept them, they failed so badly that they lost control of themselves and were hardly able to assist in managing events in a careful way.

There is no need for me to recount the rest, since it would not promote the goal of this speech. I will, however, state one of all of those things: the reason for which the emperor of that time [Michael VI, 1056–1057] and the men around him brought about the end of their dramatic play and for which our man yet again returned to his former position—to the degree, of course, that this was managed providentially with an eye to the future, so that from that position he could then be established on the patriarchal throne. My speech will be concise, setting out only the most essential aspects of the event, which caused the revolution in imperial power. And, I beg you, may no one become envious if I too become a lateral element in the narrative and, in a manner of speaking, bask in his praises. Let no one blame me for this, for I am not intruding myself into the narrative for its own sake, without it being at all necessary; rather, I too was part of the story, and so I must talk about myself.[63]

11. The military establishment was not much disposed to agree with us, the politicians, to treat us politely, or to make peace with us on even terms, but in their own way they hated us.[64] The reason for this was that when each emperor began to distribute favors he would start with the palace, namely, with us, and, as for the armies, he would either entirely overlook them or satisfy his conscience by giving them a modest amount. But they could not tolerate the fact that while they were the first to face dangers on everyone's behalf, they found themselves holding lesser honors and offices than those whom they were defending. It was because of this that they hated that emperor [Michael VI] so much, seeing as he did not give to the army commanders even a tiny fraction of what he lavished on those in the civilian administration. At that point their

63. Many works of Psellos contain similar apologies for their striking autobiographical turns.

64. An account of Isaakios Komnenos' rebellion, Psellos' embassy to him, and his accession to the throne is given also in *Chronographia* 7.3–43.

most select and distinguished leaders broke out in revolt, and immediately all soldiers in their armies joined them in severing their ties to the emperor. Then they chose one among them as their leader, so that their movement could congeal around him and the rebellion could take shape for what it was. He was a noble man who had distinguished himself in many military actions. Forging (so to speak) the imperial insignia, they acclaimed him as sole emperor over all [8 June 1057]. This man was the famous Isaakios [Komnenos], who came from the village of Komne, [101P] just as Philip came from Pella.[65] He brought honor to both his fatherland and his village through his previous military commands and later his reign, except that in some small measure he too, through what we might call an excessive love of honor, came into conflict with the state of public affairs and in the end abdicated in the way that we all know [in 1059]. But that had not yet happened.

This rebel army was unlike any other that had ever been formed. To pass over most of those events, an army was assembled on our side too, against theirs, and a terrible war was fought by both sides. The rebel won decisively.[66] The emperor's advisers despaired of continuing the resistance and decided to send to him envoys and make a treaty, if that were still an option, on the terms that he wanted. They determined to entrust this mission to their best people, and so they looked around to see who the best men were—but I now prefer to tell the truth frankly, just as the events unfolded. The emperor decided to assign the entire task to me and, taking me into his confidence, entrusted me with the secrets of his soul. For my part, I was ready to accept the position of an envoy and willing to serve the emperor in this capacity, but I feared that the man to whom I was being sent as ambassador would dismiss me empty-handed on account of his recent victories. I was apprehensive also of public opinion: in the case that I failed, many might accuse me of being a treasonous ambassador. For this reason I chose to have as my fellow ambassador a man held in high repute [Leon Alopos], so that we could conduct the embassy together, have the same purpose, and negotiate with the rebel. And then immediately the preeminent man of those in office was approved for me [Leichoudes], as if I myself had chosen him as my co-ambassador, and so he too was associated as a third man in the embassy, more distinguished than the rest

---

65. Psellos is perhaps thinking of the passage in Strabo, *Geographika* 7a.1.23, which claims that Pella was a small town before Philip II happened to be born in it.

66. The main battle was fought on 20 August 1057 by the town of Nikaia.

and suitable for our purpose.[67] And so, in turn, the man being praised here was associated with us, and became, over and against us, an argument against all the rest for having a joint embassy, or even a seal of authenticity above all the rest. Those in charge had picked out the best of the political class and did not disrupt the proper ranking among them: one of us was the first, the next was second, and the other was last, though with respect to all the others they gave us three a higher status.[68] My position was minor and marginal—[**102P**] I am not terribly interested in this matter—but they granted him the first place, for the same reasons for which he was elected above all others. Thus we set out, and we would have accomplished something, too, had not a strong north wind blown just then that threw our resolve into confusion,[69] ejected the holder of power over the rails of the chariot [31 August 1057], and placed his adversary upon that exalted platform.

12. Such is the extent of the digression in our speech, but it is necessary to say the following as well, because it demonstrates in what high regard he was held by Higher Powers. When the marvelous Isaakios received the scepters of power, he was held by all to be at the peak of his power because of his natural inclination for great designs. He wanted to approach all the parts of kingship in a scientific way so that nothing at all was overlooked. Taking care to apply this in a balanced way, he sought to find a partner in this supreme position of governance, in part to teach him, in part to effectively legislate for him, and generally to serve him in the most excellent way. Or rather, he was not opposed to most candidates, nor was he trying to discover the more reputable among many who were equivalent or interchangeable with each other, or to judge the best one through some kind of subtle criteria. Instead, no sooner had he taken the throne than he grasped our man with his hands,[70] placed him beside himself, and put him in charge of the imperial tribunal. This, then, was his second term of office, of presiding over the whole. This appointment confirmed the reputation that he had earned during his previous term and indicted the way it had ended as wrong and absurd. Seeing as he had long been retired from the science of command, some believed by that point that he

67. It may be possible to read the order in a different way, with Psellos choosing Leon, who then chose Leichoudes as the third.

68. This passage is obscure.

69. I.e., the turbulence in Constantinople, instigated in part by the patriarch Keroullarios that led to the complete overthrow of Michael VI.

70. Cf. Plato, *Protagoras* 335c.

would not govern to good effect, just like those who have neglected to swim for a certain time do not cut through the waves with the same vigor. So, too, was he regarded as one who would fall short of precise governance, with his skill shattered or grown indolent through time. But he proved them all wrong, as if currents that had been held back were suddenly released.

The emperor did not know how to make use of him, and certainly he was not the yielding type: his thinking was somewhat self-contained, and he did not want to be seen as inferior to anyone, but he would change his mind due to that man alone.[71] He admired him because he both cut sharply [103P] through the business at hand and also handled everything in an expert way, and especially because his loyalty was solid and his prudence shone with exceeding brilliance. These good qualities that God had given him had not been squandered, except he seemed to have been destined for some higher purpose from where, as from a mountain peak, he would hold up the torch of his excellent qualities.

13. That was what the emperor was thinking and planning regarding this man, but circumstances caught up with him. I will pass by all that happened in the meantime, both for the sake of the one who committed it and for the sake also of the one who suffered it (for I cannot arbitrate between the two, if not to proclaim them both winners).[72] The man who adorned the patriarchal throne at that time [Michael Keroullarios] was gathered up to God [21 January 1059], and he rose up to the Crown Giver as if he were a martyr who had endured trials, to be wreathed in a more beautiful way and seal his ascetic life with a martyr's end. The choice for a new patriarch now settled upon him,[73] just as before: it was not among many, nor did different options have to be weighed. Rather, all beasts yield the right of power to the lion, and all birds submit to the race of eagles: no beast in the forest would challenge that noble beast, nor would any bird dare to enter into a contest with the eagle. In this same way, no one stood as an alternative to the one who was being chosen over everyone else: everyone yielded to him this absolute power over every-

---

71. Isaakios' inflexible personality is described also in Psellos, *Chronographia* 7 (passim).

72. Psellos is referring here to the struggle between the patriarch Keroullarios and the emperor Isaakios in 1058, which he also recounts in *Chronographia* 7.65–66 and in the *Funeral Oration for Keroullarios*. Keroullarios died before he could be brought to trial, as Isaakios had been planning to do.

73. Cf. Thucydides, *History* 1.131.

one. Even though he had not long been ordained into the clergy, seeing as he had not been prepared for it in the usual way, still, he happened to be better prepared for it than others.[74]

Therefore, O you who were incomparable with respect to the whole of virtue—my speech will now briefly address you directly—the sacerdotal life received you no less than the political one.[75] For it is not the case, as the many suppose, that these two ranks are distinct, with the one being superior and the other inferior, and that the better sort are appointed to the one while worse types engage in the politics of the other. The difference between better and worse has to do with one's choices in life and not with career tracks. The good makes itself equally available to both careers: a man who has learned wisdom in the conduct of public affairs has thereby been purified in advance for the life that comes after that and need not, as [**104P**] if he had been pulled out of the slime, be washed clean again. One who has lived well in politics will suffice for anything else at all. At this point my speech brings together many people: if they managed to step out of this worldly life and were instantly deemed worthy of heavenly Jerusalem, why should they also not confidently step into the sacerdotal life, asking for a second occupation, prepared as they have been in the middle ground for that ultimate post? It was entirely appropriate, then, O you most marvelous man, that you were transferred to the life for which you had been destined; the judgment of your elector was impartial; and your ascent, or transfer, made perfect sense.

14. By testing this man in every public action we have found him perfect and most reliable; so now, if it seems appropriate, let us ascertain his quality in this new function too. Is it the case that he was perhaps like a Scythian who went off by sea among the Greeks and did not know the Attic language?[76] I, however, would confidently assert that he actually imported transferable things from the political life into the sacerdotal one, namely, a profundity of judgment, the ability to divide each thing into its elements, honorable conduct, a harmony of habits, and all the other qualities that testify to his divine soul. I do not know whether he was foreseeing the future or responding to

74. Leichoudes was made patriarch on 2 February 1059.

75. For Leichoudes as patriarch, see also Psellos, *Chronographia* 7.66.

76. Famous Scythians who were believed to have visited Greece were Anacharsis and Toxaris (Lucian, *The Skythian*; and *Anacharsis*), but linguistic challenges were not part of their stories (see Himerios, *Oration* 29.4, for Anacharsis' knowledge of Attic).

situations in his natural way, but he gave many signs of his later sacerdotal life to those who wanted to discern them. His modest manner, avoidance of pomp (at least no more than was decorous), self-controlled lifestyle, and refusal to enable bitter prejudice: these signs all pointed to the sacerdotal life. His plan had been to dedicate himself entirely and directly to God, but he was diverted from this plan by the fact that he could not predict the future or his life in office. But when he was separated from the life to which he had been predestined from the very beginning, he was wholly and immediately infused with spirit. Had there not been people who had known him before and who could acknowledge later that in fact it was him, he would have seemed like one placed on a candlestick which then has the hood lifted away,[77] that is, as most perfect in spiritual matters but inferior in politics, having a perfect share of the most advanced qualities but less of keenness and dynamism. In fact, these [105P] attributes of his were neither diminished nor altered in any other way, but rather his judgment was set to supervise these traits, and it selected and put its stamp of approval on those traits which it found to be appropriate for the high priesthood, while those which were not altogether suitable it did not so much drive out as dampen.

Above all, a high priest should not become too involved in public affairs nor display too much ambition regarding them. Therefore in matters where it was appropriate that his ambition not disturb him, he restrained it or reduced it and hid it; for this reason he lowered the volume of his voice, its clarion call,[78] and for a while he made its ringing echo less resonant and dimmer. Anticipating most of the concepts that people were about to propose, he did not give an immediate and resounding expression to them but allowed the others to say something confidently about them. Whatever it was that one said, even if it was not altogether sound, he neither refuted nor blamed it, but calmly corrected the error in such a way that the one who made it was not weighed down by the knowledge that he had made a slip regarding what was fitting. In this way he unobtrusively cured whatever was ailing in what had been said. This quality seems to the many to belong to their common nature, but in my view it has not been seen or manifested even in the case of the most proven people.[79] The greatest thing about him, and that which I adore the most when

77. Cf. Matthew 5:15.
78. A common allusion in Byzantine literature to Aischylos, *Eumenides* 567.
79. This sentence is obscure.

I ponder it carefully, is that in the time before his priesthood he yielded to no man at all in any matter that required the use of reason, but instead, to tell the truth, everyone yielded to him by far. No matter the aspect from which one looked upon him, he glowed with such an infinite light[80] that he required that person to shutter his eyes. But when he joined the divine tribunal and was established on that revered throne, he would trust the innermost recesses of his soul and would inquire about things that he believed he did not know.[81] He would not put on graceful airs in his speech nor earnestly practice the skills of the art [of rhetoric] or of the law, but rather terminated his study of all such things as belonging to the life of the body; he focused now solely on the spiritual life. Those who approached became more composed because of the reverence or fear that he inspired, and his desire to be equal to everyone resulted in his receiving from them the recognition that they were all inferior to him.

He gave away, for the benefit of God and the poor, all the possessions and money that came down to him through inheritance, except for a portion [106P] that he entrusted to some of his relatives. Not even in this respect was he ill-omened, as one might be, or caused aversion. For I do not praise those who have decided to overcome their nature[82] or those whose souls are abrupt, who lack empathy and refuse to associate with friends and family. Such a person seems to me to have turned his back on our world, though he also turns to higher matters. Sooner would all the Scythians and those who dwell in the lands beyond Tauros take their stand with the Higher Beings and gather into the heavenly abodes, they whose nature is so monstrous that some of them kill their infants,[83] whereas others among them who are more gentle merely sell off their offspring, and if one of them tears the nursing child from the embrace of its mother, with the teat still spirting in its mouth, she neither feels the crying child's pain nor pities it as it is torn away. Which, then, is the better choice? If one should recognize that he is both made in the image of God[84] and is himself a part of nature, he—whoever he is—will favor his family too. Even if he is devoted to God, he will not neglect his duty toward his friends nor utterly overlook what is suitable for friends and family. So let those who

---

80. Cf. Acts 26:13.
81. I.e., he did not claim infallibility.
82. Cf. Synesios, *Egyptian Oration* 127a.
83. This Scythian comparison is an extended attack on Byzantine monasticism.
84. Cf. Genesis 1:26.

fly above the air bid us farewell, and *get lost!* I join the ranks of the more empathetic and would rather accept the blame for not philosophizing in a perfect way than for being insensible and lacking feeling toward natural states.

15. Such was his character. I turn now to explain what I experienced regarding him: I admired him for all his other good qualities, though I did not immediately form a close relationship with him. Thus I did not unite myself with him, but I liked him so much that it was as if I had entered his soul. For having the same disposition leads people to grow in the same way, whereas those who seem to have the same mentality but have different habits are only affecting a merger, or are play-acting. On account of this quality, then, I would both praise him and receive along with him the joys of his soul and the praises that he earned. But as for not becoming angrily upset at anything, it was a distinctive mark of his personality that it lacked harshness, and I can bring virtually everyone as witnesses to this. As if he were a river or the sea, most people were immediately eager to have a piece of him, and they converged upon him in lines stretching [107P] from the harbors, the open seas, the air, and the mainland: they pulled him in one direction, then in the other, divided him into pieces, and most people drank from his waters two and more times. But there was enough of him for everyone: he put up no resistance when they came to him and did not take it badly; he did not push back but, with a propitious gaze and cheerful attitude, he admitted everyone together and catered to all their needs.

16. But I have forgotten one thing. God decided to purify his soul a second time[85]—or rather, to sanctify it even more. Thus, as soon as he had ascended that sacred chair, he was struck by a virulent illness: it involved a fever that consumed his innards, horribly melting and ravaging his body. He was saddened not by his suffering or the death that was expected to come from it but because he took that imminent death as a sign that he had been unworthily appointed. This grieved him horribly, his eyes released streams of tears, he sighed faintly and deeply, and the grief of his pain expressed itself in manifold ways. But when his breath began to come in short bursts and he expected his soul to be set free, God ended his anger and brought calm after the stormy waves. He strengthened his body and dispersed the illness as if it were a mist. Thereupon, a man who seemed as if he was about to breathe his last recovered his bodily vigor, acquired even greater strength, and underwent a transformation to a su-

---

85. Cf. Pseudo-Plutarch, *On Music* 1146D.

perior state. I had been warned long in advance that this would happen by a higher vision that came to me in a nocturnal apparition. One night when I was going to sleep, I thought that I was passing through his tent and reciting, with a good cadence, the hymns that we address to the Risen God. And he[86] believed that the dream was without any deceit and sought after the time at which he would recover, when that miracle would come true for him. Then he looked for a higher sign of his healing, and, as it happened, mysterious sounds and sacred icons that poured forth myrrh did herald his return to life. No sooner had he risen from the bed to which he had been confined than he offered to God the thanksgiving prayers he had promised, among them the construction of a temple. This he built with an earnest desire to honor God, and he placed a divine monastery around it. But I want to preface this with a few words.

17. [108P] It was not his intention to construct a temple to God built by human hands, only to fashion himself into a house of God not made by hands.[87] But his own father was the main reason why he built this monastery. He [his father] had built up the shrine of the martyr Kallinikos that stood there by adding another one that was dedicated to the Savior,[88] and he associated his son with him in everything that he did and planned there, before the latter became high priest [the 1050s?]. He wanted his mortal remains to be deposited there and so bound his son with many oaths not to bury him in any place but where he had built this temple for God, and also to plan some other greater project for that place. Bound by this, the man whom we are now praising did not entirely neglect this commandment, but at the same time he did not instantly conform to it as to a doctrine, either: he was torn in different directions, and pondered and considered what he might do. But when he was struck by that illness, he came to believe that he was being punished by God because he had not absolutely obeyed his father's instructions. Being convinced of this now, he proclaimed that he would no longer resist his father's will if he rose again from that bed. Obtaining his wish, he built a church to the Mother of God[89] and constructed in it a splendid dwelling for philosophy.[90] Let others praise the form of the temple, the way in which everything fit together harmoniously, the balanced and straight array of columns, the alternating variety of

86. It is not easy to identify the subject here, probably Leichoudes.
87. Cf. Leviticus 26:1; Acts 7:48; Mark 14:58.
88. Janin (1969) 275.
89. Janin (1969) 305.
90. I.e., a monastery.

slabs, the landscaping of the ground, how he arranged the colors of the stones so that they vied in brilliance with each other, the sheer height to which he raised the temple and how he made the height proportional to the width, and these and all things around the temple that he crafted with attention to detail after careful investigation, fashioning water channels in them and planting stately gardens.[91]

I leave these things for others to praise. For my part, I admire more than anything else his truly philosophical approach to the philosophy of the soul, that he made this monastery a place not for luxury but asceticism.[92] It sufficed for him to give those [109P] who chose to philosophize there only as much as sufficed for their necessities, such that they would not want to have anything redundant or even be able to obtain it if they wanted it. At first he pursued this plan in a moderate way, but as time passed his zeal for God increased, and he was propelled away from the pleasures of this life at full speed.[93] He was unable to praise what he had done and was buffeted by many considerations as he pondered whether he should not so much alter the appearance of the edifice as demolish it altogether. By removing all the material splendor that he had deposited there, he could then distribute it to the poor, and even hand over in addition the ground itself. He would have taken his stand on that decision had I not pleaded the voice of reason when he confided his opinion in me. I cast doubt on his resolve and finally caused him to abandon his purpose. I offered him an equally compelling argument: if a project is not yet finished it is better to add something to it, but, seeing as part of it was so well advanced, it would be a truly zealous vanity and a sure sign of a weak and easily reversed mind to take down what had been built up and to revisit the original plan after the end was reached. He brought forth many objections but finally admitted defeat before my arguments and therefore abandoned his plan. Still, he neglected to complete the missing parts and did not visit there often, nor did he care if the whole building would collapse,[94] nor was he was distracted by anything else.

91. In the *Chronographia*, Psellos includes such detailed descriptions of the extravagant churches built by Romanos III (3.14–16), Michael IV (4.31), and Konstantinos IX (6.185–188; cf. 6.186 especially for the wording used here).

92. In many works, including the *Chronographia*, Psellos criticized the excessive luxury in which many monks lived: Kaldellis (1999) 80–89.

93. Cf. Synesios, *Dion* 1.12 (p. 144).

94. For textual problems here, see Criscuolo (1983) 158 n. 243.

18. As for his term as high priest, before this he was eager to do many things, and it was clearly because of this that he wanted to be dissolved as quickly as possible and be with God in a pure way.[95] But as for what came after, my speech could not keep pace with it in the usual way, not even if I wanted it to, and I would not in fact have wanted to follow it to this point.[96] For how will I, in my speech, follow him who has departed, a man who, while he was alive, I never expected would die, as I said in my preface?[97] How might I recount his suffering, or by using what tone, or what approach in general, so as to endure recounting his death? Tears immediately flow from my eyes, [**110P**] my soul is shaken, and I do not know by what medicines I might completely drug myself in advance before I can describe this tragedy. O our perishable, or one might say quickly dying, composite nature! O what a faint constitution! O what a faint dissolution! The former I did not experience,[98] the latter I would not have chosen, but it still completes its work. Yet because he had been unfastened earlier and acquired an altogether more refined composition, now that he was fastened together in a more refined way he was dissolved in a more faint way. The very God who binds us together with his Creative Words,[99] when he wants to take people away from this life, unbinds his Words harmoniously and gently unties the bonds of union, so that their death, just like their life, distinguishes them from their fellow men. Death came [to him] with little or no prior difficulty, and he departed from here within the span of a single day.

While I want to avoid the tragedy of this grief, it clings tightly to me and will not allow me to end this speech before I say a few words about that man's passing. He suddenly had to lie down with a pain in his liver and burning up with a violent fever; the signs of his imminent demise were plain to see on his face. His cheeks had caved in, his nose was spent, his eyes were hollow, and his breathing was labored. I went up to his residence, found him in this—how shall I put it?—transformed condition, and was able to deduce the invisible underlying cause by the reports given to me by others. Thereupon I lost my composure: at first a trembling came upon me, as I realized that he would soon die. When I came to my senses and regrouped my inner strength, I sighed

---

95. Cf. Philippians 1:23.
96. I.e., to the point of Leichoudes' death.
97. Psellos does not say this in his preface.
98. This is obscure.
99. Cf. Psellos, *Philosophica Minora II* 13 (p. 38.2–3).

deeply, wailed aloud, poured out tears in lamentation,[100] and moved to depart with my head covered. I said only this to him, that before he died he should give thought to something more advantageous for himself than mere death.[101] Then I left, not abandoning my friend and lord, but to announce this misfortune to the emperor [Konstantinos X Doukas] so that he could visit him too [111P] and not blame me for not warning him in advance of this Father's death. At first the emperor did not believe my words, but then he immediately organized a visit to him. He saw and was amazed that the man was soon about to die. He embraced him often and powerfully with tears in his eyes, and left subdued by grief, though he often turned back to him. The emperor had not yet exited that holy temple when he [Leichoudes] departed from his body [9–10 August 1063]. It would be better to speak in that way, because he himself was all soul and was only using the body as an instrument.

19. But O, the shocking change that I experienced! I am trying to make it vividly clear to the living, as he is being conveyed to burial, that a man who I did not think would die has in fact died. Since I have managed to patiently endure my grief and resigned myself to recounting this grave matter in my own words, I will add the final farewell to his body, the words that are spoken at a funeral. Until the moment of his death, the entire City was in suspense; everyone was silent, as if sacred mysteries were being performed. But when, against every hope, the hierophant passed away and the farewell ceremony had begun, as if a higher being had been carried off, something happened that was not inferior to the miracles of old. The City's multitudes poured out for him like a stream in flood,[102] with one person following another and all calling him again and again by the sweetest names. Depending on the different phases of his life, he was named by people after opposite qualities, or, if you prefer, by the same ones, namely, those by which he named himself to those whom he benefited.[103] This outpouring was indiscriminate as the grief crossed social lines.[104] The most passionate were those who were on close terms with the deceased, or rather, with him who now lived after death more powerfully than he had lived previously while in the body. His burial took on the character of a sacred procession,[105] with

---

100. Cf. Psellos, *Chronographia* 3.26.38.
101. This is obscure.
102. Cf. Gregorios of Nazianzos, *Or.* 43.79.3 (p. 298).
103. This is obscure.
104. Cf. Gregorios of Nazianzos, *Or.* 43.79.6–7 (p. 298).
105. Cf. Gregorios of Nazianzos, *Or.* 43.80.1–7 (p. 300).

some mourning, others awestruck, and still others wanting to carry the load as if it were the Ark of the Covenant of the Lord,[106] for in this way they might receive some sanctification by touching or being in proximity to the body. Thus his death too became a sacred ceremony, and while his soul [112P] was assigned to the divine monasteries, his body, like a treasure, was preserved here in its tomb.

O, my episcopal and divine head, you attained the highest measure of all good fortune, both that which pertains to this life here and that which comes down from above and is allocated by God to holy souls. You were a match for all the virtues and revealed yourself a votive offering and ornament to them all. You vanquished the ancient models and yet are a model for no one—or rather also to all: the latter because all spiritual men must now strive to emulate you, the former because it will be impossible for them to do so. You are beyond reach and cannot be contained; you vanquished every tongue by the magnitude of your soul, astonished every soul by the rapidity of your speech, and prevailed over everyone in every respect. You are incomparable among the orators and the philosophers and hard to imitate by the high priests. You alone escaped from the tongues of all malicious people, made a direct ascent, were continually adding to your good qualities, and were growing into perfection. You cannot be compared to anyone else, for you are divided, measured, victorious, and vanquished only by yourself. You are an innovative model for life, ranked among the miraculous beings and considered to belong with the supernatural ones. You give brilliant occasions for us to deploy all the conventions of panegyric, though this has not yet been attempted by anyone because no one at all is sufficiently prepared to sing your praises. O trumpet that blared above the rest!—or rather that still blares, since still no other can be heard.

20. To whom will I compare you among all those who are now alive or who have ever lived? We would not be able to compare you to only one person, as there is no person to whom the whole of happiness flowed together. Now, if we measure you alone up against everyone else, even then we would grant you a brilliant victory. My thinking is as follows. Some of the men who are admired set out to philosophize but failed to master rhetoric, even though they wanted to, whereas those who practiced rhetoric well derived little or no benefit from philosophy. Those who set out to legislate or become judges were distinguished by those pursuits only. And others still who were allotted or chose to pursue none of those fields were praised and glorified simply because of their fathers,

---

106. Cf. Deuteronomy 31:9, 31:25; Joshua 3:14–15.

either because they decided to philosophize [113P] or chose to live exemplary lives. Another group takes pride in its fatherland alone, but have nothing to contribute of their own. But as for you, your speech, nature, family, virtue, secular qualities, and all other things are encompassed within you, as if they have there formed a chorus; or rather, some of them sprang up from the depths of your soul, others blossomed upon your body, still others came to you from above, and finally another group of them has assembled there from various sources. So it is in this way, then, that I would compare you, the incomparable one: I name you more philosophical than the philosophers, more rhetorical than the orators, greater and more revered in any one virtue than those who had many, surpassing when compared to those who are perfect and more perfect than those who are surpassing, with no rivals, and constituting a measure that no one can even hope to equal.

O, you who are desired and honored by all, and exceedingly more so by me than by the others (which is only reasonable): I speak with you as if you were alive. You yourself, before all the rest, took the initiative to open new paths for my education and, before I even entered that intellectual footrace, by some kind of imprint of character you discerned in advance that I would run as quickly as possible and would be deemed worthy of victory crowns in that race. You also admired me, exalted me to the skies before many witnesses, and, regarding my nature, you . . .—but I do not wish to say anything more about *me*. By the power of your speech you placed me above the rest. For these reasons, I honored you more than anyone else while you were still alive and, now that you have died, I lament bitterly and am unable to lighten this grief for myself or to receive any consolation from outside. Whenever I stir up my memory of you in my soul, my mind is thrown into turmoil, my body is shaken, and I am possessed by grief: I feel weak, fall to pieces, and am barely able to recover my senses. But I have dared to write this speech for you, not presuming that my praise will ever measure up to your virtues but to show you, even now that you are dead, the sweetness of my tongue, and so that you may know, now that you are stationed with God, that I have not forgotten you after your departure. Wherever you may be, surely in the more beautiful realms and in abodes beyond this world, I am devoted to you and with pleasure affixed to you by nature. For your part, do not overlook us, but look upon us from above with shining and propitious eyes: may you take no notice if we backslide, strengthen us if we hold steady, and move us along if we are advancing toward the good, pointing out to us the straight [114P] path that leads unerringly to God, to whom may there be glory for all time. Amen.

4   *Letters to Ioannes Xiphilinos*

Anthony Kaldellis

Introduction

This chapter contains translations of a pair of letters to Xiphilinos, the first of which elicited a response by the latter (which we do not have), prompting Psellos to write the second one, the long letter known as *Letter to Ioannes Xiphilinos*. For a discussion of these letters in the context of the relationship of Psellos and Xiphilinos, see the general introduction.

The first is *Letter KD* 191 (ed. Kurtz and Drexl, pp. 215–218), of which there is no published translation; there is a brief commentary in Criscuolo (1975) (with emendations proposed, 123 n. 11). The second is *Letter S* 175 (ed. Sathas, pp. 444–451), which has been reedited, with an Italian translation and commentary, by Criscuolo (originally in 1973, reissued as a second edition in 1990). There is also a German translation and discussion in Weiss (1977) 299–305. Weiss followed the Sathas edition, and his translation seems to evade some difficult passages. Some useful emendations were proposed by Maltese (1987); cf. Criscuolo (1990) 83. The bold numbers in square brackets in the translation of the first letter, such as "[215KD]," correspond to the page numbers of the Kurtz and Drexl edition. The translation of the second letter is based on Criscuolo's revised edition, and the bold numbers correspond to the section numbers in that edition.

Letter KD 191

[215KD] I do not know whether I am philosophizing, O brother dear to me and most honored, by neither speaking to you nor greeting you from a distance through a letter,[1] or whether I am committing some boorish act more suited to souls that have turned away from each other and are altogether uncommunicative. I am perplexed on this point because the chief ethos of philosophy[2] seemed preferable to some of those men whom *you* call divine, according to which they kept complete silence among themselves,[3] while to others the good of conversation both sufficed and seemed preferable for the remaining parts of wisdom. Among them, I station the silent ones on the side of contemplation, the more eloquent or more rationally debating ones on the side of the practical virtues.

But O what have I said! What a thing has slipped out through "the fence of my teeth"![4] For Gregorios [of Nazianzos] and Basileios [of Kaisareia], those instructors of the most perfect wisdom, conversed with each other in person about some matters, and also remained closely attached over great distances through letters. Yet they were not defrauded of contemplation on this count; rather, all at once, they privately associated with God and publicly with each other. Now if this distinction is not entirely accurate, let the matter be distinguished for me in such a manner anyway, allowing those men to moor themselves with two anchors, the one leading toward heaven and the [216KD] other attached to lower harbors. Whenever the supremely perfect anchorage received them, they were required to keep silent. But when they were subse-

---

1. Cf. Plato, *Charmides* 153b.
2. Silent contemplation, perhaps.
3. This could include the ancient Pythagoreans as well.
4. Cf. Homer, *Iliad* 4.350. Psellos expresses his (rather artificial) shock at the fact that he has drawn an either-or distinction, when in fact a both-and was called for.

quently separated from that place, and visited the harbor of lesser account, then they discoursed with each other using speeches that traded in virtue.[5]

What is really the purpose of all this, and what is my intention in making such a long preface? Bear with me as I prove that I am right about you. I am aware that you too are possessed by both.[6] And yet I do not know the time when the ship will arrive here from you, so that I may then send off this letter of friendship in reply.[7] [Your] soul has fastened high the cable of its own life,[8] and deems everything that comes from elsewhere to be superfluous and discordant. But see how I regulate even my schedule for you, or rather how I apportion this letter to make it fit your schedule. For if just now you have descended, let my letter give you rest, rather than the Platonic lotus or the oak tree or myrtle.[9] But if you are still uplifted by marvelous spectacles and blessed recitations,[10] the letter can wait, so that you might converse with it whenever you decide to turn toward us. Neither consider me pretentious if I do write something, nor accuse me of unfriendliness if I do not write. You should justify the letter by the divine and lofty matters in which *you* are engaged, whereas you should consider the former scenario as a most invincible proof of [our] friendship toward one another.

But what am I saying and to what end? I have been completely deprived of you, both separated from your kindred and concordant soul, and also divided within myself. For the soul can be cut into pieces just like the body. And the one spills much blood, yet the other produces extraordinary pain. For the parts of the body are not joined together in the same way as those—how shall I put it?—parts of the soul, because the former are fastened onto each other, [217KD] while the latter interpenetrate each other completely. And the former, if perhaps you recall, constitute an extension such as is produced from [the intersection of] lines, while the latter is formed from points.[11] For it remains without distinct parts even after union. For this reason, the separation of elements whose continuity is formed by interpenetration is very painful. It is therefore necessary, in accordance with this account, for divided souls to

---

5. The mercantile imagery is in the text.
6. Probably referring to Xiphilinos' dual life, i.e., both contemplative and active.
7. Presumably to an earlier letter by Xiphilinos.
8. For this obscure expression, see Philostratos, *Lives of the Sophists* 485.
9. Cf. Plato, *Phaedrus* 230b.
10. A reference to Xiphilinos' monastic life.
11. The "point" theory of the soul was of Pythagorean origin.

perish or to fly away from their bodies. But there is a certain medicine capable of giving them life even when they are divided. What is this? Memory and imagination and intellectual discourse and pure conceptions have been implanted in them by their Creator: these things make souls take flight and lead them in whatever direction they want. Nor is there anything to impose limits on them, nothing like the so-called pillars of Herakles, or hilltops raised up high. By contrast, Europe and Libya are divided by their proper boundaries, and there can be no mixing of the two. Take two men, a Libyan and a European, the one in Libya, the other in Europe: well, the Libyan has to travel to Europe, or the European to Libya, for they cannot immediately join together without any interval in some intermediate location. But the distance between Byzantion and your Olympos[12] is so great that I cannot even see you with my bodily eyes. So greatly do I entreat you not to think that I have written these things as though I were fulfilling a formal code of friendship. For I would enjoy neither philosophy nor wisdom nor the graces of friendship, if I were not attached and dependent upon you, and both rooted and present in you, and united with you.

How can I, being as I am now in this state, endure separation from you? Upon your holy soul, I am neither lying nor will I hide my deep affection from you. I still do not seem to have understood myself, whether I am some divine treasure or "a beast more complicated than Typhon."[13] [218KD] For at one moment I am enthusiastically eager to come to your side; my soul is elated and nothing can contain it. But straightaway I glimpse a very different view of the matter, according to which this impulse is not divine: regret might overtake the one who acts upon it. If, however, besides these things something else happens to me and I am distracted either by the love of practical affairs or by worldly notions, and I do not hold that the whole of happiness is more false than a figment of the imagination[14]—let my relationship to my family not be included here, so that my account may be altogether true[15]—then I should both utterly fail to achieve the divine state[16] and also not find rest in your com-

---

12. Mt. Olympos in Bithynia.

13. Plato, *Phaedrus* 230a.

14. An ascetic view of worldly happiness.

15. Xiphilinos would probably have understood this obscure reference. Psellos is suggesting that what he is saying would be falsified if he divulged the entire truth.

16. Referring to the monastic ideals practiced on Mt. Olympos.

pany, which to me would be both more desirable and yet also more awe-inspiring than anything else.

But in order to dampen the boast of virtue likely to be found in your soul, [let me say that] you bask, dear soul, in so many advantages of this kind. Winter does not trouble you, nor do criers awaken you when you are resting on your bed. You take your breakfast in a timely fashion, and your dinner similarly and in good measure. All these things are divine and extraordinary and marvelous, namely, silence, *logos*, distinctions, and ascents. But to us, life seems to be an infamous thing. For all things are in confusion here. And what is worse, they are full of suspicion and fear. There have been times when I myself (I swear this upon your marvelous soul), being either burned by the summer heat or frozen by the winter cold, when it was possible to be neither burned nor frozen, or otherwise afflicted in the outdoors or inside, am despised and neglected for the most part; and every time that I gently exclaim "O blessed Xiphilinos," I almost give you the evil eye for living such a life [the monastic one] and for having already lived that other one [the active one]. You have already reaped the benefits of second rank and will reap the superior ones in the future. As for myself, well, may I obtain both types of your blessings abundantly, and may I spend this life with you and the coming ages with God.

Letter to Ioannes Xiphilinos

1. "*My* Plato"? O most saintly and wise man! "*Mine*"?[17] O by the earth and sun![18]—there, so I too may use words from tragedy upon this debate-stage! For if it is your reproach that I often conversed with that man [Plato] in his dialogues and that I admired the style of his expression and worshipped the power that lies in his proofs, why then did you not also hurl this charge against the Great Fathers, who overturned the heresies of Eunomios and Apollinarios by employing precisely those kinds of exact proofs?[19] But if you believe that I follow his dogmas or rely on his laws, you do not think rightly about us, brother. For I read through many philosophical books and became acquainted with many rhetorical arguments; neither did Plato's teachings escape my notice (I would not deny it), nor did I overlook the philosophy of Aristotle. I am also familiar with the claims of the Chaldaeans and the Egyptians—but, upon your honorable head, why is it necessary to speak of these esoteric books?[20] For I compared everything to our Scriptures that have been handed down from God, which are pure and shining and truly excellent, and found them[21] to be impure and full of fraud.

2. *My* Plato! I do not know how to bear the weight of that word! Did I not earlier prefer the Divine Cross and now the spiritual yoke as well?[22] I fear lest

---

17. I.e., "You are saying that he is *mine*?"

18. Cf. Aischylos, *Prometheus* 90–91: "O universal mother earth, and thou, all-seeing orb of the sun, to you I call! Behold what I, a god, endure of evil from the gods" (Smyth trans.); Euripides, *Hippolytos* 601–602: "O Mother earth! O sun and open sky! What words have I heard from this accursed tongue" (Grene trans.). A potentially hostile allusion; at the least, a powerful complaint.

19. These were heretics of the fourth century who were believed to have based their ideas on ancient philosophy (or so claimed their Orthodox detractors).

20. A reference to the *Chaldaean Oracles* and Iamblichos' *On the Mysteries*.

21. I.e., non-Christian doctrines.

22. Psellos had just been tonsured.

he rather be *yours*, to attack you with your own word, you who have not refuted a single one of his beliefs. But I have refuted *almost* all of them, for they are not *all* bad. Besides, his accounts of justice and of the immortality of the soul became the foundations for our own similar dogmas. It is not as though I contracted some disease of the eyes from those studies, but rather, in a fair way, I loved what was clear in those waters and washed off what was salty. At any rate, that attack of yours I could bear with some moderation. The following, however—if you believe me—concerning Chrysippos and *my* syllogisms and the nonexistent lines,[23] and all those other things of yours [i.e., your accusations], would require an adamantine soul [to endure], or an unconscious one. Why did you not add[24] the implications of your accusation, which sound the same as the rest: "Otherwise, you will experience instruments of torture the likes of which you have never heard before"? I was bewildered by everything that you wrote and considered many possibilities, finally settling upon two alternatives: either you did not understand my letter or else you wrote yours in response to some person like Eunomios or to a follower of Kleanthes and Zenon, who, offering every sort of opinion in their arguments, did not consider that there is anything that cannot be proven with reason or that is beyond proof in general. But Plato discovered this thing, having raised himself up to Mind, and saw also that which is above Mind, finally stopping at the One.[25] But you accuse him of everything, you *Plato-hater* and *misologist*, lest I call you a *hater of philosophy*.[26]

When did you ever see me attached to Chrysippos or the New Academy? Did I not also earlier, when our habitation was not fenced around with wood but rather plated with silver and gleaming with gold, reflect upon the hide of

---

23. Alluding to Xiphilinos' attack on geometry; cf. Sextos Empirikos, *Against the Mathematicians* 3.30. Psellos had mentioned line-theory in his previous letter, *Letter KD* 191 (translated above).

24. Polemis proposes the possibility that προστέθεικας is a scribal error for προστέθεικα, thus: "Why should *I* not add" (what follows logically in your letter)?

25. I.e., the higher levels of Neoplatonic metaphysics that lay beyond rational demonstration.

26. The allusion is possibly to Eunapios, *Lives of the Philosophers* 481: Priskos "used to say that one who is beaten in philosophical argument does not thereby become milder, but rather, as he fights against the might of the truth and suffers the pains of thwarted ambition, he becomes more savage, and ends by becoming a *misologist* and a *hater of philosophy*" (Wright trans., modified). The ultimate source is, of course, Plato, *Phaedo* 89c ff.

Christ and those cloaks for the sake of which we often put our heads together?[27] Did we not then transform our plans into action, and now stand within the enclosure of the Lord? We do not adhere to Chrysippos! Are you amazed that my bile is really aboil and that my anger is shaking violently? For the body is not alone in my case lacking the guts inside, where the spirit of anger originates, so that I might endure such an insult! Upon your holy soul, had you struck me on my head, had you pulled out my remaining hairs,[28] had you drenched me in other kinds of insults, I would have endured your tirade in a more stead-fast way. But [for me] to have acted in every way on behalf of Christ and then to be indicted as "a friend of Chrysippos" and to have it thought by you, both a friend and a judge, that I have abandoned God and cling to Plato and the Academy . . . well, I do not know how to endure it for any amount of time!

3. In mentioning the lines, O you who disdain all, why did you attribute nonexistence also to them? For the first to call them "those things which do not lie anywhere" added in a highly philosophical and lofty way that "it is one thing not to exist and another not to lie in any particular place."[29] For it is not the case that the lines do not exist; rather, according to the wise, "intellectual length" is perhaps nowhere. But from both these nonexistent lines and those syllogisms that you overlook, I have gathered advantages which are hard to ex-aggerate regarding the doctrines of higher things. These nonexistent lines, you *misologist*, are the principles of the whole of natural science. And Maximos,[30] who is shared by us all—though I should rather call him *mine*, for he was a philosopher—made natural science the second virtue after action, even while not recognizing the existence of mathematical entities.[31] Whoever abandons the principles of his subject matter in making syllogisms undermines his con-clusions; and, if he does so in natural science, he rejects the totality of the whole. If these two things are thus confuted, then neither is the universe a to-tality, nor does any end or conclusion greet us anywhere on our journeys. Do you now see the nature of excess, of going beyond reason, and of ignorance of oneself, that is, of not having turned oneself around and used discursive rea-

---

27. Referring to the plans Psellos and Xiphilinos had made to leave the court of Kon-stantinos IX Monomachos by becoming monks (wood), when they were still at the court (silver and gold).

28. I.e., the ones that remained after monastic tonsure.

29. Cf. Proklos, *On Plato's Timaeus,* vol. 1, 227–228.

30. I.e., Maximos the Confessor, *Various Chapters on Theology and Economics* 5.93–94 (*PG* 90.1388–9).

31. As did, for example, Neoplatonists such as Iamblichos and Proklos.

son, but of gulping down mounds of suppositions uncritically and without subtle technical discrimination?

If now you trust me at all, to address you in your own manner up to this point,[32] then do not think too highly of your life upon the mountain, nor give yourself airs about the fact that you do not delight in discourse; but if there is a plain anywhere, or a deep valley, or a sundered gorge, or a hidden corner of the earth, secret and mysterious, go and hide yourself down there, and take a close look into all books, both our own and the profane ones. And, by first training yourself in reasoning, you can then ascend to the knowledge that makes no use of logic. For every virtue, when it is accompanied by arrogance and false notions, my dear brother, becomes an extreme evil and is the off-spring of a state of wilful ignorance, which *my* philosopher [Plato], as you think, doubly condemns.

4. But since that word [that you used] stings me again, lend me your ear for a moment and listen to what a Platonic philosopher is telling you. My dear brother, I have been made worthy of the divine name of Christ by the previous generations of Fathers and was the student of the crucified one (assuming no one reproaches me if that the word is too daring);[33] I was instructed by the holy Apostles and fashioned into a most suitable vessel, I dare say, of the great and mysterious doctrine concerning the divine. As for the Platos and Chrysip-poses whom you mention, I have loved them—how could I not?—but only for their beauty and surface smoothness.[34] Of their doctrines, some I imme-diately passed over, while those others that complement our suppositions I readily took on and mixed with our holy doctrines, just as once Gregorios [of Nazianzos] and Basileios [of Kaisareia], the great luminaries of the Church, did. As for syllogisms, I have never despised their form [*eidos*]—I would in fact prefer to despise them, however, if it allowed me to see the Lord "face to face [*eidos*], but not through riddles"![35] For reasoning, my brother, is neither

32. Cf. Plato, *Gorgias* 467b.

33. I.e., the word "student."

34. I have accepted the emendation proposed by Maltese (1987) 430; cf. Criscuolo's note at (1990) 83.

35. Cf. Numbers 12:8; and 1 Corinthians 13:12, where Paul compares the knowledge of God available to us in this world, including the teachings contained in his epistles, to riddles. For the contrast between true knowledge and riddles (the latter including the writings of the Fathers), see Pseudo-Dionysios, *Letter* 9.1. Christian writers used the word "riddle" in reference to scriptural passages. It would be interesting to know exactly what "riddles" Psellos intends to reject.

a dogma foreign to the Church nor a paradoxical position of the philosophers, but rather it is only an instrument of the truth for the discovery of any sought-after thing. But if someone should *not* want to accept the Orthodox doctrine in a spirit of more rational inquiry, *nor* feast on solid nourishment, but if he preferred rather to only drink milk like a Corinthian,[36] for that reason should we too, who toil after exact reasoning, be indicted and accused?[37]

Since you use mountains and plains to distinguish between virtue and vice—I do not, but my starting point was the common faculty of human choice, and I now sail upon a different sea[38]—mountains and cities neither remove contrary attitudes nor invite them. See here. I, a city-dweller, concede the victory in virtue to you and throw reason into the ring, too, because I have chosen it, and it alone, for myself, and I blame my soul for being untested in virtue. I have borne witness in your favor regarding all the chief virtues, and have even added a certain rhetorical grace, as much of it as the law of friendship does not reject. But you, the mountain-dweller, have not behaved in this way at all, but immediately grew arrogant against us, and modesty, which you ought to have praised, you made into a reproach against us. Because we assigned a certain portion of reason also to ourselves, you regarded this as an insult to *you*,[39] and, darkly intimating to us that you stand on higher ground in all things, you thundered your boasts in your letter. And this man [Xiphilinos] who has attacked syllogisms, then resorts to proof by witness, now citing Stephanos,[40] now Gregorios, as though sufficient proof can be found in them alone.

5. Next you pounced on geographical ideas as well. But you are ignorant of some details: for instance, the south, but not Asia, lies opposite to the north, and also whether we place the Europeans in the north or the Libyans. But if I am to be slandered by you with respect to the knowledge of geography, then let the zones of the earth be divided in whatever way you see fit. Except I did not write my earlier letter with the intention of discussing geography or of dividing the entire earth into parts, but to bear additional witness to your inflexi-

---

36. Cf. 1 Corinthians 3:2.

37. Γραφαῖς (Scriptures) should be γραφαῖς (indictments).

38. I.e., toward secular learning rather than monastic retreat.

39. I have accepted here the emendation proposed by Maltese (1987) 431; but see the response of Criscuolo (1990) 83.

40. Possibly the "first martyr," in Acts of the Apostles 6–7, an exemplar of the martyr-as-witness. Or else Stephanos of Alexandria or of Athens, a philosopher of the late sixth and early seventh century, though it is not clear why Psellos would cite him here.

bility toward anything whatever that can soften a man. I endowed you with this from an abundant store[41] and as an inheritance from your fathers, and traced its pedigree from your fatherland.[42] On both counts I ascribed a more yielding nature to myself,[43] perhaps not speaking the truth, dear friend, but I wanted to form the image of the monk and fulfill the requirements of friendship. But that different parts of the world produce different types of character, this you should learn from the secret philosophy.[44] If they vary partially and in some small measure, then this will not contradict the general discussion of characters. For matter everywhere produces minor variations, by resisting the heavenly revolutions and through the mixing of the atmosphere.[45] And if you were not ignorant of the Chaldaean Oracles, which you attack with gibes even though you do not know what they are, from them you would know which one is the unmixed and unadulterated manifestation, and which the one that holds true for the most part.

But you think that these things are superfluous for the road that lies ahead of you![46] Nevertheless, if someone both travels upon that same path and yet knows these things, is he not much better than the one who has happened upon only one of these two? I say this not with reference to myself, but only in case some other may seem to be in that position. Sinai—so that I may philosophize to you about this as well—did not, like some physical mountain, lead Moses up and God down, but rather, it is a symbol for the rise of the soul up from matter. Our kind is not seized in rapture when we dwell on mountaintops and woodland vales, but when, by moderating the passions and purifying ourselves—for this is the second and more intellectual life—we advance the goals of contemplation. Or rather, we move even beyond Mind and are elevated to the highest sphere, I mean the one of illumination. This is both a mountain and a darkness and a silence that follows straightaway after a great motion, and a cessation of all intellection. Once there, we *see*, we do not think, or rather we do not think that we think. For discursive thought is an inferior form of knowledge and the perception of a partial being. For he who knows

41. Cf. Plato, *Theaetetus* 154d–e.

42. Psellos is possibly alluding to qualities of people from Trebizond, a provincial corner of the empire.

43. This clause is obscure.

44. It is not clear what secret philosophy Psellos means, unless this is an ironic reference to Xiphilinos' spiritual contemplation.

45. Cf. Iamblichos, *On the Mysteries* 1.8, 3.10.

46. I.e., the monastic life.

that he knows is divided between two parts of knowledge,[47] but division is a certain turning away from the best[48] and a descent.

6. Having learned these things from the Chaldaeans, I subordinated them to the doctrines of *our* wise men. I have written many such books, the off-spring of my soul, and this kind of knowledge reaches many people, through both writing and speech. Nor do I despair of ever seeing God, even in this "vale of tears"[49] in the city. For the mountain about which I stopped speaking earlier rises *everywhere* above all the parts of the earth.[50] Should I ever con-template going up to *your* mountain, this will be done with great eagerness, so that I might find some rest in my toils. For what lazy ease is lacking to those who inhabit that divine mountain? Once one has lived there and endured its hardships, would he then not be more likely to give up the desire to return? Therefore, dear friend, that is how I arbitrate between mountains[51] and cities, following my God and Lord for whose sake I have taken up his yoke[52] and put on this very hair shirt. He was often in the marketplace and rarely drew near to mountains. And those around the famous Gregorios, as you yourself know, went to the angelic life right from the midst of crowded squares. For if "the kingdom of heaven is within us,"[53] then what inner mountain remains?[54] For this kingdom is the ultimate sphere above all mountains and every ascent.[55] You should not wonder what I have suffered to speak to you in this way and such length. For that which moved me to speak also furnished me with an abundance of motives and reasons to speak.

7. Plato *is* mine, brother, and so is Chrysippos! But Christ, with whom I have been crucified,[56] whose is he? On his account did I not symbolically cut off the superfluity of my hair? On his account did I not exchange one way of life for another? If I completely belong to Christ, surely I will neither repudiate

47. I.e., the knowing part of him and the part that is known.
48. The "best" is absolute unity.
49. Psalm 83:7.
50. I.e., intellectual ascent can be practiced anywhere.
51. I.e., the spiritual "mountains" of intellectual ascent.
52. Cf. Matthew 11:29.
53. Cf. Luke 17:21.
54. Presumably after the inner ascent to the kingdom of heaven.
55. By using the word "sphere" to describe both the Christian Kingdom of Heaven and the highest level of Neoplatonic reality (in his discussion of Sinai), Psellos is imply-ing that they are the same.
56. Cf. Galatians 2:19.

wiser literature[57] nor cast off the knowledge of beings, both those that are intelligible and those that are sensible. Yet through a prayer I will petition God for as much as my abilities merit, and I will be seized and taken up,[58] should this be granted to me. But when, because of the endless motion of nature I have descended from those heights, I will walk through the meadows of rational discourse, now plucking the saying of an elder father as though it were a beautiful flower, and now gathering some other teaching of ours, thereby culling the best for my soul. Leaving this place in turn, I will then engage in syllogisms, concern myself with natural reasoning, seek the causes of events, inquire into Mind and that which lies beyond it, and I may even make some minor investigation concerning form. You think that we carry on in the same way as before, and that all those things are but shadows of the truth. However, I do not now philosophize about forms in that manner, for I have discovered from that source a doorway to,[59] and an ascent leading toward, higher things.

Thus I entirely cleanse my mind of matter, leading it up to wherever I can—for who can philosophize about everything?[60] I also smooth off the unevenness of speech with elegance and euphony, with compounds and harmonies and with the so-called periods or periodical forms. I have persuaded myself that these things pose no obstacle to virtue, and when I come to a standstill at the uttermost depth of this descent,[61] I quickly depart from there to again attain a higher state of consciousness. But do not think, dear brother—for you *are* dear, even if you have separated us from Christ and ranked us with Plato—that these words have been written by me in a spirit of hatred toward you. No, by Jesus who is *both* mine *and* yours! But because I was suddenly wounded by the word you applied to Plato [i.e., *yours*], I did not know how to bear my grief. For this reason I immediately composed this letter, to defend myself against the insult and to prove, as far as I could, that I

57. Wiser than what? Note that in the main autobiographical section of his *Chronographia*, Psellos presents genuine philosophy, intellectual culture, and scientific and rhetorical knowledge as derived entirely from ancient authors (6.37–43). Accordingly, the wisest emperor in his *Historia Syntomos* is Marcus Aurelius (32), whereas Leon VI is presented as wise only to the extent that he knew the ancient authors (100).

58. An allusion to 2 Corinthians 12:2?

59. The image of the gateway (*thyra*) is significant because the Byzantines referred to ancient, i.e., non-Christian, learning as "lying outside the threshold of the gate": *thyrathen*.

60. Cf. Psellos, *Chronographia* 6.40.

61. "Descent" because rhetoric is inferior to philosophy.

consider the whole of Greek wisdom, as much of it as antiquity cultivated—
and add to that the wisdom of the Chaldaeans and the Egyptians, and any
other secret *gnôsis*—to be completely inferior to that of the old men [i.e.,
monks]. And with that, I further express my regret to you—which is customary according to your[62] upbringing—and I seek forgiveness for the fact that I
neither bridled my reasoning nor checked my language, yet I was acting under
the assumption that to be ranked with Plato was equivalent to being separated
from our divine men.

---

62. The editor rightly suggests that this should read "our" instead.

5 Funeral Oration for the Most Blessed Patriarch Kyr Ioannes Xiphilinos

Ioannis Polemis

Introduction

The Life of Xiphilinos. Ioannes Xiphilinos was born in Trebizond around the year 1010.[1] His family seems to have been of humble origins. At an early age he moved to Constantinople to pursue higher studies. There he became a friend of Ioannes Mauropous and Konstantinos (later Michael) Psellos; the latter secured his appointment in the imperial chancellery, as Psellos tells us in the oration. Xiphilinos was at first active as a judge in Constantinople, but in ca. 1045–1047 the emperor Konstantinos IX Monomachos founded or officially recognized the *Didaskaleion ton nomon* ("School of Law") and appointed Xiphilinos its head, with the position of *nomophylax* ("Guardian of the Laws"). However, the fall from power of Konstantinos Leichoudes, Monomachos' prime minister and the patron of the circle of Psellos, along with the controversies stirred up by the accusations of a certain Ophrydas (possibly a derogatory nickname), a rival judge, forced Xiphilinos to abandon his position and to join a monastery on Mt. Olympos of Bithynia, where he was tonsured in ca. 1050–1053. We know virtually nothing about his life there, other than that he seems to have been happy and was briefly joined by Psellos in 1055 (who, however, quickly returned to the capital and the court of Theodora, 1055–1056).

---

1. For Xiphilinos in general, see Bonis (1937).

Psellos claims that it was he who persuaded the emperor Konstantinos X Doukas (1059–1067) to appoint Xiphilinos patriarch after the death of Leichoudes, in early 1064. However, Xiphilinos' relations with Psellos became strained due to his opposition to the Platonic and paganizing intellectual tendencies of his friend. Xiphilinos seems to have taken a rather conservative and intransigent position toward those wishing to free themselves, even if moderately, from the yoke of the official positions of the Church. A testimony to this is the famous letter sent to him by Psellos (translated in chapter 4), in which he seeks to defend himself against the accusations of his friend. Xiphilinos died in 1075. He was the author of some minor legal scholia and hagiographical works. Psellos, as a friend of the late patriarch, composed this funeral oration, as he had done for his predecessors, Michael Keroullarios and Konstantinos Leichoudes. It is among the last of Psellos' datable works.[2] For more on Psellos and Xiphilinos, see the general introduction.

The Funeral Oration for Xiphilinos.   The structure of the funeral oration is linear. In the first part of his speech, Psellos describes Xiphilinos' career: he started as a young official in the imperial secretariat and was promoted to the position of *nomophylax*. In the middle part of the speech, Psellos describes Xiphilinos' loss of the emperor's favor and his retreat to a monastery on Mt. Olympos. In the last part of the speech, he describes Xiphilinos' elevation to the patriarchal throne. Accordingly, the text is structured around the two ascents of Xiphilinos in a symmetrical way. His bureaucratic ascent is contrasted to his ascent to the most elevated spiritual dignity of the Orthodox Church, and these are bridged by the "hiatus" of his monastic retreat. It is noteworthy that we encounter again the Platonic motif of descent-ascent that we came across in Psellos' *Funeral Oration for Keroullarios*. Xiphilinos is reluctant to accept the patriarchal dignity, stressing his view that for a monk to become patriarch is in fact a descent (19). In the case of both ascents, Psellos plays a crucial role: in the first part of the speech, it is he who manages to appoint Xiphilinos as an imperial servant, while in the second part, it is he again who persuades the emperor Konstantinos X to appoint Xiphilinos as patriarch. Xiphilinos' character displays the same traits in both parts of the oration: in the first part he courageously rejects the accusations of the emperor Konstantinos IX that he is conspiring against him, while in the second part he stubbornly resists the efforts of the emperor to accomplish his wishes through him.

2. Kaldellis (2011).

The oration seems to have been delivered on the occasion of a memorial service for Xiphilinos some time after his death. According to Sideras, the speech was too long to have been prepared in time for the actual funeral service of Xiphilinos in 1075.[3] Anastasi argued that the oration is a patchwork of two independent texts, the first being a praise of Xiphilinos and the other an indictment of him![4] No further comment would be required if this strange theory had not been partially adopted by Ljubarskij in his book on Psellos.[5] Suffice it to say, there is no such problem. From section 22 onward, Psellos gives a description of the various intellectual subjects that Xiphilinos dealt with during his life. It is a pedantic enumeration of the basic studies of a Byzantine scholar, similar to the one that Psellos inserts into the *Encomium for His Mother*, describing his own scientific interests.[6] In some passages, Psellos attacks Aristotle directly for pagan theories that cannot be accepted by Christians, but this has nothing to do with an alleged attack on Xiphilinos (one of the bases for the mistaken reading of Anastasi).

The *Funeral Oration for Xiphilinos* was first published by Konstantinos Sathas in 1874 on the basis of MS Parisinus gr. 1182.[7] It is preserved incomplete in that manuscript. The end of the oration is found in MS Barberinianus gr. 240 ("B"), a highly damaged copy of the speech, from which it was published by Sideras in 2002.[8] The present translation is based on the new edition of the speech I have prepared for the series Bibliotheca Teubneriana (*Orationes Funebres I*, ed. Polemis, pp. 115–169). Although my edition is based on the same manuscripts as the previous ones, its text is not identical to that of Sathas' edition. No translations of this funeral oration have been published before. The bold numbers in the translation correspond to section numbers in my edition; the bold numbers in square brackets, such as "[115P]," correspond to the page numbers.

3. Sideras (1994) 146.
4. Anastasi (1966).
5. Ljubarskij (2004) 392–393.
6. Psellos, *Encomium for His Mother* 27–30.
7. Sathas (1874) 421–462.
8. Sideras (2002).

Funeral Oration for the Most Blessed Patriarch
Kyr Ioannes Xiphilinos

1. [115P] It is necessary, for those who wish to praise men who flourished in virtue and who surpassed nature, to offer an encomium that is truly transcendent and more precious than mere words, so that matters most valuable and divine are not degraded by the impression that they are being eulogized by men of inadequate power. Progress toward beauty is unrestricted and has no limit at all, for God, from whom it proceeds, is its sole limit and he cannot be reached by anything[9]—but the measure of a speech is the ingenuity of the orator. Therefore, it is impossible even for the most perfect rhetorical skill and power to put itself on a par with the perfection of the best men. But if for this reason we refrain from honoring with our words those things that surpass us, none of the things that are beyond praise will be praised at all, and their sheer magnitude will cause them to be deprived of all praise. Thus we will praise neither the sun nor the rotation of the universe, to say nothing of supernatural and pure disembodied Powers. How can anyone decide to praise things that he cannot fully comprehend? Taking the argument a step further, we will deprive even the celebrated wisdom of God of the smallest possible praise. Thus, we must not avoid thinking about and praising matters divine, and we must find a method by which to contemplate and praise them. It is in this way that the sciences and the arts have become admirable, for the former investigate things that are loftier than our mind, while the latter find proper concepts for those things that surpass conceptualization.

Therefore, our soul should not be discouraged from attempting either to praise [116P] or to investigate higher matters. The soul is a link between the two extremes on either side of it, I mean Intelligible Being and mere sen-

---

9. Cf. Pseudo-Dionysios, *On Divine Names* 4.10 (p. 154).

sation,[10] and so it is in a position to know sensible things, being superior to them and functioning as their archetype, while, on the other hand, it obtains a picture of Intelligible Essence through certain postulates of nature: imitating it as far as possible, the soul explores it, receiving its impression. I hope that the man whom we are now about to praise will forgive our speech if it falls short of his dignity and virtues. But my speech does not approach him with the intention of contending with him. Its purpose is not to put itself on a par with him or even to surpass him with its praises. If it is permitted for me to say so, the intention of my speech is to offer something to the whole world by praising the life of this man. The universe is imperfect, if it is not a composite of every nature, both higher and lower ones; thus, the whole structure and order of the beautiful will suffer the greatest loss if someone fails to offer to it a speech composed of all elements. Lack of sensation is lack of knowledge of things sensible, and if God had not created human nature to have intellect, things intelligible could not have been grasped. How then does our life not suffer the greatest loss, if something beautiful is deprived of all praise? If someone takes away the beautiful prototype from those who are trying to imitate the true good by imitating the highest good, he will certainly cool their ardor for noble things.

2. My speech has adequately proved so far that it is necessary for us to praise not only those things that are within our reach, but also those that cannot be grasped by our mind. I personally have two reasons for praising the great bishop: my ardor for the beautiful and the discharge of a just and necessary debt to him. Is there anyone else more suitable as a model of the perfect life? And is there anyone else to whom I am more indebted to offer a speech as a reward on those terms? But I do not know [117P] how to approach my subject, and from which point to start my speech. Shall I start as if fulfilling my duty to present a speech for him, or by necessarily elevating him as an example for all those who want to look upon him and sculpt their lives according to his model? If I deal with each of them in good time, one by one, my speech will be split, and their combination will be a failure;[11] generally speaking, they will be incompatible with each other. On the other hand, it is very difficult to opt for both of them, weaving them together as my speech goes on, but I will try to do exactly that as adequately as possible.

10. Cf. Psellos, *Philosophica Minora I* 47.68–70 (p. 171).
11. Cf. Psellos, *Oratoria Minora* 37.189–190 (p. 143).

In case the subject itself causes my speech to lose its balance, then we will ask for well-disposed listeners, that they not demand a continuous success by all means, but be content with whatever the nature of speech can accommodate. I know that I will not handle every matter according to the wishes of this divine man, as I abide by the laws of rhetoric, which he despised, being a superb philosopher; I am trying to bring glory to him in every respect, and to find every excuse to gather praise for him. But let us praise him not only for his own virtues, but also for the virtues of his kinsmen and ancestors, so that we might not create the impression that we hold the art of rhetoric in contempt, as if we do not have what to say. If we manage to praise him through those things he rightly despised, we will prove that he did not look down on them because he was deprived of them but because he did not regard them as important; as a courageous and prudent man he flew above them because they were humble and low-lying. He had no desire to be adorned by any colors but by the nobility of his body, and he did not even boast of that either, but took pride in the virtues of his soul instead.

3. [118P] The line of our ancestors is twofold, since we are made of two natures, being a mixture of two opposite components, a nobler one and a worse one.[12] Therefore, let that nobler part of him wait for a while—in any case, the greatest part of my speech will be devoted to it. Let us spend some time instead with that lower part of him for a while. Other people boast of their origin from the Orient and of having Egypt or Babylon as their country, or some other celebrated city and nation, even if they are deficient in other respects. How then can it not be considered significant by him, or rather by my audience, that his country is the first to greet the rays of the sun? That city enjoys a climate which is not to be found in any other renowned city. It is built on the boundary between the whole land and the whole sea; it is established precisely at the boundary of the whole land and the sea, at the end of the one and the starting point of the other, or vice versa: the beginning of the first is the end of the other. Being a colony of that blessed empire of Athens, it surpasses its own metropolis.[13] Athens has thin soil and does not produce much wheat,[14]

---

12. I.e., body and soul.

13. In reality, Trebizond was a colony of Miletos (more accurately of Sinope). But Miletos was founded by Neileos, son of Kodros, the mythic king of Athens. Thus Psellos could argue that it was a colony of Athens.

14. Cf. Strabo, *Geographika* 8.1.2.14.

but this country produces much wheat and is especially conducive to the vine. Athens has vanished, having withered with time,[15] but his country, as if recently planted, is flourishing full of beauty, adorned with all the elements and blooming with youthful beauty. Its name indicates its happiness: it is not only the hearth (*trapeza*) of cities,[16] it is also a true banqueting hall and a place of all sorts of entertainment. Is there anyone who has not heard the name of Trebizond?[17] Is there anyone who, departing from this city, will not realize that everything is inferior to it? Who, coming from all other countries and seas abroad, whether by land or sea, will not award to that city the prize of victory over all other places on earth? Who will not exceedingly admire the way it appropriates all seas and all lands, being full of ambition to surpass the virtues of its first aspect by the virtues of the other? Its defeat is its own victory, and its victory is its own defeat as well. Its successes are due to its nature, [**119P**] but its failures are due to the power of the word.[18] Enjoying so many good qualities such as no other city possesses, Trebizond bows to this citizen of hers. Although it is more highly esteemed than any other nation, in the case of that man it is proved superior to any other country and city, but at the same time inferior as far as its other virtues are concerned. Therefore, it boasts more of its failures than of its successes over other cities.

4. As I have said, his native land surpasses all others and wins the pageant-prize by its magnitude and beauty. As for his parents, they had virtue as an inheritance;[19] their happiness consisted in being noted for their good deeds. They vied over who would approach the Good first. The rest of his family too was prosperous from of old. But let me pass over his father, who was admired in all respects but died prematurely. His mother lived longer than her husband, and she was recognized by all people as vigorous even in old age, because of her ardent desire for the Good. Her life was devoted to God and she was numbered among those celebrated for their virtues. She had such an overabundance of higher qualities and was so tightly united with God that she was

---

15. The praise of cities since late antiquity often called for a comparison to Athens, so that Athens was both the ultimate standard for comparison and usually found to be inferior.

16. A typical Byzantine paretymology.

17. Cf. Demosthenes, *On the False Embassy* 312.2.

18. I.e., the virtues of Trebizond, which were more physical, were overcome by Xiphilinos' spiritual qualities.

19. On the parents of Xiphilinos, see Bonis (1937) 12–13.

blessed with the gift of prophecy. She predicted that her child would in the future attain perfection in all respects. She foretold it to many people, not as if predicting the future or prophesying what was to come, but clearly seeing in advance what would happen.

My speech, however, in trying to fulfill its purpose, has no intention of dealing with them much longer. It discusses them only so as to put before the man praised by me some unrivalled examples of virtue, taken not from outside or far from his family, but kin to him from within it. My speech will later examine him on the basis of those examples, comparing what came next to what happened before, in order to show to everyone that, although this man had to compete with two invincible families as if in a mighty contest, [**120P**] he managed to surpass his parents to the same extent that they had surpassed all others who excelled in virtue. I ask only this of anyone who comes across my speech, not to think that any exaggerations that might occur in it give an accurate picture of this man. As I said, exaggeration is here limited by the measure of my speech, but his virtue resembles an immense and boundless sea: it cannot be confined by either words or thoughts. If this is understood and settled, my speech is encouraged to accomplish its task and is going to deal passionately with the admirable story of that man.

5. Two things are the subjects of our praise, words and deeds. He [Xiphilinos] started his life[20] advantaged in both respects. However, he clearly showed forth the first one, I mean, his education in matters of speech, while he made only a shadowy outline of deeds. In any case, both approached him, intertwined with each other. He wanted to extol his own country as far as was possible within his power, and to repay it for his birth with his noble deeds and progress; however, divine providence transported him to a place where he would shine more fully, enlightening the entire world. So providence transferred him to Byzantion;[21] his education was still imperfect and his virtue was yet unknown to many, although he already vied with superior men, being evenly matched with the best of them. But how am I to describe that man? How am I to lay the foundations of his virtue,[22] describe his character, make

20. Xiphilinos was born ca. 1010–1013, or earlier, according to Bonis (1937) 10–12; Rosenqvist (1966) 28.

21. According to Bonis (1937) 23, Xiphilinos moved to Constantinople in the reign of Romanos III Argyros (1028–1034). The same move was made by another native of Trebizond, Athanasios of Athos, whose life presents many similarities to that of Xiphilinos (see *Life of Athanasios of Athos* A10, p. 7).

22. Cf. Xenophon, *Memorabilia* 1.5.4.

known his ardent desire for learning, or declare with my speech any other of the virtues that he had by nature? I am going to speak about them all, neither taking my information from his acquaintances, nor being myself acquainted with the man in a merely passing way. Rather, I am an eyewitness of all these things, and I have an accurate knowledge of each. I praised them at first, then later [121P] I admired them exceedingly, and was overwhelmingly overcome by his superlative qualities. If I take some credit too in my speech, either in praising this man or narrating his acts, let no one take offence at it. I will not combine my own story with his on purpose, but rather because I am constrained by the story itself. And if after death he becomes the cause of my own praise, let no one envy me, since, even when he was alive, he made a great contribution to my progress toward virtue.[23] Let me say something more audacious: we had grown together. Each of us vied with the other and, through whatever good qualities he had, each of us measured himself by the measure of the other. We were neither opponents nor, worse still, adversaries: being of equal character and evenly matched, we vied with each other in our progress toward higher ideals.

We separated from each other at the beginning, dividing between ourselves the realms of discourse and the arts: I devoted myself to the art of rhetoric, philosophy, and the mathematical sciences, not learning them from someone else, as the torch of learning had gone out. I kindled it once more, spreading its flame to those who wished to learn those things.[24] For his part, he [Xiphilinos] took for himself the science of law, studying it before me. At a later stage, we exchanged scientific realms: he studied the art of rhetoric beside the law and turned his attention to philosophy as well; he also occupied himself with the mathematical sciences, taking what was nobler after having acquired what was inferior. Conversely, I moved to something inferior after obtaining what was nobler. In this way, we came together gradually, completing our education, although we set out from different starting points; thus we came from imperfection to perfection. We were not of the same age, but he was not much older than me.[25] When we came to know each other and became friends, I had only begun to grow facial hair, while he already had a full beard.

---

23. Cf. Plato, *Phaedo* 61d.

24. Cf. Psellos, *Chronographia* 6.36.1–43, where the author gives a brief account of his early studies and makes the same claim about the extinction of higher learning.

25. Psellos was born in 1018: Volk (1990) 1–2; Ljubarskij (2004) 41; so we may confidently say that Xiphilinos was born no earlier than 1010.

6. Having mentioned the laws, his own subject and one of which he was proud, and his legal education, I want [**122P**] to devote part of my speech to this subject for the sake of two reasons: I want to explain what kind of a scholar he was when it came to this discipline and to highlight its qualities, which are not approached by students in that way.[26] I also wish to express my admiration for his ability in that, before studying philosophy in depth, he approached the laws in a philosophical way. He had not yet learned the highest science of dialectics, but he managed to discover it by studying the laws; he even discovered First Philosophy. As I maintain, to all arts and logical sciences one must apply the philosophic methods of division and reduction, of definition and demonstration. What is beyond them is metaphysical and supernatural, and we must abandon it. This man, after mounting the chariot of law, realized the full scope of the forensic science: he separated what was old from what was new and understood that the former part of that science was immense and without boundaries, while the latter was confined, having proper measures; the first defies rational apprehension, but the second is in need of it. Each is divided into parts, one higher, another inferior: the first one is qualified by fullness and indefiniteness, the second by half-fullness and limitation. Therefore, he put each one right with the help of the other: he enclosed what was full by imposing a limit, and he applied fullness to what was limited.[27] Afterwards he drew each of them together to a common peak, most of them that were lesser than most,[28] and drew many lines from there as if it were a single point or the center of a circle. Thus he bound those many things together into one knot, but immediately he also unbound them, permitting them to return to the previous multitude. Whenever it was necessary to make one those that were many, he tied them together in a prudent manner; and whenever there was need of making the one many once again, he let them return to their previous multitude. Thus he became a law to the laws, functioning as an example of a proper education.

A person should not admire me, who turned my attention from the study of philosophy to the study of the laws, learning that science accurately, as I proceeded from what was higher to what was inferior, and had already ac-

26. This is a criticism of the students of law in Psellos' time who approached law in a partial and inadequate manner, paying no attention to the principles of that science. For the study of law in eleventh-century Byzantium, see Weiss (1973) 28–37; Wolska-Conus (1976) and (1979).

27. I use readings πλῆρες . . . πλήρει of B, not included in the critical apparatus.

28. The meaning of this passage is obscure.

quired there the method of scientific investigation. I admire him [Xiphilinos] instead, who approached what was inferior first, though he had not yet been raised above the clouds; [123P] however, he managed to speak as if from the celestial arch.[29] Most students of the law nowadays do not make the proper distinction among the various laws, but simply pull them to pieces[30]—I am not referring to the perfect jurists, of course. But now they do not divide them in the way that they should be divided, but shred them. One person gives the impression of surpassing another simply by the great number of the legal chapters he knows. It is as if the value of the philosopher lies in accumulating various syllogisms, without any knowledge of their origin or how they may be combined, and not in the knowledge of their figures or in the ability to put each one of them under its proper heading. Far from doing this, he [Xiphilinos] applied the rules of philosophy beforehand to the study of the law even though he learned those rules afterward; therefore, what he learned after abandoning the study of the law, when he became a philosopher, was in fact a recollection of what he had already learned beforehand.[31] He despised Plato and his doctrines, but he admired and praised him for eulogizing the method of division.[32]

7. That was how he studied law. My speech has omitted most of the details, but later on, coming to the other sciences, it will deal with the art of law once more. But let those things wait for a while. As it is our intention to elevate that man from the foot of the mountain to its top, let us ascend slowly. He had completed this course of education, and he was shining, surrounded by a multiform fire. However, he had not yet been put on the lampstand:[33] I do not mean the higher and more important one, on which he was put later on, shining like a torch;[34] I am referring to the lesser office, whose job is to regulate the affairs of the state. It too is admirable, especially when its holder exercises it in a just manner in exact accordance with the law. My speech, having reached the point when he [Xiphilinos] took office, seeks another office, by which both he and no less I [124P] were known and much admired. It came about as follows.

The political situation needed a change for the better [in 1042]. Let us begin from the highest office, that of our emperor, and everything will come

29. Cf. Plato, *Phaedrus* 274b.
30. Cf. Aristotle, *Prior Analytics* 26a–b.
31. Cf. Plato, *Phaedo* 72e–73b.
32. For the method of division, see Plato's *Sophist.* For Xiphilinos and Plato, see Psellos' long *Letter to Xiphilinos*, in this volume.
33. Cf. Matthew 5:15.
34. I.e., the patriarchal throne.

to its proper end. And a change took place indeed: the man who was predestined for the imperial throne by God many years before, but had been hidden in obscurity in the meantime, at last was promptly placed upon it. He became emperor at the right time and was like a light placed upon the imperial disk in order to shine its rays upon the entire world. All who know understand that I am referring to Konstantinos from the family of Monomachos.[35] No emperor dared to compete with him: his virtue was unsurpassable, no enemy could defeat him. As soon as he became emperor, he gathered all sorts of virtuous people around him: he did not pursue only one particular virtue, neglecting the others; nor did he show zeal for a group of virtues, while bidding farewell to the set of all others. He did not praise only a powerful body, without admiring a brave heart; he did not strive after the passionate and vigorous spirit, while despising the sweet and gentle temper.

And what seemed better to him than rational discourse? What did he praise or admire more? But reason is multiform: one type flows from the tongue, while another resides in our soul. Therefore, the emperor was divided: making a distinction between these two sorts of *logoi* [i.e., rhetoric (speech) and philosophy (thought)], he occupied himself with both. It is not possible to say which one he loved more: the one with which he happened to be occupied at a certain time seemed to him to be more important. But if he managed to find a certain fountain of it gushing out both from below and above, making a perfect and harmonious mixture of opposites, he either took pains to drink both, each one in turn, or he drank only one, the one that was offered to him, absorbing it all with his soul. But I do not know how to use speech to describe all this. I want to compose this part of my speech as a history, safeguarding its reliability. However, realizing that I myself am [125P] involved in the whole affair too, I am afraid lest most people consider me self-absorbed and so unsuccessful, believing that I am doing this with the perverse intention of glorifying myself with the praises of another person. In order to safeguard the coherence of my narrative and avoid the accusations of most people, I will mention my own affairs in a cursory manner, only to the extent that this is reasonable; but as far as his [Xiphilinos] virtues are concerned, I will, by contrast, give a detailed account of them.

8. This emperor decided not to promote public officials and courtiers in accordance with their family lineage, nor to fill the senate only with members of the aristocratic families; the same applied to the bureaucracy and to all concerned with laws and decrees. He wanted to appoint men of lower status to

35. I.e., Konstantinos IX Monomachos (1042–1055).

those offices as well, provided they had given proof of their ability to hold such offices, being more competent than the aristocrats.[36] He thought that it was absurd not to appoint to military office men whose fathers had been generals, army officers, or common soldiers, but only men of proven personal ability in the military life, but on the other hand to appoint as senators only men of noble lineage, as if this had been a hard and fast rule that permitted only those who had glorious ancestors to approach the imperial palace, even if they were mentally disturbed and arrogant, their only recommendation being their boasting of their glorious family. Therefore, the emperor decided to appoint men to those offices not on the basis of an irrational habit but after a proper consideration of their merits. I was appointed to the court before the man I am praising, after undergoing an examination that was not at all easy. I was tested many times, and my knowledge of every subject was scrutinized. I was examined in all sorts of disputes and in improvised composition. [126P] Thus, after this ordeal I made my way in;[37] it was difficult even to recollect myself after that. After a short time, he took these exams too.[38] I could not bear to have a prestigious job in the palace knowing that he, with whom I shared my industrious studies, was deprived of such an advantage.[39] That, then, is the part of the story relating to me, so let me stop here.

9. He was introduced to the imperial palace in a magnificent manner:[40] while still standing at the threshold, he was promoted to the tribunal and was awarded an exalted office and station. He was not head of the jury yet, sitting under the presiding judges, but he was more admired and esteemed than they. He had a most eloquent tongue, and the teaching of the law was gushing from it, so to speak. As if from a fountain, the words welled out of it, and his apprehension of a given subject was not based on the consultation of books, but memory kept everything inside his soul. As I said, having become acquainted with all the subdivisions of philosophy, he proceeded to the proper division into chapters of all knowledge. He was delivering various speeches and reading the relevant handbooks at the same time, if there was need to consult them. He did not acquire a loud voice through exercise, but was fortunate

36. See also Psellos, *Chronographia* 6.29.1–28, and *Orationes Panegyricae* 1.92–95 (p. 5).

37. Between 1038 and 1041; see Volk (1990) 11; Ljubarskij (2004) 44–46.

38. On the exams taken by those who were to be appointed as judges, see Weiss (1973) 31.

39. Psellos confirms this in *Chronographia* 6.192.14–17.

40. See Bonis (1937) 38–43; Ljubarskij (2004) 86. At first Xiphilinos was appointed *krites tou hippodromou kai tou velou* and *exaktor*.

to be granted such a voice in an almost supernatural way. When he spoke on behalf of the emperor, or on another subject assigned to him, his speech resembled thunder heard in the sky. He was standing in the middle, or rather he was surrounded by the crowd; he resembled a solid and fixed column, neither disturbed nor losing his head by what was said by those around him; rather, he kept his composure and showed the stability of his character.

As soon as he began speaking, using a prolific but honey-sweetened speech, he made a proper division of the chapters of his subject: he went up to its most important point, making it the starting point of his speech. At the beginning and middle of his oration he was thoughtful and pensive, but at the end of his discourse he became pleasant and beautiful. Through his harmonious, flowery style he made clear that his speech had come to its conclusion smoothly. [127P] As for the opposition—was there any possibility that we would not be envied and attacked? I dig up my own affairs once more! He was not in haste to answer his opponents, as if he wanted to reduce them to silence. He let them speak as much as they wished. After their arguments ran dry, he examined each one of those arguments thoroughly according to the canons of rhetoric, and thus he was able to point out their fallacy in a gracious manner. His opponents were stricken with amazement: they kept their mouths shut, but went on murmuring in an undertone. I alone was more than an adequate compensation for him, standing in the audience and loudly clapping my hands at his achievements. Of course I received no less in return from him, when I took part in rhetorical competitions and won them: he remunerated me in full with his applause and praise.

10. We emulated and measured ourselves against each other in this way, as far as our common endeavors and attainments were concerned. We were both united and likewise divided from each other. Here is what I mean: There were schools of the arts and sciences in our City in the past, as well as illustrious chairs not only for the art of poetry that is accessible to all, but for the art of rhetoric and the most admirable philosophy as well. On the other hand, most people neglected the science of law. But circumstances changed, the situation became gloomy, and the torches of education almost went out.[41] Public rhetorical performances had continued, and there was a president of these games as well as able performers of the declamations, but the name of

41. Psellos frequently deplores the decline of education during the period of his youth: *Chronographia* 6.43.1, and *Letter S* 7 (p. 233); see Kriaras (1972) 56–57. For the expression, see Gregorios of Nazianzos, *Or.* 19, in *PG* 35, 1045.

those rhetorical games did not agree with the facts: people were basically just whispering some speeches in obscure places. There were many dancers, but there was no leader of the chorus. The company danced without keeping order [128P] or rhythm; they were unable to perform either the strophe, or the antistrophe, or the epode while singing harmoniously. It was just a rapid, irrational motion. This was due to the fact that none of the orators who took part in those contests was superior to the others; so there was no one able to become the King of Speech, as happened in the old Ethiopian story,[42] as no one was exceptional and more powerful than the others in speech. All the wrestlers and boxers were equal to each other.

But as soon as *I* prevailed in the arts and sciences and *he* in the science of law, all serious students were divided between us: those whose only care was to adorn the state with their service chose him [Xiphilinos] as their leader, coming to him all together and appointing him their general, while those who were lovers of the nobler lessons separated themselves from the others and sided with me.[43] How did the emperor react? He was indignant at being forced to act, but in any case he *was* forced to act because of the torments suffered by the students. Not thinking of himself, he surrendered us,[44] as it were, although we were unwilling to obey either him who was trying to persuade us or those who were pressuring us.[45] But it is very difficult for anyone in the middle to

42. For this reference, see the *Funeral Oration for Keroullarios* 11.

43. On the reestablishment of the so-called University of Constantinople, which was divided into a School of Philosophy (with Psellos as its head as Consul of the Philosophers) and the *Didaskaleion ton nomon* (under Xiphilinos as Guardian of the Laws, or *nomophylax*), with a dating of ca. 1045–1047, see Weiss (1973) 65–76; Markopoulos (2008) 790–791; for the offices, see Volk (1990) 12; Bonis (1937) 53; Ljubarskij (2004) 86. Other scholars date the establishment of the *Didaskaleion* as late as 1047: Karpozilos (1982) 31 n. 61 and 40. The imperial decree establishing this institution, composed according to some scholars by Ioannes Mauropous, is preserved and deals with the organization of that school: Karpozilos (1982) 31–32.

44. I.e., the two friends were freed from serving the emperor in the palace.

45. Wolska-Conus (1976) 223–243 argues that Xiphilinos and Psellos shared a common private school, which was subsequently taken under the patronage of Konstantinos IX Monomachos, who transformed it into a public school, dividing it into two branches: the *Didaskaleion ton nomon*, under the directorship of Xiphilinos, and the School of Philosophy under Psellos. Lemerle (1977) 205–206 is reluctant to accept Wolska-Conus's conclusions, limiting himself to the affirmation that Monomachos entrusted Xiphilinos and Psellos with the reformation of education in law and philosophy in Constantinople; see also Weiss (1973) 65–76.

resist those who surround him from both sides, especially if they are stronger than him. Thus we had to abandon our studies and choose the active life. But we were separated from it once more,[46] coming to a union that was no union at all: we were both separated and united. We were the only educators in Byzantion, and we were separated with regard to the highest studies. I was advocating the two opposite disciplines [rhetoric and philosophy] to those who wanted, while he [Xiphilinos] was opposed to the one part of my lessons, but with regard to the rest he was closely attached to me as an equal adversary.[47] We were not totally opposed to each other, as most people believed: each of us was proclaimed teacher of one particular branch of science, but both of us were equally studying that branch supposedly belonging only to the other. Therefore, the streams of rhetoric, philosophy, and, no less, of law gushed out from both of us. Our offices were different, but our common job united us.

What happened next? I am wondering if [**129P**] I should impute the reversal that took place to the emperor or impute the imperial decision to us. Having appointed us to salaried posts as educators, he summoned us to himself once more,[48] after we had accomplished the joint task of helping those to whom we were previously surrendered. We became tutors for him as we had been for other people before: I was training him in the art of rhetoric, mixing in some small instruction in philosophy as well, while he [Xiphilinos] was initiating him into the science of law, as if initiating him into the Eleusinian mysteries.

11. But my speech has gone off its prescribed course. So I will add just one final detail, which will contribute to his being admired and will prove my dignity, though it will seem unbelievable to most people. Having learned that the philosopher-king Marcus attended a school and carried a tablet with him,[49] he [Konstantinos IX] envied this man for his wisdom and did something more

---

46. The train of Psellos' thought is the following: Psellos and Xiphilinos were devoted to the contemplative life. Then they were forced to abandon it, entering the service of the emperor. But the emperor decided to make them change their way of life once more, by appointing them as teachers.

47. The meaning of this passage is obscure.

48. Lemerle (1977) 206 interprets this as a reference to the return of Xiphilinos and Psellos to their previous posts in the palace. The emperor asked Psellos and Xiphilinos to offer him private instruction in rhetoric and law.

49. I.e., the emperor Marcus Aurelius Antoninus (161–180). A version of the anecdote can be found in *Souda*, s.v. "Markos Antoninos"; cf. also Psellos, *Chronographia* 3.2.5–9.

important than that philosopher-king: he made me sit on a chair and took notes while I was speaking, and was listening to my teaching with as much vigilance as possible. But what is the value of this episode, if we compare it with his manifold soul? When a plotter who wanted to kill him was caught, he reproached him a bit, but afterward, recovering his composure and being re-morseful for that, he embraced him with both hands and gave him many kisses, placing on his own eyes the hand that had been armed with a knife to assassinate him.[50] But my speech has lost its way, like a river; it resembles the river Nile evading its mouth by the city of Herakles,[51] meandering along its course and forming many bays. Let it now return to its original source. My de-sire would be not to mix my story with the story of this man, but it is [**130P**] impossible for me to isolate him. I give my audience leave to decide what the truth is.

12. The law of nature did not permit us to be led astray; we were forced to follow the road that leads to the Good.[52] In the beginning, we made some hints to each other about our plans. As time passed, we fully revealed our common plan to each other: our desire was neither to confine our philosophi-cal investigation to the search for certain proofs and to the accurate percep-tion of abstract notions, nor to embrace geometry while neglecting to meas-ure the ethereal realm or the dimension of Being beyond that as well, whether it is a bodily entity or an immaterial one. We wanted to turn our attention to the philosophy of our faith, too, which urges each of us to carry his cross and follow in Christ's footsteps.[53] No one can follow in the shadows of theory if he does not first humiliate the body of degradation.[54] In the beginning, we did not pay great attention to what we were hearing from one another, but after-ward, pondering over our thoughts, we fanned the small spark into a great fire. Finally, through the divine fire we both became like a torch shining to-ward that purpose. But our thought was still indefinite. Our love for God was burning but lacked a fixed point. The torch needed a more divine gust, so that its flame might be raised up high in the air and become unrestrained.

50. Cf. Psellos, *Chronographia* 6.145–147.
51. I.e., Herakleopolis. The god Harsaphes, identified with Herakles by the Greeks, was worshipped there. See Heliodoros, *Aithiopika* 1.1, a text on which Psellos had writ-ten an essay.
52. Psellos is referring here to their eventual escape to monasticism.
53. Cf. Matthew 16:24; Mark 8:34; Luke 9:23.
54. Cf. Philippians 3:21.

Something happened then that gave us wing, so our impetus was unrestrained. Someone attacked us in the back with the bitter shafts of spiteful envy.[55] My view is that such a thing might be more or less indifferent for a courtier at the beginning of his career, who is going to make progress in the palace, but for someone who is at the peak or at the end it is rather malicious and harmful. That was the case with us: the wound was deep, festering within. Is there really a need to disclose the identity of the man who attacked us or his reason for doing so? My speech is not an invective but an encomium.[56] Anyway, he attacked us while being himself invisible, since he could not shoot at us from the front. In any case, we still had the impression [**131P**] that our standing was untouched, since the emperor did not change his behavior toward us at all nor showed any sign of displeasure on his face. He expressed only his astonishment to those whom he trusted that we too had been compromised.

But as nothing on earth remains hidden, at last we were informed about the kind of attack that had been made against us. As soon as I heard it, although I had no appetite for laughing, I smiled a bit, despising both the attacker and the attack. However, although he [Xiphilinos] was a gentle man and knew how to restrain himself in daily affairs, at that particular time he did not keep his composure as usual. He reproached my lack of anger,[57] and, angry as he was, stormed off to the emperor and reproached his readiness to listen and even pay attention to our detractor instead of exposing his maliciousness immediately. He was so angry that he dared to say that he would have been less indignant had he been slandered at another time; but now the accusation itself was offering a great service to those who had been accused![58] At that time he said nothing more; he calmed down and fell back on the same grips as the wrestlers of old used. But after a short time, he reminded me of our previous

---

55. Psellos is referring to an old judge, Ophrydas: Weiss (1973) 84–86; Ljubarskij (2004) 86–87. According to Ljubarskij, the incident took place around 1050. Psellos composed a long and virulent defense of Xiphilinos: *Orationes Forenses* 3; see Lemerle (1977) 211–212. Ophrydas seems to have disapproved of the reforms of Monomachos and Xiphilinos in the study of law; for the issues, see also Angold (1997) 63–67. The fall of the *mesazon* Konstantinos Leichoudes (see the *Funeral Oration for Leichoudes*) created many difficulties for the circle of Psellos, Mauropous, and Xiphilinos: Karpozilos (1982) 36–38. Psellos had to write defenses against his own detractors, who were arguing that philosophers had no business running affairs of state: *Oratoria Minora* 6–12.

56. Cf. Hermogenes, *On Types of Style* 1.1 (p. 242).

57. Cf. Psellos, *Chronographia* 6.190.3–4.

58. The meaning of the passage is obscure.

thoughts and was eager to fulfill his holy purpose.[59] However, we kept post-poning the realization of our intentions. Then a second calamity struck him, and a third one, and a fourth as well. Not all arrows were shot from behind; some of them were shot at his chest, so to speak. They did not cause any harm, but the fact that he was targeted and that the arrows were shot one after the other annoyed him. When he was hit, he was reminded of his higher purpose, but when arrows ceased to be shot, he would forget it, alternating between his eagerness and then subsequent neglect. How did he remedy this situation? He decided to bind himself with a solemn, ineffable oath to God that he would carry out his plan, and he urged me to do the same, since my wish [132P] was to take part in all his enterprises, whether inferior or superior and divine.

13. Thus we were preparing for our departure. We made it look like an effort to prepare proper attendants for the emperor, but our hidden plan was to abandon this composite world in order to reach the most reverent sim-plicity.[60] After a short time God smoothed out his path, so that he could fulfill his promise. There was no way for him [Xiphilinos] to escape easily, because he respected the emperor who had honored him and because he was intimi-dated by the prospect of such a momentous change in his own way of life. What was his immediate cause for leaving? At the beginning he was thought to be gravely ill, even to the point that his soul would abandon the body, with which it was united. Being caught between his earlier desire and this later ill-ness, he decided to act immediately and started to prepare himself for be-coming a monk, offering himself as a total and not partial sacrifice to God. Then he asked the emperor to be merciful and permit him to take up the monastic habit. Is there now anyone who will not admire this emperor? He was struck by that man's words as if by an arrow, and did not know how to react. At the prospect of losing that man, he seemed like a man who had lost his hands or tongue, or had suffered something even worse.[61] So he behaved in an unusual way and was overcome with a very strange emotion.

As he [the emperor] could neither bring himself to his senses nor put the other man off from his plan, he used my tongue as a last resort, in order to persuade him to change his mind. Here I will accuse myself a bit, or rather I will take full responsibility for it, since I stood up to the emperor immediately

---

59. I.e., to become monks.
60. Cf. Psellos, *Theologica I* 10.31–32 (p. 38).
61. Cf. Psellos, *Chronographia* 6.195.7–9.

and did not help him carry out his plan. When he started advising me what to say to the man [Xiphilinos] and how to persuade him to restrain his ardent desire, [133P] I answered: "O emperor, find someone else to give him such advice. If you send me to him, I will encourage him to follow his course. Let me confess to you the desire of our souls: we are *both* planning to change the course of our lives for the better. We have already taken an ineffable oath to God to abandon this world and to go over to him." As soon as he heard this, he raised his voice, crying: "What you have schemed is treason; this is a sufficient proof of a conspiracy. You have given clear proof of your ingratitude, confessing that you hold the emperor in contempt." Hearing this, I thought it was tantamount to a dismissal from my post at the palace and to the striking of him [Xiphilinos] off the register and permission for him to act as he wished. But how admirable was the heart of the emperor! He was neither resentful nor prone to anger. His eyes filled with tears and he said: "Both God and nature deprived me of this man, who was like the right hand of my kingdom. Replace him at least partially, and try to function as the only hand that still works, as much as you can." In this way, he [Xiphilinos] sacrificed himself to God and was numbered among the best. I did not follow him, and did not keep the agreement with him; as a result, he became a monk first, while I adopted the monastic habit only later on.

14. As he was destined to be sacrificed to God not only once but many times, and to become a most holy sacrificial offering, that sacrifice caused the healing of both his soul and body. He was healed as soon as he renounced this world and, taking divine wings, he could not be restrained any longer; he could not bear to creep upon the earth anymore rather than fly. So he flew aloft on light wings,[62] leaving Byzantion[63] and migrating to Olympos,[64] the divine mountain: Olympos, the dwelling place of holy souls [134P] since ancient times, which at that time became the house of a most holy man who was above human nature; Olympos, the name of a place much desired by me in the past, which then became more desired than heaven itself;[65] Olympos, which

62. Cf. Plato, *Phaedrus* 246d.

63. Bonis (1937) 77 dates the departure of Xiphilinos to 1054. Sideras (1994) 145 proposes 1055, but this seems too late.

64. This is Mt. Olympos in Bithynia, the mountain backing Prousa. It was an important monastic center in the eighth to tenth centuries. We do not know in which of its numerous monasteries Xiphilinos was tonsured. Ioannes Mauropous departed from Constantinople at the same time: Ljubarskij (2004) 52–53.

65. Cf. Gregorios of Nazianzos, *Or.* 24.5 (p. 48).

was transformed into a new paradise by the conduct of this admirable man. It was not guarded by a sword of fire, prohibiting men from entering;[66] everyone could easily enter it. It was irrigated by ineffable rivers,[67] I mean, his golden speeches. He not only thrived in technical matters and shone through his beautiful orations; he not only excelled in the art of law among all men of the past; he not only rivaled the best philosophers; he not only became an exemplary administrator, distinguishing himself as a judge above all others; but now, as soon as he chose the better life, he also managed to be not inferior to those admirable men who distinguished themselves as monks.

He did not become equal to the most distinguished monks only as far as some particular virtues were concerned, falling short of them in another respect. Nor was he seen exercising the practical part of virtue by following the example of *other* monks, yet failing to become himself a model of it for other people or to make himself perfect by creating an example for himself and teaching others, too, as far was as possible, through the outline of virtue he fashioned for them. Not at all. Even after he had changed his life, he employed the same method as before, even though his subject had changed. As the philosophers claim, this takes place at the time of the creation of beings: their leader [Plato] mixes the material for souls in the same mixing vessel,[68] but distinguishes the different sorts of creatures. This is, of course, a pagan belief, far removed from our doctrines and the true faith. The same happened with him [Xiphilinos]: he handled each public affair with a proper measure [**135P**] and in the same way that he ordained the affairs of the spirit.

What I have said is only a shadow-outline and prelude for what I am going to narrate later. He made tremendous progress toward the good, beginning at the starting line and moving toward perfection.[69] He was taught the elementary lessons, but at the same time he taught those who were more advanced than him the lessons concerning what is above perfection. He was offered an instruction in the practical aspects, but he was guiding others to the divine good in a more abstract way; he was both initiated and initiating others. He resembled a torch upon a high mountain, raised up into the air and seen by everyone from afar. All sorts of virtuous men came to him: those who were beginners in the ascetic life came to consort with him; those who were found

---

66. Cf. Genesis 3:24.
67. Cf. Genesis 2:10.
68. Cf. Plato, *Timaeus* 41d.
69. Cf. *Corpus Paroemiographorum Graecorum* vol. 1, p. 210.3 (Diogenianos 2.83).

by the divine spirit in the middle of the road came to benefit from his teaching; and those who had already reached the end of the road to perfection visited him in order to share with him their experience, so as to teach him something more. No one was disappointed, as he addressed each one in a suitable manner. To those who were willing to listen, he gave a lesson for advanced students, but he was listening with the outmost attention to all who opened their mouth in order to give him a lesson in spiritual matters. In this way, he was both a teacher and a student. He made all his students more virtuous, and at the same time he was initiated into the mysteries of divine contemplation.

15. So abundant was goodness in him. His life advanced on the road toward God without difficulty, and the change in his way of life took place without storms. However, my soul was in turmoil, or rather it was assaulted by waves and deeply agitated. I did not know where to turn for help, having lost such a friendly soul. Whenever I recalled the agreement I had come to with God, and the fact that he [Xiphilinos] had kept his promise while I had not yet done so, my mind became inflamed in an ineffable way: I burned up and that ineffable fire was immense. Therefore, I was trying to find a pretext for changing my life too and joining him. God created such a pretext. How? He lit a fire in my heart[70] and then [**136P**] caused pain in my intestines. The pain was not great, but at last I had found an excellent pretext. I exaggerated the illness and its symptoms, and I was crying loudly as if I were on the verge of death, asking to become a monk immediately. I was unrestrained in this ambition, but no one fulfilled my wish because all were afraid lest they do something contrary to the emperor's wishes. But as soon as the news reached him, he immediately guessed my intention. Though he did not visit me while I was ill, he did whatever else he could to dissuade me. He made great declarations. He promised to cure my illness, so to speak. He begged me, cried loudly, and sent me letters written not in ink, but in tears. Finally, he resorted to threats against things he knew I loved greatly. He added curses and even asked for the intercession of God. He sent emissaries in order to pressure me, to persuade me, to beg me.[71]

But should I not mention what was more important and unbelievable? Sending me letters from afar, he prostrated himself at my feet, reminding me through these letters of our friendship, his benefactions, our lessons, my teaching him, his intellectual intercourse with me, our serious discussions, and our

---

70. Cf. Gregorios of Nyssa, *Life of Moses* 2.257.6 (p. 282).
71. Cf. Psellos, *Chronographia* 6.198.3–16.

common philosophical investigations.[72] The man I am now praising [Xiphilinos] had offered powerful resistance to all this, but when I began to yield to the emperor, who brought great pressure to bear upon me, my soul was disturbed and gave way to his demands; yet as soon as I turned my mind to the man who had adopted the superior life before me, I found myself moving toward him under full sail and with genial breezes.[73] In the end, this latter inclination prevailed.[74] Looking down on everything else, or rather resisting all others bravely, I devoted myself to God and renounced the worldly habit.[75] This caused an immediate stir in the palace: [137P] that deed was rumored by some, while others announced it in a loud voice. The news reached the emperor and he almost lost his voice, so oppressed was he by what happened to me. His soul was full of anger and despair, and he did not know what to do. In the end, however, he displayed his habitual mercy and benevolence.[76] Changing his mind, he sent me an imperial letter, as if by his order I had been restored to health. I thought that I was half-united with my friend now, as I had taken the monastic habit like him, though I was still far away from him. I would have remained on the threshold between my love for him [Xiphilinos] and the violence exerted by the emperor, had God not taken to himself the man who exercised violence upon me because he loved me.[77] I say this while omitting many details, being afraid that I may be accused by many of being self-absorbed. I also do not wish to give more attention to what is a subordinate business here than to the main one.

16. The life of the emperor came to its end [1055], and all good things ended with him, like the leaves of a tree that is cut, which fade and fall down. Then my desire to abandon this world grew stronger. Accordingly, before I

72. In his *Encomium for His Mother*, written roughly at this time, Psellos asks the emperor to allow him to depart, offering an apology for his decision to become a monk: Kaldellis (2006) 33.

73. Cf. Synesios, *Letter* 5 (p. 13).

74. In his *Chronographia* (6.191.13–17) Psellos attributes his decision to become a monk, abandoning his illustrious career in the palace, mainly to the instability of the emperor's character, admitting that his illness was feigned: Kaldellis (2006) 32. In his *hypomnema* (court memorandum) concerning the breaking off of the engagement of his daughter with a certain Elpidios, he argues that the only reason for his tonsure had been his illness: Kaldellis (2006) 32, and 151 n. 12.

75. This happened a short time before Theodora's accession to the imperial throne in early 1055: Ljubarskij (2004) 53 n. 35.

76. Cf. Psellos, *Chronographia* 6.199.5–10.

77. Cf. Gregorios of Nazianzos, *Or.* 4.33.1 (p. 130).

had even completely recovered, before my body was completely restored to strength, I forced it to abandon its bed where it was lying under medical treatment, and climbed to Olympos,[78] both in order to visit that mountain which I had never seen before and to see my friend and partner. As soon as I beheld him who had already taken on the shape of all virtues, being an exact replica of beauty itself, without the slightest hesitation, not respecting his magnificence and forbidding appearance, I embraced him wholeheartedly. I washed him first with my tears, then touched his whole body and admirable head, which gave off a spiritual odor, and my own body and even my soul were then completely healed. It was as if I had heard a divine voice. I do not know if any other moment of my life was happier than this.

The mountain itself resembles [138P] the heavenly meadows where the souls of the best men dwell, according to the pagans.[79] They place those meadows somewhere between the clouds and the ether; and it is adorned by the stars of the sky above as if by flowers.[80] Olympos consists of unlike parts and its surface is rough, but all these are combined in a harmonious way, and each part can give a spectator sufficient joy. One part of it is flat, another mountainous, and they vie with each other. If one takes a walk in the flat part, he will consider that region much better than the mountainous one, but if he climbs to the hills, he will despise all regions that are fit for horsemanship. No peak of that mountain is bare: sometimes the sweat of the earth becomes rivers;[81] sometimes they give birth to several plants, watering them. The planes, cypresses,[82] and all sorts of towering trees are arranged in rows, as if by command, while others grow together in clusters. Their tops converge, transforming the places underneath into a new, imperishable paradise. Many wild bushes grow there, and there are also some small trees: their foliage is not slender but very thick.[83] All sorts of waters gush out there: some are self-flowing, very clear and cold, moving in all directions. Others resemble the waters of artificial wells: they gush out from below and, when they reach the outer ring, stop there as if by a royal order. If one takes shelter under the junipers, the myrtles, the mastic trees, and their

---

78. According to Ljubarskij (2004) 53, this happened in January 1055.

79. What follows is a typical Byzantine *ekphrasis* of a *locus amoenus*. Four descriptions of Olympos by Psellos are preserved separately in certain manuscripts (*Oratoria Minora* 36, pp. 134–137).

80. A reference to the Elysian Fields.

81. Cf. Aristotle, *Meteorology* 357a25.

82. Cf. Plato, *Phaedrus* 229a.

83. Cf. Achilles Tatios, *Leukippe and Kleitophon* 1.15.3.

fruits, they refresh him with the gentle breeze blowing through them, and the songs of the birds sitting on their branches give him a great pleasure at noon, when the birds, hidden in the leaves, speak in the Attic dialect.[84] [**139P**] Only the language of Plato could praise the thick shade of the chaste-tree.[85]

So far we have described the material aspect of the mountains, omitting most details. What about the spiritual aspect? There are natural, hollow caves in them and some small churches, built by men but in a rudimentary way. There are also hermitages, some built on the mountain peaks and others in the ravines. They are made to be brilliant, like big or small torches planted all over the mountains. Some of the fruitful trees are to be found in special gardens, while others grow together with trees that do not produce fruit; they either grow by themselves or are planted by men. All this applies to the mountain ridges, and one can only guess at its superb grace, which offers an ineffable pleasure. The meadow, which seems fit for horsemanship, looks like a different world altogether, being completely opposite to the mountainous area. There is plenty of fresh pasture, irrigated by waters; most of it is suitable for horses and cattle, sheep and goats, if someone wishes to graze animals. Some animals graze in herds, while others graze alone, without any fear of being caught, since no one either shoots at them or hunts them. So they are not afraid and hidden, but live together with men, eating the same food, if they so wish.

Some of those men enjoy the divine ascetic life—leading such a life is a real pleasure. They form a chorus of their own and are filled by the spirit in unison. They live under the guidance of the chorus leader, who is their guide toward virtue. They all sing together, share a common meal, and all things are common among them. Some others live alone, but they dwell in a common hermitage: they meet together at the time of the holy service, but each of them has his own way of life. Still others are utterly separate from the rest, surpassing human nature, which has a downward tendency. [**140P**] These are the ones who have defeated the demon of indifference. They do not do any manual labor; in fact, they do nothing, being dedicated only to God, enjoying an ineffable union with him.

17. Such, as described, is this mountain. But if one wishes to make it his dwelling place and live in the company of those spiritual men as if they were angels, he will consider it that blessed land, promised to those worthy of it. I enjoyed an additional pleasure, in that I had the opportunity to live with my

---

84. Cf. Synesios, *Letter* 114 (p. 200).
85. Cf. Plato, *Phaedrus* 230b, a classic description of a *locus amoenus*.

friend and share his philosophical investigations concerning both visible and invisible beings. I wanted to fly like him, who was like a high-flying eagle,[86] rising up into the air with him. But while I seemed to be of the same species with him, I was still an eaglet and resembled a tender young bird that could not yet fly. I was eager to rise up like him, but was proved his inferior, not being able to follow the right road. Therefore, I acquitted myself of my desire to go to him: I had many philosophical discussions about what we could see with the eyes of our body, but not with the eyes of our soul, which are hidden. And then I departed from him, crying loudly. I was turning my head back to see him. When natural affection pulled me back to my family and their needs, I abandoned his company, but whenever I felt the need for a superior kind of freedom, I took wing and went to my companion. My path had two directions, one to the left and the other to the right.

18. My speech, having reached this point, wants to deal with another, more important part of his life. So it makes a new beginning, going up, so that by following the road from that point onward it might reach the end. Not everything is up to us; not all things can proceed according to our desires. We depend not only on our inclination, but there is another, supernatural [141P] Power that directs our own affairs in whatever way it desires. I am not about to include among these powers the nature of the world, which spins the wool of our fate,[87] directing our affairs, as some pagans argue. We are in fact governed by two powers, first by divine providence and second by our own inclination.[88] In some cases these two must act together, in others divine providence suffices by itself. I call inclination the power of our soul to lead us toward what is better, defeating the opposite desire. Therefore, I can confidently claim that where our inclination works, providence works too, but our inclination does not always obey divine providence. Our inclination proceeds jointly from both reason and appetite, and not from just one of these two. The same applies to opinion and desire.[89] Let us say nothing more about these matters, for my speech turns to another direction now.

In any case, the rationale behind divine providence does not always follow the direction of our inclinations and desires: something different from

---

86. Cf. Homer, *Iliad* 12.201.
87. Cf. Lucian, *Charon* 16.2.
88. Cf. Psellos, *Philosophica Minora II* 47 (p. 162.22).
89. Cf. Aristotle, *Nicomachean Ethics* 1139a29–32.

what we want or desire may happen. He [Xiphilinos] had fallen in love with the quiet monastic life, and was already devoted to contemplative quietude. He took the path toward good things, and that was his aim. Is there anything more desirable for a soul than a separation from everything natural and bodily, as far as that is possible? Defeating the passions that disturb it, the soul turns to itself and contemplates the orderly arrangement of the whole soul. Then, turning to things more divine, it contemplates the life of the intellect and grasps those noble things without employing human syllogisms. Then, from there, it goes beyond all power and energy, reaching the apex of its own life. [**142P**] Setting before itself the unity of nature, it is united with the One, becoming Spirit, Mind, and God.[90] Having reached that point, he [Xiphilinos] did not pay any attention to the affairs of this world. He ignored them. This is the union of the particular one with the whole One. This is known to all who have become perfect in virtue and have surpassed human nature. Most people will not believe what I am saying as a philosopher about that which is beyond Intellectual Indivisibility. I can confidently claim that he would reach his goal. I am not referring to his opinion and desire. However, God had other plans for him. The pagans believe that souls come down from the higher spheres so as to lead a nobler life on earth. I would never accept such a doctrine.[91] Human souls are created together with their bodies, and those that surpass the limits of human nature are given by God to those who need a better way of life.[92] The cycle of the seasons is due to the movements of the sun up and down, but spiritual improvement is due to those higher souls. As soon as divine providence realized that the man being praised here had become perfect in all sorts of virtues and had become able to govern human souls, it proceeded to carry out its preordained plan in the following way.

The sacrificer of the holy sacrifice, the great archbishop of Constantinople, was sacrificed to the Lord and departed from this life to a higher one.[93] The

90. This description corresponds to the stages of the soul's journey toward the One as described by the Neoplatonists, e.g., Plotinos, *Enneads* 4.7.13.14–19. See also Psellos, *De omnifaria doctrina* 54.11–12 (p. 39); his long *Letter to Xiphilinos* 40–42, in this volume; *Chronographia* 6A.8.13; *Philosophica Minora I* 7.63 (p. 24).

91. An obligatory rejection of the doctrine of reincarnation; cf. Psellos, *Philosophica Minora II* 38 (p. 132.20–25).

92. Cf. Psellos, *Philosophica Minora I* 40.6–8 (p. 144).

93. The patriarch of Constantinople Konstantinos Leichoudes, a close friend of Psellos, died in 1063: see the funeral oration for him in this volume.

throne of the archbishop was left vacant for a while, not because the emperor of that time [Konstantinos X Doukas, 1059–1067] neglected the matter, but because many men made a name for themselves as qualified for the office of archbishop, though no one surpassed the others so as to gain all the votes for himself. The reason was that the candidates were clergymen of Constantinople, not outsiders. [143P] All sorts of men leading a life devoted to God were proposed as candidates. Even those who were leading a life between that of a layman and a monk, or who had distinguished themselves as imperial officers, were examined, but the emperor wanted neither to be misled by fallacious reasoning nor to be led astray by mere appearances; rather, he wanted the whole affair to be conducted with true judgment and knowledge. But no one was absolutely perfect in all respects: one of them might have led a perfect life for a short time, while another had more years of experience. The latter might have led such a life for more years, but the former might have been more earnest than the first one. One might have had an ability to instruct through his lectures, another might have provided his own life as a shining example for his students. It was difficult to find someone who combined all the qualities required for a successful, virtuous life, I mean, his life, mind, speech, and all the rest. Therefore, no one appeared to be better than another for being the chief bishop.

At that time, he [Xiphilinos] decided to help the emperor to choose an archbishop by bringing to his attention some spiritual and holy men who lived on the mountain. And indeed he brought them to Constantinople. So great was his desire not to become a priest; he did not place anything above his quiet and noble life. He wanted to fill the position with other people, but God had already elected him. It was I who brought his name to the emperor's attention many times, but he [Xiphilinos] ordered me to stop doing that as soon as he learned it, saying that he would never agree to such a thing. However, the emperor could not find anyone more perfect than him, with respect to his speech, his great virtue, and his manifold knowledge. So, setting all the others aside and inspired by a divine spirit, he inclined toward him and exerted much pressure upon him through many letters. In the end he just barely managed to persuade him to accept this offer, after God moved him too. Therefore, the man who had transferred his dwelling place to the palace of God now entered the imperial palace.[94] But he did not abandon the palace of God; rather, like

---

94. At the end of December 1063: Bonis (1937) 97.

the angelic, superior powers, he was both above and below, walking together with the crowd. He entered the palace and [**144P**] admired the magnitude of the imperial City, just as if he were seeing it for the first time. He had almost forgotten that he was brought up in and nourished by that City. However, he did not admire the way of life of its inhabitants.

19. How could I accurately describe his entrance into the palace, narrating it in detail for the sake of the majority of my audience? I witnessed the whole of it and was examining everything carefully with my soul; I have such an aptitude. It was morning. Someone came to the emperor announcing that the man whom he had asked for had arrived, standing before the gates of the palace. Immediately the emperor came out, accompanied by very few men of his entourage and his guard. He met him while he was entering the palace and embraced him. However, he [Xiphilinos] behaved as if he had forgotten his good manners completely; anyone who knew him from before would say that he had a different man in front of him, not the one he knew before. He did not bow down before him and did not address him in a humble manner. He did not care at all, not even if the emperor had been crowned with all the crowns of this world and was adorned with all sorts of ornaments. The emperor himself, his entourage, and all the servants of the palace who happened to be present thought that this man was unpolished and unsociable. But as soon as he saw me, abandoning all the others, he gave me his hand and kissed me, saying, "Is this really what I urged you to do? Did I ask you to use your influence with the emperor to achieve this thing? Did I not warn you in advance? Did I not protest that I would never abandon the quiet life voluntarily, descending into this world to such an extent?"[95]

"But this is not a descent," I immediately answered. "You will be elevated to the most prestigious office of archbishop." He [Xiphilinos] said, "That's exactly a descent. Is there something beyond God, who initiated me into the most ineffable mysteries?" [**145P**] I replied, "To be initiated is a passion, not an action.[96] Initiating is nobler than being initiated. You are going to initiate us into the mysteries and introduce us into the divine realm." While we were speaking, the emperor came to us, interrupting us in the middle of our exchange and ending our conversation. But he stubbornly persisted in resisting our proposal. While we were all of a like mind on this question, upholding his

95. Cf. Plato, *Republic* 539e.
96. Cf. Psellos, *Theologica I* 30.15–26 (p. 122).

nomination, he kept having strong unilateral, or one-sided, reservations. Finally, he could not resist our pressures or our arguments, or rather the inexorable decision of God, so he surrendered himself to us and the Holy Spirit; being anointed, he received the grace of an archbishop.[97] He was anointed with spiritual unction, which did not fall only upon his chin and beard, but washed over his entire body, and before that his soul too.[98] The man himself bore testimony to all his other virtues, but a sanctification and perfect cleansing of his soul were given to him by all people as a prestigious office through universal consent. Thus a pure man was offered as a sacrifice to the Pure One:[99] he put on both the garment and the undergarment, was crowned with the mitre and headdress, and wore the belts much more aptly than had Aaron and Samuel,[100] as these two were adorned with material ones, whereas he was wearing spiritual ones.

20. So far my speech has dealt with the man in his political and monastic capacities, praising him for his achievements in each of those lives. As far as his political life was concerned, it has focused on his knowledge of the art of law, on his lawgiving, and judicial activity; as far as his monastic life was concerned, it has focused on his practical and contemplative virtues, his spiritual progress, the beauty of that life, and all the things beyond them that contribute to our union with the First Good.[101] Let us now examine him as archbishop. That office is superior to both statesmanship and the monastic way of life; however, it is related to both, and its difference with them is somehow [146P] mitigated. He did not abandon the contemplative life when he took the responsibility for the salvation of most people. Nor did he neglect the governance of other people just because he enjoyed a blessed, quiet life and spent his leisure time with God. He did not devote part of his time to what was higher and another part to what was lower, but he did both at the same time: he raised himself up to God through his prayer, and there was taught by God how to instruct his people down on earth. On the other hand, while he was initiating them into the more perfect mysteries, or was dealing with them in any other way, at the same time he was raising his mind up to God secretly,

97. On 1 or 2 January 1064: Bonis (1937) 100.
98. Cf. Psalm 132:2; Exodus 28:31.
99. Cf. Plato, *Phaedrus* 67b.
100. Cf. Exodus 28:33–39.
101. Cf. Psellos, *Oratoria Minora* 21.72 (p. 78).

although his body was with his people. At first, he did not dare to come into contact with the crowd, as if it were a wild beast, and he was totally inaccessible to them. Instead, he devoted himself entirely to God and was very slow to withdraw from that position.

But as soon as he forced himself to deal with the affairs of this world, knowing that his mind was unwilling to come down with his body but remained above even at the time of the change of his life, he devoted himself to us too: his change of life did not make him upset anymore, as his habits remained the same. Therefore, he did not consider his new task as secondary, but divided himself into as many parts as he could, adapting himself to the needs of various persons: he became benefactor to some people and life-guide to others. He cleared up the doubts of some and at the same time bound others with spiritual bonds. Some he admonished to choose a nobler and better life, while he even interceded on behalf of others. He defended some with candor, doing that not only in front of magnates and arrogant judges, but also in front of that emperor who had appointed him archbishop, or rather who had pressured him to accept that office. Although he loved him, because he was a mild and good emperor, he did not refrain from opposing him if he saw him doing wrong. I saw that many times myself: when his entreaties failed to persuade him to do what was right and the emperor remained adamant and unyielding to all efforts, he [Xiphilinos] was filled with just anger and stood up from his throne. He castigated the emperor vigorously and reprimanded him again and again, not giving any ground until he saw that [**147P**] the emperor had given way to his wishes. His requests were just, but the emperor too was right not to grant them. He put in front of the emperor God himself as an example, but the emperor hastened to do what was safe for his kingdom. The words and the desires of each were appropriate to their station in life. But in the end the emperor gave way not so much to his own benevolence, but to the arguments used by the archbishop in favor of benevolence.

Was this man absolutely perfect only in this respect, being deficient in others? Not at all. All of his components were magnificent in themselves and even better as a whole. The same happens with the elements of the universe: each one is beautiful in itself, but they are all more beautiful when combined in an orderly way,[102] and I know that the same applies to the separate parts of our body, the whole earth, and the ether, and to everything capable of being

---

102. Cf. Psellos, *Theologica I* 71.104–106 (p. 320).

constructed harmoniously. The separate parts of his benevolent activity were magnificent, considered each in itself, but more magnificent when considered as a whole. What is more important is the following: his task was to offer sacrifices to God and to perform the Great Sacrifice, but he did not perform this task rarely, once in a week or a month, or at the beginning of the month or the Sabbath,[103] but he celebrated mass every day, in every feast and celebration. He did not neglect any established liturgical practice, and even added new tasks to be performed. In that particular respect, he was adamant. He annoyed many of his bishops with that habit, and they went away from him, as if unable to follow a bird in flight. Festal processions from the Great Church [Hagia Sophia] had been preordained for the archbishop on some particular days, and previous archbishops used to follow the procession only as far as the narthex. But he, being filled with ineffable ardor, followed the whole procession, dripping with sweat and breathing laboriously when he came back. He would have gladly departed from this [**148P**] life in performing such a spiritual task. In the intervals between those solemn ceremonies, he performed other tasks, even better ones: he gathered the dependents of the Great Church around him and, forming them into an admirable chorus, read holy books to them, particularly the canons written by the Fathers. He explained the difficult passages and clarified the meaning of some ambiguous ones. He also expounded upon the meaning of the terms of our religion and clarified the meaning of our doctrines, which have many forms in accordance with the various heresies we have had to fight.

21. All these things were proper to his station in life, and his predecessors possessed these virtues too. But what I am about to say came to me totally unexpectedly. What am I talking about? Even when he was a layman, he held in contempt all aspects of material life: he did not in any way partake of ostentation, did not wear grand clothes, did not possess either a luxurious residence or fields, meadows, and gardens; he did not pursue any of those things. He lived without material goods; his life was frugal. He preferred what was at hand over what was luxuriously prepared. His only adornment was reason: he loved the logical arts excessively, and he accurately understood the principles of the sciences. After he became archbishop, he kept his habit as a law over himself, but when it came to other people he did not act in this way. First, he took care to adorn the sanctuary of the Great and Holiest Church of the Wis-

103. Cf. 2 Kings 4:23; 2 Ezra 5:52.

dom of God; the greater part, including the sanctuary, of that church had been left unadorned, and the apse and the roof high up were cracked, and altogether in bad shape. He adorned both parts and contrived solutions to their problems: he surrounded the upper part of the apse with golden crowns and honored it with well-crafted images, while he repaired the other parts in a splendid manner, making the new construction more beautiful than the previous one.

But did he pay attention only to that church, neglecting the others? Far from it. He repaired those that were cracked, rebuilt others that were in ruins, and embellished others that had been deformed, making them better than before. Some were partly repaired to a greater or lesser extent, [**149P**] others built all over again. He did not keep anything for himself so as to live luxuriously, [instead] offering everything to God and to his worshippers. He enjoyed his lack of enjoyment,[104] nourished himself only enough in order to remain alive, but let flow fountains of pleasure for the others. Generally speaking, he did not pay any attention to his kinsmen. I do not know why he did that, probably to avoid accusations of selfishness. But he took care of all others as if they were parts of his own body.

Realizing that the situation had taken a turn for the worse, and that the rich could hardly get by on their patrimony, on the fortunes they had amassed, or on the imperial gifts they received, while poor people had no income at all because the fountain that irrigated them had dried up, one man now met all their needs. He did not limit himself to nourishing them and giving charity just once. There were many installments in each week and month, and how could I count the annual ones? One may wonder where he found all those sums that he gave to so many people. Let me remind you that the Lord—who fed many people with just a few loaves and showed clearly that what had been left was much more than what had been given before, as we read in the Gospels[105]—once more through the hands of this man's servants provided poor people with a charity that was half-full indeed.[106] However, that charity was sufficient for the masses, and with what was left over the Lord provided them with a second course.

---

104. Cf. Gregorios of Nazianzos, *Or.* 43.61.8–9 (pp. 256–258), and in other texts of his.

105. Cf. Matthew 14:19; Luke 9:16; John 6:11.

106. Cf. Isaiah 58:7.

But was he really so generous toward those men who were gathered around the church, those frequenting the market, and those from farther away, while neglecting the clergymen who received communion with him? Was he less generous or less benevolent toward those who were in the churches, the servants of the holy altar, those carrying the vessels of incense, and those who belonged to the ultimate chorus? I invoke here the testimony of the Holy Synod and the other orders of the Church: he was generous to all, both individually and as a whole. [150P] He did not rebuke anyone who asked for seconds; in fact, he offered a gift greater than the first. If someone was grateful, well, it was likely that he would shrink back from asking for more sooner than he [Xiphilinos] would stop giving it. Who could give an account of what he added to the annual and monthly gifts, to the gifts offered during the general celebrations? He was also concerned [. . .] He revered the martyrs and Apostles [. . .] and all who were servants of God he honored brilliantly and took care of them. He was particularly devoted to the Virgin Mother of God. I do not know if he had a vision of her, but it is certain that he honored her magnificently and loved her, as if he saw her with his own eyes in front of him, just as if she gazed upon him. Her miracles gave him the opportunity to organize special feasts for her.

22. I realize that my speech has become too long. However, I have covered none of the aspects of his life adequately, but have given only a short account of them, as if writing a simple narrative; I have avoided the usual excesses of panegyric. Since I have not yet trumpeted his secular or ecclesiastic (and so superior) learning, nor mentioned his painstaking composition of speeches, both oral and written, nor yet said how deeply he was immersed in the mathematical sciences,[107] I want now to make a new start in order to deal with all these. I am not going to speak about them in detail—for who is able to count the sand in the sea?[108]—but will give a synoptic account of each, defining it properly.[109] I will touch on some of them individually but on others as a group. Having related all these circumstantially, I will finish my speech concerning him. Before that I will say a few things about his departure from this

---

107. The so-called *mathemata* (*quadrivium*): arithmetic, geometry, astronomy, and music.

108. Cf. Sirach 1:2.

109. A concise praise of Xiphilinos' erudition is found in the treatise of Psellos against his accuser, Ophrydas: *Orationes Forenses* 3.128–184 (pp. 129–131).

world. I am well aware that he does not want to be praised on account of what others did for him or even on account of his own deeds, being filled as he is with supernatural qualities. He already contemplates the archetypal images, having left the shadows behind.

[151P] However, if I do not give a short account of all the rich gifts he enjoyed, my speech would be incomplete. Having started with the study of the law, he tried to find its prior source and what was before that source, out of which the laws gushed like rivers. He proceeded with the exact method applied by students of First Philosophy:[110] they try to explain each thing on the basis of a thing prior to it, gradually reaching the highest peak. They do not regard either the undergirding reality or the initiator as a beginning,[111] but only Mind, Power, the Father, or the One above everything; they proceed from what participates to the one that is participated in, and from there they rise up to the one that cannot be participated.[112] However, even that is considered by them multifarious, so they proceed finally to the Original Unity. In the same way did he [Xiphilinos] explain laws through other laws; he asked after their origin and found it. Then he proceeded by using the method of those who examine the powers of the soul: initially they distinguish many parts among them, then, cutting down their number, they reduce them to four or even to two. He did exactly the same: at the beginning, he distinguished many parts of the laws, then he cut down their number, imitating the procedure followed by Aristotle in his treatise on winds, where, after arguing that there are as many winds as sectors of heaven, he cuts their number down to four and then reduces them to just two.[113] He had taken this theory from Hippokrates of Kos.

Was there any man more precise in cutting down than him [Xiphilinos]? Was there anyone more apt at discovering things, or more philosophical at reducing multiplicities to higher unities, or more dialectical at dividing the one into many?[114] It is true that division and reduction belong to both sciences,

110. Cf. Psellos, *Philosophica Minora II* 13 (p. 37.32).

111. Cf. Psellos, *Philosophica Minora II* 39 (p. 146.16–19). Psellos' interest in the interpretation of the *Chaldaean Oracles* was well known and a matter that required him to be defensive.

112. Cf. Psellos, *Philosophica Minora II* 10 (p. 21.3–7).

113. Cf. Pseudo-Aristotle, *De mundo* 349b13–36; *The Situations and Names of Winds* 973a1–973b25; and Psellos, *Philosophica Minora I* 22.60–65 (p. 85); *Poemata* 59 (pp. 424–426).

114. Cf. Psellos, *Philosophica Minora I* 13.32–37 (pp. 41–42).

that is, First Philosophy and dialectics, but the former searches mainly for the unique principle behind the various things, while the latter examines things in their multiplicity. Who cross-examined those things opposite to each other, realizing that what was opposite was just an appearance and not a real being? [152P] Who brought the *actiones*, which are many, out of the *enochai*, the number of which is much smaller, just as he brought the *enochai* out of that which has the same name? Who subordinated the *actiones* to the matrix of the *enochai*, making a proper distinction between things that nevertheless shared the same name?[115] That was unknown to most other scholars. Who gave such manifold form to what lay in the middle, giving it many names, thereby distinguishing things that are akin to each other from those that belonged to a different kind? Who else like him traced the common origin of some of them, while postulating that others were unoriginated? In the same manner, our theology exalts someone of our co-religionists above the highest order, not because this was so in fact, but because this has been handed down to us by the historians.[116]

Who elevated the science of law as high as he did? He united it with rhetoric, subordinated it to philosophy, and thus managed to adorn it through these two sciences, or rather to adorn these two fields sufficiently through the science of law.[117] My intention was to say more about the laws, and I could indeed do so. But the art of rhetoric draws me to itself. He was more enthusiastic about that art and managed to surpass all others in it. He did not divide rhetoric in the manner that most orators do. He did not reduce its infinite power, as if he were writing a synopsis of it, imitating those who cut off the sea from the great rivers. He examined all its powers and found its principles, and he himself made an important contribution to it: he did not compose synoptic textbooks of rhetoric for the sake of some commoners or idle and indolent emperors.[118] Instead, he gave a complete account of its essence. He did not reduce the prefatory concepts to distinct principles; he did not apply just a few terms to cover the multitude of the literary forms;[119] he did not behave as a legislator giving in-

115. Cf. Psellos, *Poemata* 8.93–108 (pp. 127–128), where a brief exposition of these legal terms can be found.

116. This passage is unclear. Is Psellos referring to Melchizedek (cf. Hebrews 7:3)?

117. Cf. Psellos, *Orationes Panegyricae* 17.232–242 (pp. 151–152).

118. Psellos himself had composed such a synopsis for the idle emperor Michael VII Doukas! See Psellos, *Poemata* 7 (p. 103).

119. A reference to Hermogenes, *On Types of Style*.

structions by fiat concerning the parts of a speech. Rather, he explained the cause of everything and [153P] gave an account of this art in a geometric fashion.[120] He made distinctions among the prefaces of speeches[121] on the basis of those belonging to the same *genus*, namely, those that exhibit accidental similarities. He also proceeded to make a proper division of the demonstrative proofs of rhetorical syllogisms[122] and of the dialectic proofs[123] that are prior to them, on which the discussion of a given subject is based.

Who else discovered their causes, peculiarities, quantities, and qualities more successfully than he [Xiphilinos]? Who discovered their contrasts, parts, and totality, how something proceeds out of its unity and reverts to it? Who combined the several forms of rhetorical speech[124] into a harmonious whole? He united some of them with each other without any intermediary, while others were combined with each other through a tie he placed between them,[125] binding them together and creating an organic whole, both divisible through its contrasts and indivisible because of the similarities of its parts to each other: it is indivisible because its parts are combined to each other harmoniously, but divisible through an accurate division. Who classified speeches in order to examine them more aptly? He did not look for an archetype of both outside of himself but, like the creator of the world described by Plato, he possessed an archetype in himself.[126] The Platonic creator had life in itself inside him,[127] and on the basis of it created the various parts of the world. Likewise, he [Xiphilinos] put the idea of the ideas into his soul in advance, and afterward proceeded to the creation of the whole art of speech. Let the gods and other fantasies of the pagans go to hell, and let the followers of Plato stop

120. See Psellos, *Poemata* 7.87–126 (pp. 106–107), where a brief exposition of the ancient theory of rhetoric is to be found; and see later in the same poem for other terms mentioned below. On the legal writings of Xiphilinos, see *ODB* 1054.

121. This is done in the treatise of Hermogenes, *De inventione*, book 1.

122. The term enthymeme refers to a rhetorical syllogism, and it was used by Aristotle in his *Rhetoric*. In Hermogenes, *De inventione* 3.8, a theory about the distinction among the several kinds of enthymemes is introduced, which was modified by later commentators.

123. The term *epicheirema* is found in Aristotle's *Topics*, referring to a dialectical syllogism. The term was discussed in detail by Hermogenes, *De inventione* 3.5–7.

124. Another reference to Hermogenes' *On Types of Style*.

125. For Psellos's view of intermediacy, see Jenkins (2016).

126. Cf. Plato, *Timaeus* 28a–c.

127. Cf. Psellos, *Philosophica Minora II* 33 (p. 111.26).

boasting about First Ideas, whether they consider them as substantial thoughts of the Creator or as entities, distinct from this world, independent and transcendental.[128] Let Plato stop claiming some advantage over us, dealing as he does with the ideas. He applies various terms to them, but does not regard them as the cause of all things.[129] But the ideas we discovered through the art are true and can be successfully grasped, even if they lack the magnificent name of an unreal existence. [154P] He [Xiphilinos] distinguished the three fields—rhetoric, sophistry, and statesmanship—and gave to each its own, just like Plato distinguished the politician, the sophist, and the philosopher.[130] Emulously desiring the several styles of speech, he used them in the proper place in his writings: in some cases he employs a sublime style, while in others he employs the language of everyday life. In any case, he adapted the style of his speeches to the requirements of his subject and the various circumstances in a magisterial way.

23. In this way he examined in depth both the science of law and rhetoric; he adorned them and magnified himself by them. He also placed himself between our own, pure philosophy and the secular one, thoroughly examining and clarifying both of them. He not only discovered the deeper meaning of Christian philosophy, but he put it into practice too. He also screened what was involved in secular philosophy, or rather he divided it into two parts, rejecting what was poisonous and keeping what was nourishing for the soul. Who distinguished the boundaries of the several branches of knowledge and found the paths leading toward the highest good to a greater extent than he? He started from the world of nature and proceeded to the supernatural one. Who built that highest ladder of virtues?[131] He began from the material world of composites and moved toward the point where the souls tended to return; and, from there, he easily flew up to the highest level. Others thought that there he had already achieved perfection. But he then proceeded to the apex, where the limits of all knowledge are to be found and from where the streams of wisdom flow. Who came to such a rest like him? He had climbed so high that there was nowhere to go or fly any more.

He resided there for a long time, many Sabbaths passed by,[132] but in the end he was installed in a place where all action ceases and only passion occurs in-

---

128. Cf. Psellos, *Philosophica Minora II* 33 (pp. 112.2–113.20).
129. Cf. Plato, *Parmenides* 130d.
130. Cf. Plato, *Sophist* 217a.
131. Cf. Gregorios of Nazianzos, *Or.* 43.71.14–18 (p. 284).
132. The meaning is unclear.

stead.[133] [155P] Therefore, the good can have no end: anyone who comes there does not need to act anymore or activate his powers. Who managed to discover that which is beyond us, finding it both inside unity and in its parts? That was strange indeed. Who examined thoroughly the mixture of those opposites, being and nonbeing, safeguarding both the unity and the differences much better than does the dialogue on the *Sophist*? I am referring to that composite god of Plato.[134] Who set the ends of the ladder on appropriate boundaries and put each of the more general virtues into its proper place on the ladder, giving a correct interpretation of it? Who defined more accurately the body and the bodiless?[135] Who explained better the various names of Being, giving a most wise interpretation of the terms "immaterial," "otherness," and "not multiplied"? He even managed to give a safe definition of intelligible entities; their meaning is very obscure indeed. He safeguarded the indivisibility of the soul inside the body, which is composite, explaining how the soul, while remaining by itself, illuminates the entire body.[136] He preserved the motionlessness of the mind,[137] while finding the motion of the soul, as it exists below the indivisible realm.[138] He also divided the parts of the various powers according to the unity or the differences of their subjects. Who, starting his investigation from the Primary Good itself, ended up in the world of bodies and of their parts?[139]

But afterward he took the opposite approach, and reached, through his analysis, the world of the primary essences.[140] He was in a position to subordinate something to its cause, to then trace its way out of that cause, and to understand the way of its return to it.[141] Who took the measure of the beings-in-themselves and the secondary ones? On the basis of what is prior to them, he defined what was major for those that were only fractal.[142] He recognized

133. Cf. Psellos, *Theologica I* 110.24–25 (p. 434).

134. Cf. Plato, *Sophist* 241d and 250e.

135. Cf. Psellos, *Theologica I* 52.41–54 (p. 200).

136. Cf. Plotinos, *Enneads* 2.3.9.33–34, and Psellos, *De omnifaria doctrina* 60.7–8 (p. 41); *Philosophica Minora II* 23 (p. 99.1–2).

137. Cf. Psellos, *De omnifaria doctrina* 23.7–11 (p. 27).

138. Cf. Psellos, *Theologica I* 89.18–32 (pp. 350–351) and 97.29–34 (p. 379).

139. Cf. Psellos, *Theologica I* 49.125–129 (p. 189).

140. This Neoplatonic theory is also expounded by Pseudo-Dionysios, *On Divine Names* 4.15 (p. 161.1–5); see also Proklos, *Elements of Theology*, for the discussion here and below, esp. 37, 55, 92–95.

141. Cf. Psellos, *Theologica I* 57.95–96 (p. 223).

142. Cf. Proklos, *Elements of Theology* 55 (p. 52).

double eternity and the infinity that is beyond power, placing it between the Good and Being. He also recognized true unity and the unity that exists only in our mind, the double power, and [**156P**] the manifold infinity.[143] Is there any other who managed to examine the causes of beings, revealing the name of the initial cause? In my view that was his greatest philosophical achievement. Who gave reasons for the partaking of lower beings in the essence of the higher beings, discovering the way of this participation? Who discovered what came first, isolating it from what came next? Also: how providence operates among those secondary beings too, but at the same time is distinct from them.

He found out the number of the divinities of beings and, concerning the middle orders,[144] he recognized how many there are and how they stand and the relations of each to those two extremes between which it is found.[145] He discovered what their conflagration is and their growing manifold feathers. He realized what the hymn was, the way it was sung, the way it was divided, and the way it started again.[146] He realized what the thrones of fire were, what the meaning of wheels in succession, and what the other, more complicated figures symbolized.[147] He recognized the intelligence of the Divine Mind and the Second Mind,[148] realized what will and action were,[149] and how many and of what sort were the signals that come down. He understood the meaning of the first conflagration and of that which was utterly consumed; how God comes into contact with man and vice versa;[150] and that secondary beings cannot absorb the powers of prior beings in their entirety. He understood what substance, power, and energy are, and how substance and energy might be identical in some particular cases; the subdivisions and the unity of substance; what mind is; whether it is filled with species,[151] or a whole comprising many parts, and, if divisible into many parts, how it remains undivided at the same

---

143. Cf. Psellos, *Philosophica Minora II* 35 (p. 119.16–18).

144. Cf. Psellos, *Theologica I* 51.62–66 (p. 197).

145. Cf. Proklos, *On Plato's Parmenides* 951 (pp. 151–152).

146. Cf. Pseudo-Dionysios, *Letter* 9.2 (p. 200.3–4).

147. Cf. Pseudo-Dionysios, *The Celestial Hierarchy* 2.1 (p. 10.5–6).

148. Cf. Psellos, *Philosophica Minora II* 32 (p. 111.10–11) and *De omnifaria doctrina* 27.3–7 (p. 28).

149. Cf. Ioannes of Damascus, *Exposition of the Faith* 59.6–20 (pp. 144–145).

150. Cf. Psellos, *Theologica I* 59.97–159 (pp. 232–234), where that problem is discussed on the basis of some passages of Gregorios of Nazianzos.

151. Cf. Psellos, *De omnifaria doctrina* 27.2 (p. 28) and *Theologica I* 62.36–37 (p. 244).

time.[152] He found out what the three ways of the soul's return are, and whether all things are included in it. Who else made soul an image for both the first and the second orders, transforming it into the bond binding the two parts of the world?[153] He taught that it is through the soul that we go up and down, now being able to grasp what is divine with our mind, and now [157P] with our imagination, by conjecture, or with thought. He contemplated all these with his superb wisdom previously, and afterward[154] he was able to observe them from above, having acquired a higher order by nature.

But let me not harm him by omitting his other preoccupations. Who realized the deeper meaning of our two Testaments, recognizing that the Old Testament had only the figures and shadows, while the New Testament had truth itself; the former gave only an advance notice of them, while the latter presented their outcome. Who praised the Lord from the fountains of Israel,[155] slept in the middle of the two covenants, and contemplated the silver wings of the righteous pigeon, realizing that its back was golden-shining, however that is to be understood?[156] I think this text signifies the various energies of the Holy Spirit. Who managed to transmit to the mind the data of our vision through the senses? He understood the meaning of the ark, the mercy-seat upon it, the cherubim on either side, the sanctuary, what came before it, the veil dividing the two parts of the temple, the symbolic garments of the priests, the tributes, bathing tub, cups, sacrificial offerings, and altars.[157] Let me not enumerate them all. Who managed to bring all these into the mixing vessel of the Gospel, especially the inscriptions of the Psalms[158] and the prophetic readings? He interpreted the Gospel as referring to our future state, finding the images of the images, the ideas of the ideas, and the paradigms of paradigms.[159]

152. Cf. Psellos, *De omnifaria doctrina* 24.2–5 (p. 27); see also 31.2–7 (p. 30) and 53.7–12 (p. 39) for the discussion here.

153. Cf. Psellos, *Orationes Hagiographicae* 3.113–122 (p. 121). This theory is taken from Gregorios of Nazianzos.

154. Presumably, after his death.

155. Cf. Psalm 67:27.

156. Cf. Psalm 67:14.

157. Cf. Exodus 25:16–22, 26:31–33, 29:28, 30:18–28. Cf. Psellos, *Theologica I* 109 (pp. 430–432), where he interprets the relevant passages of Exodus in detail.

158. Psellos had composed two treatises, *Theologica II* 1–2 (pp. 1–16), and a whole poem, *Poem* 1, explaining the inscriptions of the Psalms.

159. Cf. Synesios, *Hymns* 2.68 (p. 62).

24. Such was his philosophy. My speech has omitted most of it. But as for you,[160] will you keep talking in all that barbaric vaunting, or rather chicanery: the *iynx, teletarches, hypezokos, ameiliktos,* or, if you want, even the *drakonto-zonos, trikarenos,* [158P] *angelides,* the etherial connector, the fathers belonging to the primal source, and Hekate placed between the two fathers?[161] Then paint her in a more bodily way and in diverse colors, draw down her flowing hair, and compose her elbows.[162] If you are ashamed of those things, let me examine your more admirable and magnificent mysteries, your strange evocation of gods[163]—you use that word to designate false phantoms—namely, the *strophalinx* of Hekate,[164] the multifaceted oracles, and strange penetrations.[165] You enjoy them, being proud of them, but I gladly mock them, believing them to be just a performance and a show. If you do not wish to be made a show of, try to base the stage of nature in reason, about which you boast. You believe that you have discovered the mysteries of nature, which you claim are the cause of rest and motion.[166] But you do not take into account the fact that some bodies in nature neither rest nor move, although you move to a hasty interpretation, enumerating the poles and axes of the celestial sphere.[167] Try to speak about the three causes of being, which later become two![168] Whenever you wish, you conflate the two causes into one. You whirl the privation around as you wish, now casting it offstage or considering it a substance too,

160. "You" seems to refer to an anonymous pagan philosopher, but later that invocation is mainly used as a reference to Aristotle.

161. These are technical terms associated with the metaphysics of the *Chaldean Oracles*. Psellos was fascinated by these esoteric matters, and often had to defend himself against critics who suspected his involvement was too personal. Cf. Psellos, *Philosophica Minora I* 36.106–107 (p. 123), 46.39 (p. 166); *Philosophica Minora II* 38 (pp. 135.9–12 and 145.23–28), 39 (p. 146.9–20); *Theologica I* 23A (p. 92.9–14), 51.85–90 (p. 198); and *Orationes Forenses* 1.599–604 (p. 24); see also Michael Italikos, *Letter* 28 (p. 190.11–12). A similar passage is found in Psellos' *Encomium for His Mother* 28 (p. 148). Cf. also Gregorios of Nazianzos, *Or.* 5.5.8–12 (p. 302).

162. In a similar passage, Psellos, *Oratoria Minora* 24.84 (p. 87), warns his students not to approve the most extreme elements of the "Chaldean" theories.

163. Cf. Psellos, *Philosophica Minora I* 3.218 (p. 11).

164. Cf. *Chaldaean Oracles* 50.1 (p. 79), with Psellos, *Philosophica Minora II* 38 (p. 133.16).

165. Cf. Psellos, *Philosophica Minora II* 23 (pp. 98.16–99.12).

166. Cf. Aristotle, *Physics* 253b8–9; Psellos, *De omnifaria doctrina* 57.2–11 (p. 40).

167. Cf. Pseudo-Aristotle, *On the World* 391b24–26.

168. Cf. Aristotle, *Physics* 191a12–22.

associating it with matter, which you transform into something bad. You mix together the object and what comes out of it and then distinguish them once more.[169]

Add, if you wish, the differences between the mathematical and the physical sciences.[170] These are necessary and important, if one is to understand what being is. I would accept what you say about the causes of beings, except for the instrument, which is useless, and the paradigm, which is impious.[171] I do not enumerate them because of my wish to refute them all; my intention is to get rid of what is strange [**159P**] and useless for our doctrines. But you did not accurately specify the terms "time" and "infinite" in your *Physics*.[172] The opposition of substances is contrary to common sense;[173] that thought is hard to explain, and ends up in anonymity in a systematic way. So as to avoid mentioning either conjunction or continuity,[174] I make fun of your theory about timeless, endless, and thus eternal motion, and the strange hypothesis that is based on it. I ridicule your theory about the perpetual generation or eternity and endlessness of heaven,[175] as well as your opinion concerning the void that is supposedly above it and opposite to it. I deride the way you attribute to heaven the possibility of action, maintaining that it possesses a rational soul, and the way you account for its irrational movements, arguing that soul and nature do not move it in the same way. Your theory about generation and passing-out-of-existence[176] is inferior to that of Hippokrates, the doctor. He managed to explain these in both a symbolic and literal sense in several passages of his treatise on food.[177] Your treatise on meteorology is false, as is demonstrated by the fourth book. Your explanation of the nature of the Milky Way is inconsistent,[178] because it is not a perfect comet. Your theories concerning seasons are also mostly false. False also are your theories concerning the

---

169. Cf. Aristotle, *Categories* 3b10.
170. Cf. Aristotle, *Metaphysics* 1026a13–17.
171. Cf. Aristotle, *Metaphysics* 1013a26–27, 1069b32–34, 1070b18–19; *Physics* 192a3.
172. Cf. Aristotle, *Physics* 204a8–30, 217b29–34.
173. Cf. Aristotle, *Categories* 3b24–25.
174. Cf. Aristotle, *On the Heavens* 226b7–9, 287a24–25.
175. Cf. Aristotle, *On the Heavens* 269b7–9, 287a24–25.
176. Cf. Aristotle, *On Generation and Corruption* 314a1.
177. The meaning is obscure.
178. Cf. Aristotle, *Meteorology* 345a21–25, and Psellos, *De omnifaria doctrina* 123.2–14 (p. 66).

halo and the rainbow.[179] Those who comment upon your works correct these errors, repaying you for nourishing them.

Some people even deny that his [Aristotle's] mathematical knowledge was accurate. You [a pagan] may reply that all these books deal with the material world and their mistakes are due to the instability of matter, arguing that your theological treatises are blameless. I answer, first, [160P] that their foundations are in natural science too. Also, you repeat the same point many times. The garrulity of those strange doctrines is immense. Most of these books do not answer the questions: What is being qua being?[180] Are its attributes essential to it? Are they to be found in the mind or in the senses?[181] What is the science that deals with all these matters?[182] That science is not identical with any other partial knowledge. What is the meaning of those multiple subdivisions of essence? What is this distinction among beginnings, causes, and divisions among the elements?[183] What is their original cause? The philosopher does not clarify that thing anywhere. What is the meaning of the cause of beings? Why is the division of being into many subdivisions necessary? I do not understand why the science of mathematics is sometimes considered as a bridge[184] for scholars moving from the study of nature to the study of theology, but at other times one is led from physics to theology without any intermediary (that is why First Philosophy is called *Meta-physics*).

I praise Aristotle only for the following reason, namely, that he organized the whole body of philosophy for us and dealt with all other sciences as well. Nor is your [the pagans'] great Parmenides to be considered a great philosopher, nor Melissos, nor Zenon. Some were led to false conclusions, because the way they investigated them was false; others regarded only the ideas as true beings.[185] Pythagoras with the long beard, so esteemed by you, is to be blamed as well because he turned everything into number.[186] Aristotle exposed his mis-

---

179. Cf. Aristotle, *Meteorology* 371b18, and Psellos, *De omnifaria doctrina* 142.1–143 (pp. 73–74).

180. Cf. Aristotle, *Metaphysics* 1003a21.

181. Cf. Aristotle, *Metaphysics* 995b31–34.

182. Cf. Aristotle, *Metaphysics* 995b4–19.

183. Cf. Aristotle, *Metaphysics* 998a20–25.

184. Cf. Nikomachos of Gerasa, *Introduction to Mathematics* 1.3.6.21.

185. Cf. Aristotle, *Metaphysics* 988b1–6.

186. Cf. Aristotle, *Metaphysics* 987a19–28, 1083b8–13, 1091b1; *On the Heavens* 268a11–12.

takes at the end of his own theology.[187] But as far as the nature of man is concerned, I must admit that the doctor from Pergamos [Galen] dealt with that subject in his treatise on the utility of the members of the body more accurately than Aristotle.[188] The latter's treatises on animals are just collections of stories from the works of other authors.[189] I prefer drinking water directly from the Nile itself to drinking from a jar containing water pumped from that river.

25. [**161P**] I wish I had the liberty to refute all these doctrines here, so that I might deploy all the arguments at my disposal. On the other hand, the funeral purpose has a claim on my speech. But let it wait a while longer. I do not always find fault with pagan philosophy nor do I target its every article. For example, I could greatly praise its demonstrative art, which constitutes the completion of the system of Logic.[190] The *Topics* and *Sophistical Refutations* do not come first. I praise the principles of syllogism,[191] their enumeration and division, and whatever is composed of them, either a simple phrase or something more complicated. I approve the division of syllogisms into three groups, their figures, middle terms,[192] analysis, and summary principles of sophistry and dialectic. I approve also logical demonstration and the category of beings-in-themselves and qua beings,[193] except that I draw a distinction between these two terms. I would also praise the deduction of the universal out of what applies to all, and what is discovered first.[194] I agree that quite often this lacks a name, and this is a reason why some people are led astray.[195] I take the view that each science has its own characteristics, but necessarily it shares some with all other sciences.[196] I approve of the double foreknowledge,[197] and the definition of the superlative degree.[198] I agree that all learning has to do

187. I.e., the *Metaphysics*.

188. Cf. Aristotle, *History of Animals* 486a5 ff.; the reference is to Galen, *De usu partium*. Psellos refers to that work in his *Philosophica Minora I* 2.29–34 (p. 2).

189. He is referring to the various relevant treatises of Aristotle (*History of Animals, Motion of Animals, Parts of Animals, Generation of Animals*).

190. A reference to Aristotle's *Posterior Analytics*.

191. Cf. Aristotle, *Prior Analytics* 46a10.

192. Cf. Aristotle, *Prior Analytics* 66b1–3.

193. Cf. Aristotle, *Prior Analytics* 24a10–15; *Posterior Analytics* 73a25–27.

194. The meaning is unclear.

195. Cf. Aristotle, *Posterior Analytics* 74a4–12.

196. Cf. Aristotle, *Posterior Analytics* 76a37–41.

197. Cf. Aristotle, *Posterior Analytics* 78a22–28.

198. Cf. Aristotle, *Posterior Analytics* 78b28–29.

with forms,[199] not with any particular objects, and that the ideas are mere sounds,[200] like those that are emitted by a stringed instrument being tuned.

Aristotle was esteemed by him [Xiphilinos] in these respects, too, so long as he was involved in political affairs. He derived from there much that was useful for refuting false doctrines, especially for making a distinction between a true philosopher and a sophist; [. . .] of absurd doctrines [. . .] reasoning in an unscientific way against the truth. [**162P**] Is there anyone else—to use his own words now—who better understood and grasped the meaning of the logical demonstrations of each science,[201] arranging some of them in a linear and others in a cyclical way?[202] [. . .] He constructed many syllogisms that lead to impossibilities[203] [. . .] Likewise, on the basis of the science of dialectics, he discovered accidental properties, syllogisms, and their properties. What is much more admirable is that he gave an accurate description of order and the dialectic question.[204] He admired Aristotle's ethical treatise on virtues,[205] and, after washing many of his theories with the pure and more potable waters of the Gospel, he confidently incorporated them into the teaching of the spirit.

26. That was his attitude toward the study of logic. As for astronomy, he [Xiphilinos] rejected its astrological part as an abomination or an incurable illness, throwing it far away from the body of the Church. He did not even crown it with woolen fillets, as Plato did for Homer,[206] but he left it completely unadorned, throwing away all the strange terms of the astronomical tablet, I mean, the evidence by aspect of the stars, the satellite orbits, the convergences of the planets and their counteractions, and all the other nonsense, as well as the nativity that follows from all that, the powers of the cardinal points of the ecliptic, [**163P**] the system numbering twelve parts [the zodiac],[207] and all the

199. Cf. Aristotle, *Posterior Analytics* 79a7–8.

200. Cf. Aristotle, *Posterior Analytics* 83a32–35; Psellos, *Orationes Panegyricae* 4.5–8 (p. 55).

201. Cf. Aristotle, *Metaphysics* 1087b21.

202. Cf. Aristotle, *Prior Analytics* 28a10–17; *Posterior Analytics* 72b25–35; also Psellos, *Philosophica Minora I* 11.27–28 (p. 36).

203. Cf. Psellos, *Philosophica Minora I* 11.68–69 (p. 37).

204. Cf. Aristotle, *Prior Analytics* 24a25.

205. A reference to Aristotle's *Nicomachean Ethics*.

206. Cf. Plato, *Republic* 398a; also Psellos, *Encomium for His Mother* 28.

207. Terms probably taken from Vettius Valens, *Anthology* 3.3.41 (p. 131.28); 1.1.40 (p. 4.26); 9.12.33 (p. 342.8); 4.16.21 (p. 177.1); 2.18.5–6 (p. 76.14–20); 1.4.1 (p. 18.15–19).

other babbling of Rhetorios,[208] Hephaistion,[209] Valens,[210] and the other members of that company. As far as the *Syntaxis* of Ptolemy was concerned, that is, his compilation of general inferences, he did not reject those geometric demonstrations that established the length of the lines of a circle,[211] but he rejected from his philosophy the principles of the casting of horoscopes.[212] He considered the theorems referring to the movements of the stars useful to us, but he regarded all theories referring to the influence that the stars exercise upon the births of men and upon chance accidents[213] as blasphemous and impious. That was his attitude toward astronomy.

As for arithmetic, geometry, and music, he praised and admired most of their theorems, if not all, especially when he saw that all the parts of a number were discovered inside objects in a harmonious way, having been derived from equality, and returning to their original sources, coming out of their opposites. He admired how the various forms of uneven numbers fall out like seeds from a sieve, and how square and not square numbers are found in a certain immutable order, keeping their qualities in mathematical proportion.[214] He approved how the principal mathematical sciences received one thing in exchange for another from each other.[215] He regarded geometry as the most magnificent of them all, because its demonstrations are undeniable. However, he disapproved of circles complete in themselves, which were to be found in human souls and morals; also of the so-called intelligible axes and their non-existent poles,[216] thinking that these were inventions of an ill-starred mind. However, he calculated the angles in various figures on the basis of their sides. In the same way he calculated the dimensions of the sides of those figures, [164P] by using the theorems as starting points for the calculation of their dimensions.

208. A sixth-century AD astrologer from Egypt.

209. A late-fourth-century AD astrologer from Thebes, who composed a treatise in three books called *Apotelesmatika.*

210. A second-century AD astrologer from Antioch.

211. Cf. Ptolemy, *Mathematical Systematic Treatise* 1.1 (p. 31.19–20).

212. Cf. Ptolemy, *Apotelesmatika* 1.2.18 (p. 8.23–26).

213. Cf. Ptolemy, *Apotelesmatika* 3.4.1 (p. 112.13–16).

214. Cf. Plato, *Theaetetus* 148a–b.

215. Cf. Psellos, *Oratoria Minora* 37.349 (p. 148); *Orationes Panegyricae* 4.389–393 (p. 72).

216. Cf. Ptolemy, *Apotelesmatika* 2.4.5–6 (p. 123); Aratos, *Phainomena* 1.24–26.

In optics, he admired how symmetry was found through geometric calculations, because wise men managed to discover in solid bodies what nature did not allow to exist as in the case of numbers. Many times he mentioned the figures that were sketched and those that had sides about the equal angles reciprocally proportional, the extreme and the mean ratio;[217] but he considered the lesson referring to lengths and powers, and to their ratio, to be secret.[218] He admired the stereometry of Plato,[219] and thought that it is impossible to find any different method from the same principles than that one. As for music, he discovered the difference between high- and low-pitched sounds in the type of quantity, and from there, as if from a citadel, he proceeded toward theories about spoken sounds. Thereafter, he examined intervals and scales in their variety. Proceeding in an orderly fashion, he spoke about *genera* and pitches, about modulations and musical composition. He defined sound as a noise of just one pitch,[220] and consonant chords as those none of which gives the impression of being high or low when they are struck,[221] while he described dissonant ones as those one of which gives the impression of being high or low. He defined homophonic chords as those having a different power, but a common pitch.[222] He also examined in detail notes that were close-packed, and those that were not. He accused the Pythagoreans of giving an inaccurate explanation of consonant systems,[223] and the opposite party, the Aristoxenians, of defining symmetry on the basis of intervals, not pitches.[224] But let me say something further, making a subtle distinction: Who found the measures of the fourth interval, defining it as less than two [165P] tones and a half [...] ?[225] Even if he found the interval and the abridgment [...] Who distinguished the harmonic, the chromatic, and the diatonic genus,[226] who found how the tetrachords in the middle are linked together and divided from each other?[227] Who devised a

217. Cf. Euclid, *Elements* 6, def. 2–3.
218. Cf. Plato, *Theaetetus* 147d; also Psellos, *Encomium for His Mother* 27.
219. Cf. Pseudo-Plato, *Epinomis* 990d8.
220. Cf. Aristoxenos, *Elements of Harmonics* 3.69 (p. 87.4–6); Ptolemy, *Harmonics* 1.9 (pp. 19.16–20).
221. Cf. Ptolemy, *Harmonics* 2.7 (p. 58.7–20).
222. Cf. Aristoxenos, *Elements of Harmonics* 1.17 (p. 22.5–7).
223. Cf. Aristoxenos, *Elements of Harmonics* 1.24 (p. 31.3–5).
224. Cf. Ptolemy, *Harmonics* 1.9 tit. (p. 19).
225. Cf. Ptolemy, *Harmonics* 1.10 (p. 23.19–24).
226. Cf. Ptolemy, *Harmonics* 1.5 (p. 11.14), 1.12 (p. 29.5–6).
227. Cf. Ptolemy, *Harmonics* 2.6 (p. 55.15–22), 1.16 (p. 38.23–33).

measuring rule for the consonant systems [. . .] finding the positions, the marks, the indivisible time, and all that follows from the various rhythms?[228]

27. As I have pointed out many times, as long as he was involved in the affairs of the state, he paid attention to the technical aspects of all these sciences, but as soon as he was freed and was independent, he was initiated into the lessons referring to the powers of the soul, the intelligible accounts, the unity of the soul with the body through the body itself, the unity of the sky with itself, and with what is above. Since many things constitute plurality and each of them is derived from that plurality, he discovered their differences and brought them into unity. In the same way he examined virtue, that which is beautiful in itself, and all other sorts of unity. He made himself an example of learning both to the laymen, the lower order, and to clergymen, the higher one: he displayed his learning of higher matters to bishops and monks, while explaining to laymen how they should approach the political life.

He would receive the crown for total victory, if one wanted to compare him to other men. [**166P**] One would have to examine the words and deeds of the other men first, and then proceed to the comparison of each of them and then of all together with him [Xiphilinos]. In his speech he surpassed the prominent orators; in his philosophy and his scientific knowledge he surpassed those who studied philosophy in depth; in his perfect conduct as an archbishop, he surpassed all who wore those robes that reached down to the feet and the mitre, because he was bright, whereas the others were mere shadow.[229] But he also surpassed most Christian clergymen. If my claim is not too audacious, I would say that he became equal to Gregorios [of Nazianzos] and Basileios [of Kaisareia], the luminaries of the Church. He admired the style of their speech and their philosophy. He took the same road, and he was awarded the same crowns as them.[230] Although he had learned the whole of philosophy and had gathered in himself all sorts of virtue, he did not boast about it. He was not unapproachable to common people; rather, he was more accessible than anyone else. He walked together with the people, explaining the divine laws to them, especially during the ceremonies of the Church. The only thing I can reproach you with, you who are the only one beyond reproach, is your zeal for the holy services, although you took care to avoid being praised excessively.

228. Cf. Aristoxenos, *Elements of Harmonics* 2.34 (p. 43.15–19).
229. Cf. Exodus 28:4.
230. Cf. 2 Timothy 4:7–8.

28. Who might now lend me streams of tears,[231] how can I bewail myself for the accident that befell you, depriving me of you suddenly, beyond all expectation? How can I enter upon the last chapter of my speech, how can I explain to the audience the reason for your departure? As the epic poet says, your own temper destroyed you.[232] As there was no possibility that you would be crowned a martyr in front of impious and bad rulers,[233] you were elevated to that rank all by yourself. O my audience, he devoted himself to the holy services more than was necessary, but his body was not made of steel or something harder; so it suffered a stroke and started trembling. That attack did not last very long. His deformed face was soon restored to its previous state. He realized what had happened, but did not restrain himself as he ought to have done; rather, he pushed himself even harder, fighting against [**167P**] all the odds. But what had happened was the seed of his death and the beginning of his gradual paralysis. The illness was not so bad at the beginning, because it made its appearance suddenly and then suddenly disappeared. But it would never fully depart. It attacked the head which governed his body, but did not affect his mind at all, because God had ordered it, like the bad spirit that attacked Job, not to touch his soul,[234] namely, his morale—that is how I understand that passage.

But his tongue was damaged and his speech was affected: he started mumbling a bit, and mixed up the order of the letters. Then the impediment of his tongue became stronger: it was as if it had been bound by a strong rein. However, he did not withdraw from the governance of spiritual matters; he went on steering the helm of the ship of the whole Church. Then after his speech, he lost his breath too, and departed from this life to join that immaculate and true one. He had prepared himself for that departure while he was still healthy. He had added wings to his thoughts, in order to be able to fly together with the angels who would lead his soul toward God [...]

29. But now, O great archbishop, you enjoy the true archetypes, having left their shadows behind, which you had contemplated in the past down here. O, you traveled up from night into light, from what was faint to what was bright. I do not know if your knowledge is still increasing. Probably there are some

---

231. Cf. Jeremiah 9:1.
232. Cf. Homer, *Iliad* 6.407.
233. Namely, because the emperors were pious and good.
234. Cf. Job 1:12.

limits on acquiring superior knowledge set upon the souls of the dead. O, you were a perfect philosopher on this earth, who always contemplated death with joy, was not afraid of the separation of the soul from the body, was not frightened at the prospect of your departure. O, you killed off bodily passions, [**168P**] confronted your natural death bravely, giving way quietly to the laws of nature regarding separation. What songs may I sing over the change in your life, what harmonic sound may I employ for the peaceful dissolution of the harmonious bond uniting your soul and body? That harmony sang a holy song to God at the time of its dissolution. You contended in all aspects of virtue with all dead men of the past, and you surpassed them all. I am referring not only to the priests but to all those who were philosophers in a good sense. You surpassed the men [of the Old Testament] who lived in the shadows and among the images: the light of your truth shone brightly upon them. I am referring to the likes of Samuel[235] and the great priest Joshua.[236] You surpassed those belonging to the true light [of the New Testament] also because you had made a greater progress in contemplation.

O, you did not leave behind anything of yourself except for your body, but you had worn it down too. O, you slept without a small couch, without a soft, precious blanket, almost without a bed. You paid attention only to the treasures above, which you also amassed while you were alive. You were poor, and you earned Christ in place of anything else. You bought the precious pearl,[237] which illustrious, rich men do not know how to get. Your achievements raised you up to God, borne in a straight line. Poor men held your coffin high up, and their hands tried to touch you at the time of your funeral. As soon as the body was carried out of the Great Church, held up by the hands of priests, all who enjoyed gifts from his hands, having been given by him not only what was necessary but what was superfluous too, both men and women, old and young, and persons of all other ages, surrounded the new Jerusalem, the Great Church of the Wisdom of God, preventing the bier's exit out of the church and blocking the road of the procession. It was the most pitiful and heart-wrenching sight of all: one person asked for the man who fed him, another for the one who dressed him, another for the one who cured him frequently when he was ill, and still another for the one who comforted him in his grief. Even

---

235. Cf. 1 Samuel 3:19–21.
236. Cf. 2 Ezra 2:2–13.
237. Cf. Matthew 13:46.

the babies carried by mothers in their arms were unrestrained at the time of this common misfortune. They tried to slide out of their mothers' embrace in order to reach him.

30. [169P] How is one to properly address you? You surpassed all philosophy and approached divine wisdom. So all our names for referring to virtue do not apply to you anymore; you left all composite words behind you, reaching divine simplicity. You kept the faith, finished your path with Paul, and now you have been crowned.[238] You stand by the King of All, from whom everything proceeds and to whom all things return according to their nature and order. You have now kept inside you all the powers of your soul [. . .] I do not know what to say [. . .] despite the troubles that I take studying books I am not in a position to see the immaterial God with my material eyes. But if you reveal to me some aspect of that mystery while I am still on earth, showing me the substance without form, you will do what I expect from you and desire. But if you guide my life on earth from on high and lead me toward a virtuous life, which is a precondition for the contemplation of beauty in itself, and at the time of my death—whenever God wishes—you give me a place near your supernatural abode, even though this is something audacious to say, you will then give me the opportunity to partake of the Good itself by being near it. But if I am placed far from you, I hope you will take care of me there too,[239] O my divine and holy leader, whom I honored more than anyone else, after whom I admired no one else, and toward whom I steer my life!

238. Cf. again 2 Timothy 4:7–8.
239. Cf. Gregorios of Nazianzos, *Or.* 43.82.6–17 (pp. 304–306).

Bibliography

The bibliography does not include easily accessible classical texts cited in the notes.

Ancient and Byzantine Texts

Aristoxenos. *Elements of Harmonics.* Edited by R. da Rios, *Aristoxeni Elementa harmonica.* Rome, 1954.

Attaleiates, Michael. *History.* Edited by Th. Tsolakis, *Michaelis Attaliatae Historia.* Athens, 2011.

Chaldaean Oracles. Edited by E. des Places, *Oracles chaldaïques, avec un choix de commentaires anciens.* Paris, 1971.

Corpus Paroemiographorum Graecorum, vols. 1–2. Edited by E. L. Leutsch and F. G. Schneidewin. Göttingen, 1839–1851.

Galen. *De usu partium.* Edited by G. Helmreich, *Galeni de usu partium libri xvii,* 2 vols. Leipzig, 1907–1909; repr. Amsterdam, 1968.

Gregorios of Nazianzos. *Or.* 1–3. Edited by J. Bernardi, *Grégoire de Nazianze: Discours 1–3.* Paris, 1978.

―――. *Or.* 4–5. Edited by J. Bernardi, *Grégoire de Nazianze: Dicours 4–5.* Paris, 1983.

―――. *Or.* 6–12. Edited by M.-A. Calvet-Sebasti, *Grégoire de Nazianze: Discours 6–12.* Paris, 1995.

————. *Or. 24–26.* Edited by J. Mossay, *Grégoire de Nazianze: Discours 24–26.* Paris, 1981.

————. *Or. 28–31.* Edited by P. Gallay, *Grégoire de Nazianze: Discours 28–31.* Paris, 1978.

————. *Or. 38–41.* Edited by C. Moreschini, *Grégoire de Nazianze: Discours 38–41.* Paris, 1990.

————. *Or. 42–43.* Edited by J. Bernardi, *Grégoire de Nazianze: Discours 42–43.* Paris, 1992.

Gregorios of Nyssa. *Life of Moses.* Edited by J. Daniélou, *Grégoire de Nysse: La Vie de Moïse ou Traité de la perfection en matière de vertu.* Paris, 1968.

Hermogenes. *De inventione.* Edited by H. Rabe, *Hermogenis opera,* 93–212. Leipzig, 1913; repr. Stuttgart, 1969.

————. *On Types of Style.* Edited by H. Rabe, *Hermogenis opera,* 213–413. Leipzig, 1913; repr. Stuttgart, 1969.

Himerios. *Orations.* Edited by A. Colonna, *Himerii Declamationes et orationes cum deperditarum fragmentis.* Rome, 1951.

Iamblichos. *De communi mathematica scientia.* Edited by N. Festa, *Iamblichi De communi mathematica scientia liber.* Stuttgart, 1975.

Ioannes of Damascus. *Exposition of the Faith.* Edited by P. B. Kotter, *Die Schriften des Johannes von Damaskos,* vol. 2, 3–239. Berlin, 1973.

Italikos, Michael. *Letters.* Edited by P. Gautier, *Michel Italikos: Lettres et Discours.* Paris, 1972.

Komnene, Anna. *Alexiad.* Edited by D. R. Reinsch and A. Kambylis, *Annae Comnenae Alexias.* Berlin and New York, 2001.

Life of Athanasios of Athos. Edited by J. Noret, *Vitae duae antiquae sancti Athanasii Athonitae.* Turnhout, 1982.

Nikomachos of Gerasa. *Introduction to Mathematics.* Edited by R. Hoche, *Nicomachi Geraseni Pythagorei introductionis arithmeticae libri II.* Leipzig, 1866.

Proklos. *Elements of Theology.* Edited by E. R. Dodds. Oxford, 1963.

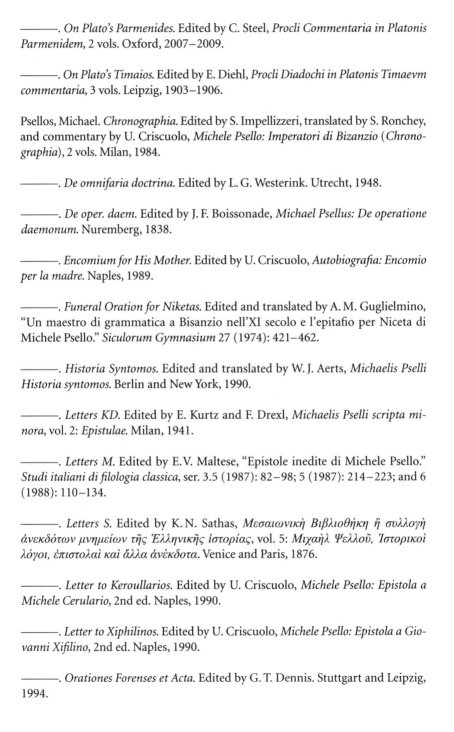

―――. *On Plato's Parmenides*. Edited by C. Steel, *Procli Commentaria in Platonis Parmenidem*, 2 vols. Oxford, 2007–2009.

―――. *On Plato's Timaios*. Edited by E. Diehl, *Procli Diadochi in Platonis Timaevm commentaria*, 3 vols. Leipzig, 1903–1906.

Psellos, Michael. *Chronographia*. Edited by S. Impellizzeri, translated by S. Ronchey, and commentary by U. Criscuolo, *Michele Psello: Imperatori di Bizanzio* (*Chronographia*), 2 vols. Milan, 1984.

―――. *De omnifaria doctrina*. Edited by L. G. Westerink. Utrecht, 1948.

―――. *De oper. daem*. Edited by J. F. Boissonade, *Michael Psellus: De operatione daemonum*. Nuremberg, 1838.

―――. *Encomium for His Mother*. Edited by U. Criscuolo, *Autobiografia: Encomio per la madre*. Naples, 1989.

―――. *Funeral Oration for Niketas*. Edited and translated by A. M. Guglielmino, "Un maestro di grammatica a Bisanzio nell'XI secolo e l'epitafio per Niceta di Michele Psello." *Siculorum Gymnasium* 27 (1974): 421–462.

―――. *Historia Syntomos*. Edited and translated by W. J. Aerts, *Michaelis Pselli Historia syntomos*. Berlin and New York, 1990.

―――. *Letters KD*. Edited by E. Kurtz and F. Drexl, *Michaelis Pselli scripta minora*, vol. 2: *Epistulae*. Milan, 1941.

―――. *Letters M*. Edited by E. V. Maltese, "Epistole inedite di Michele Psello." *Studi italiani di filologia classica*, ser. 3.5 (1987): 82–98; 5 (1987): 214–223; and 6 (1988): 110–134.

―――. *Letters S*. Edited by K. N. Sathas, *Μεσαιωνικὴ Βιβλιοθήκη ἢ συλλογὴ ἀνεκδότων μνημείων τῆς Ἑλληνικῆς ἱστορίας*, vol. 5: *Μιχαὴλ Ψελλοῦ, Ἱστορικοὶ λόγοι, ἐπιστολαὶ καὶ ἄλλα ἀνέκδοτα*. Venice and Paris, 1876.

―――. *Letter to Keroullarios*. Edited by U. Criscuolo, *Michele Psello: Epistola a Michele Cerulario*, 2nd ed. Naples, 1990.

―――. *Letter to Xiphilinos*. Edited by U. Criscuolo, *Michele Psello: Epistola a Giovanni Xifilino*, 2nd ed. Naples, 1990.

―――. *Orationes Forenses et Acta*. Edited by G. T. Dennis. Stuttgart and Leipzig, 1994.

————. *Orationes Funebres I.* Edited by I. Polemis. Berlin and Boston, 2014.

————. *Orationes Hagiographicae.* Edited by E. Fisher. Stuttgart and Leipzig, 1994.

————. *Orationes Panegyricae.* Edited by G. T. Dennis. Stuttgart and Leipzig, 1994.

————. *Oratoria Minora.* Edited by A. R. Littlewood. Leipzig, 1985.

————. *Philosophica Minora I.* Edited by J. M. Duffy. Stuttgart and Leipzig, 1992.

————. *Philosophica Minora II.* Edited by D. J. O'Meara. Leipzig, 1989.

————. *Poemata.* Edited by L. G. Westerink. Stuttgart, 1992.

————. *Theologica I.* Edited by P. Gautier. Leipzig, 1989.

————. *Theologica II.* Edited by L. G. Westerink and J. M. Duffy. Munich and Leipzig, 2002.

Pseudo-Dionysios. *The Celestial Hierarchy, The Ecclesiastical Hierarchy, The Mystical Theology, and the Letters.* Edited by G. Heil and A. M. Ritter, *Corpus Dionysiacum II: Pseudo-Dionysius Areopagita de Coelesti Hierarchia, de Ecclesiastica Hierarchia, de Mystica Theologia, Epistulae.* Berlin, 1991.

————. *On Divine Names.* Edited by B. Suchla, *Corpus Dionysiacum I: Pseudo-Dionysius Areopagita, De divinis nominibus.* Berlin, 1990. 107–231.

Pseudo-Kaisareios. *Questions and Answers.* Edited by R. Riedinger, *Erotapokriseis.* Berlin, 1989.

Ptolemy. *Apotelesmatika.* Edited by F. Boll and E. Boer, *Claudii Ptolemaei opera quae exstant omnia,* vol. 3.1, 1–213. Leipzig, 1940; repr. 1957.

————. *Harmonics.* Edited by I. Düring, *Die Harmonielehre des Klaudios Ptolemaios,* 2–111. Göteborg, 1930.

————. *Mathematical Systematic Treatise (Syntaxis mathematica).* Edited by J. L. Heiberg, *Claudii Ptolemaei opera quae exstant omnia,* vol. 1.1–2. Leipzig, 1898.

Simplikios. *Commentary on Aristotle's "On the Soul."* Edited by M. Hayduck, *Commentaria in Aristotelem Graeca,* vol. 11. Berlin, 1882.

Skylitzes Continuatus. Edited by E. Th. Tsolakis, *Ἡ Συνέχεια τῆς Χρονογραφίας τοῦ Ἰωάννου Σκυλίτση (Ioannes Skylitzes Continuatus).* Thessalonike, 1968.

Skylitzes, Ioannes. *Synopsis of Histories.* Edited by I. Thurn, *Ioannis Scylitzae Synopsis Historiarum.* Berlin and New York, 1973.

Souda. Edited by A. Adler, *Svidae Lexicon,* 5 vols. Leipzig, 1928–1938.

Synesios. *Dion.* Edited by J. Lamoureux, *Synésios de Cyrène,* vol. 4. Paris, 2004.

————. *Egyptian Oration.* Edited by J. Lamoureux, *Synésios de Cyrène,* vol. 4. Paris, 2008.

————. *Hymns.* Edited by C. Lacombrade, *Synésios de Cyrène,* vol. 1. Paris, 1978.

————. *Letters.* Edited by A. Garzya, *Synesii Cyrenensis Epistolae.* Rome, 1979.

————. *On Kingship.* Edited by N. Terzaghi, *Synesii Cyrenensis opuscula,* 5–62. Rome, 1944.

Timarion. Edited and trans. by R. Romano, *Pseudo-Luciano: Timarione.* Naples, 1974.

Vettius Valens. *Anthology.* Edited by W. Kroll, *Vettii Valentis anthologiarum libri.* Berlin, 1908.

Modern Studies

Agapitos, P. A. 1998. "Teachers, Pupils, and Imperial Power in Eleventh-Century Byzantium." In *Pedagogy and Power: Rhetorics of Classical Learning,* edited by Y. L. Too and N. Livingstone, 170–191. Cambridge.

Anastasi, R. 1966. "Sull'epitafio di Psello per Giovanni Xifilino." *Siculorum Gymnasium,* n.s. 19: 52–56.

Angelidi, C. 2006. "The Writing of Dreams: A Note on Psellos' Funeral Oration for His Mother." In *Reading Psellos,* edited by C. Barber and D. Jenkins, 153–166. Leiden and Boston.

Angold, M. 1997. *The Byzantine Empire, 1025–1204: A Political History.* 2nd ed. Harlow.

Bonis, K. G. 1937. *Ἰωάννης ὁ Ξιφιλῖνος. Ὁ Νομοφύλαξ, ὁ μοναχός, ὁ πατριάρχης καὶ ἡ ἐποχή του. Συμβολὴ εἰς τὰς Βυζαντιακὰς σπουδὰς τῆς ΙΑ΄ ἑκατονταετηρίδος.* Athens.

Cheynet, J.-C. 1990. *Pouvoir et contestations à Byzance (963–1210).* Paris.

————. 2003. Notes to *Jean Scylitzès: Empereurs de Constantinople (texte traduit par B. Flusin et annoté par J.-C. Cheynet).* Paris.

Criscuolo, U. 1975. "Sui rapporti tra Michele Psello e Giovanni Xifilino (*ep.* 191 Kurtz-Drexl)." *Atti della Accademia Pontaniana*, n.s. 24: 121–128.

————. 1981. "Tardoantico e umanesimo bizantino: Michele Psello." *Koinonia* 5: 7–23.

————. 1982. "πολιτικὸς ἀνήρ: Contributo al pensiero politica di Michele Psello." *Rendiconti dell'Accademia di Archeologia, Lettere e Belle Arti di Napoli* 57: 129–163.

————. 1983. *Michele Psello: Orazione in memoria di Costantino Lichudi. Introduzione, traduzione, commento e appendici.* Messina.

Dagron, G. 2003. *Emperor and Priest: The Imperial Office in Byzantium.* Translated by J. Birrell. Cambridge.

Garzya, A. 1967. "On Michael Psellus' Admission of Faith." *Ἐπετηρὶς Ἑταιρείας Βυζαντινῶν Σπουδῶν* 35: 41–46.

Gautier, P. 1974. "Éloge funèbre de Nicolas de la Belle Source par Michel Psellos moine à l'Olympe." *Βυζαντινά* 6: 9–69.

Hondridou, S. D. 2002. *Ο Κωνσταντίνος Θ΄ Μονομάχος και η εποχή του (ενδέκατος αιώνας μ.Χ.).* Thessalonike.

Janin, R. 1969. *La géographie ecclésiastique de l'empire byzantin. Première partie: Le siège de Constantinople et le patriarcat oecuménique, Tome III: Les églises et les monastères.* Paris.

Jenkins, D. 2016. "Michael Psellos." In *The Cambridge Intellectual History of Byzantium*, edited by A. Kaldellis and N. Siniossoglou. Cambridge. Forthcoming.

Kaldellis, A. 1999. *The Argument of Psellos' "Chronographia."* Leiden and Boston.

————. 2005. "The Date of Psellos' Theological Lectures and Higher Religious Education in Constantinople." *Byzantinoslavica* 63: 143–151.

————, ed. and trans. 2006. *Mothers and Sons, Fathers and Daughters: The Byzantine Family of Michael Psellos* (with contributions by D. Jenkins and S. Papaioannou). Notre Dame, IN.

————. 2007. *Hellenism in Byzantium: The Transformations of Greek Identity and the Reception of the Classical Tradition.* Cambridge.

————. 2011. "The Date of Psellos' Death, Once Again: Psellos Was Not the Michael of Nikomedeia Mentioned by Attaleiates." *Byzantinische Zeitschrift* 104: 649–661.

————. 2012. "Byzantine Philosophy Inside and Out: Orthodoxy and Dissidence in Counterpoint." In *The Many Faces of Byzantine Philosophy,* edited by K. Ierodiakonou and B. Bydén, 129–151. Athens.

Karpozilos, A. 1982. *Συμβολὴ στὴ μελέτη τοῦ βίου καὶ τοῦ ἔργου τοῦ Ἰωάννη Μαυρόποδος.* Ioannina.

Kazhdan, A. 1983. "Hagiographical Notes. 3. An Attempt at Hagio-Autobiography: The Pseudo-Life of "Saint" Psellus." *Byzantion* 53: 546–556.

Kolbaba, T. 2000. *The Byzantine Lists: Errors of the Latins.* Urbana and Chicago.

Kriaras, E. 1972. "Ὁ Μιχαὴλ Ψελλός." *Βυζαντινά* 4: 53–128.

Lemerle, P. 1977. " 'Le gouvernement des philosophes': L'enseignement, les écoles, la culture." In P. Lemerle, *Cinq études sur le XIe siècle byzantin,* 193–248. Paris.

Ljubarskij, J. N. 2004. *Ἡ προσωπικότητα καὶ τὸ ἔργο τοῦ Μιχαὴλ Ψελλοῦ. Συνεισφορὰ στὴν ἱστορία τοῦ βυζαντινοῦ οὐμανισμοῦ.* Translated by A. Tzelesi. Athens.

Maltese, E. V. 1987. "Un nuovo testimone dell'epistola di Psello a Giovanni Xifilino (*Paris. Gr.* 1277)." *Byzantion* 57: 427–432.

Markopoulos, A. 2008. "Education." In *The Oxford Handbook of Byzantine Studies,* edited by E. Jeffreys et al., 785–795. Oxford.

Moore, P. 2005. *Iter Psellianum: A Detailed Listing of Manuscript Sources for All Works Attributed to Michael Psellos Including a Comprehensive Bibliography.* Toronto.

Musso, O. 1977. *Michele Psello: Nozioni Paradossali.* Naples.

ODB = The Oxford Dictionary of Byzantium. Edited by A. P. Kazhdan et al. 3 vols. Oxford, 1991.

Papaioannou, E. N. 1998. "Das Briefcorpus des Michael Psellos: Vorarbeiten zu einer kritischen Neuedition." *Jahrbuch der österreichischen Byzantinistik* 48: 67–117.

────. 2013. *Michael Psellos: Rhetoric and Authorship in Byzantium.* Cambridge.

Polemis, D. I. 1968. *The Doukai: A Contribution to Byzantine Prosopography.* London.

Riedinger, J.-C. 2010. "Quatre étapes de la vie de Michel Psellos." *Revue des études byzantines* 68: 5–60.

Rosenqvist, J. O. 1966. *The Hagiographic Dossier of St Eugenios of Trebizond in Codex Athous Dionysiou 154: A Critical Edition with Introduction, Translation, Commentary and Indexes.* Uppsala.

Sathas, K. N. 1874. *Μεσαιωνικὴ Βιβλιοθήκη ἢ συλλογὴ ἀνεκδότων μνημείων τῆς Ἑλληνικῆς ἱστορίας*, vol. 4: *Μιχαὴλ Ψελλοῦ Ἑκατονταετηρὶς Βυζαντινῆς ἱστορίας.* Athens and Paris.

────. 1876. *Μεσαιωνικὴ Βιβλιοθήκη ἢ συλλογὴ ἀνεκδότων μνημείων τῆς Ἑλληνικῆς ἱστορίας*, vol. 5: *Μιχαὴλ Ψελλοῦ, Ἱστορικοὶ λόγοι, ἐπιστολαὶ καὶ ἄλλα ἀνέκδοτα.* Venice and Paris.

Shepard, J., ed. 2008. *The Cambridge History of the Byzantine Empire c. 500–1492.* Cambridge.

Sideras, A. 1994. *Die byzantinischen Grabreden: Prosopographie, Datierung, Überlieferung. 142 Epitaphien und Monodien aus dem byzantinischen Jahrtausend.* Vienna.

────. 2002. "Der unedierte Schlussteil der Grabrede des Michael Psellos auf den Patriarchen Johannes Xiphilinos." *Göttinger Beiträge zur byzantinischen und neugriechischen Philologie* 2: 113–132.

Siniossoglou, N. 2011. *Radical Platonism in Byzantium: Illumination and Utopia in Gemistos Plethon.* Cambridge.

Snipes, K. 1981. "A Letter of Michael Psellos to Constantine the Nephew of Michael Cerularios." *Greek, Roman, and Byzantine Studies* 22: 89–107.

Strauss, L. 1952. *Persecution and the Art of Writing.* Chicago.

Tinnefeld, F. 1973. "'Freundschaft' in den Briefen des Michael Psellos: Theorie und Wirklichkeit." *Jahrbuch der österreichischen Byzantinistik* 22: 151–168.

────. 1989. "Michael I Kerullarios, Patriarch von Konstantinopel (1043–1058): Kritische Überlegungen zu einer Biographie." *Jahrbuch der österreichischen Byzantinistik* 39: 95–127.

Treadgold, W. 1997. *A History of the Byzantine State and Society*. Stanford.

Volk, R. 1990. *Der medizinische Inhalt der Schriften des Michael Psellos*. Munich.

de Vries-van der Velden, E. 1996. "Psellos et son gendre." *Byzantinische Forschungen* 23: 109–149.

———. 1997. "Psellos, Romain IV Diogénès et Mantzikert." *Byzantinoslavica* 58: 274–310.

Weiss, G. 1973. *Oströmische Beamte im Spiegel der Schriften des Michael Psellos*. Munich.

———. 1977. "Die Leichenrede des Michael Psellos auf den Abt Nikolaos vom Kloster von der schönen Quelle." *Byzantina* 9 (1977): 219–322.

Will, C. 1861. *Acta et scripta quae de controversiis ecclesiae graecae et latinae saeculo undecimo composita extant*. Leipzig and Marburg.

Wilson, N. G. 1971. *An Anthology of Byzantine Prose*. Berlin and New York.

———. 1983. *Scholars of Byzantium*. London.

Wolska-Conus, W. 1976. "Les écoles de Psellos et de Xiphilin sous Constantin IX Monomaque." *Travaux et Memoires* 6: 233–243.

———. 1979. "L'école de droit et l'enseignement du droit à Byzance au XIe siècle: Xiphilin et Psellos." *Travaux et Memoires* 7: 1–107.

Index

The index does not contain entries for Psellos, Keroullarios, Leichoudes, Xiphilinos, Constantinople, or authors mentioned in the notes to the translations. Indexes locorum accompany the original editions of the texts.

Anthony Kaldellis

is professor of classics at The Ohio State University.

Ioannis Polemis

is professor of Byzantine literature at the University of Athens.